The Harmony of Science and Soul

Also by Art Bobrowitz

Each Human Spirit: The Transformation of the American Workplace

The Harmony of Science and Soul

Finding Meaning in the Twenty-First-Century Workplace

Art Bobrowitz

Compass Rose Consulting Inc.
Keizer, Oregon

*The Harmony of Science and Soul:
Finding Meaning in the Twenty-First-Century Workplace*
Copyright © 2012 by Art Bobrowitz
Compass Rose Consulting Inc.

All rights reserved. No part of this book may be used, distributed, transmitted or reproduced, in any form or by any means, including photocopying, recording or any other electronic or mechanical methods, or any informational storage or retrieval system without prior written consent. Brief quotations may be used. This includes critical reviews and certain other non-commercial uses permitted by copyright law. Permission for any other requests must be obtained in writing from the author.

Compass Rose Consulting Inc.
P.O. Box 20997
Keizer, Oregon 97307

We gratefully acknowledge the many people who contributed to the creation of this book. If we have forgotten to mention you, we deeply apologize and wish to let you know it was not intentional.

Printed in the United States of America

Cover Design: Bruce DeRoos, Portland, Oregon
Layout: Jennifer Omner, ALL Publications, Portland, Oregon

ISBN 978-0-615-47013-9

Business — Science — Spirituality

Author of *Each Human Spirit: The Transformation of the American Workplace*

Acknowledgements

Writing a book is a calling. It is an exciting process and the reward comes in knowing that what you have to say is presented with a sense of purpose and meaning.

It is with a deep sense of gratitude that I dedicate this book to my wife Roseann. She is truly the "Rose" in Compass Rose Consulting Inc. Her support and insight have nurtured me through endless hours of thought and reflection. I would like to extend endless gratitude to my parents, Andrew and Cecelia Bobrowitz. Each is a perfect example of what it is to be a message and messenger.

This finished product could not have happened without the incredible skill of Lauren Ruef, Janet Bassett, Gail Wayper and Bruce DeRoos. Their gifts are too numerous to mention. If my mind is a ball in a soccer stadium, they made sure everyone was sitting in his assigned seat. Their organization and talent are a wonder to behold.

I would also like to recognize a person for whom I have immense respect, Chuck Whitlock. His insight, challenges, and support have been a critical component in the success of this manuscript.

Early thoughts and continued counseling came from Kristi Negri. Her help gave me focus and a fundamental plan. Her assistance is deeply appreciated.

And to all employees looking for a sense of purpose and meaning in their work and their lives, you are the DNA of the human spirit. My wish is for the day when each of you will be able to sing *your individual song.*

"The individual song held inside each human spirit
is beautiful beyond words, unequalled
in lyrics, and most likely never to be played."
—Art Bobrowitz

Contents

Preface

We are undergoing nothing less than a revolution in how we look at work and how it gets done. Like all revolutions, it isn't easy or clean. The victim is the human spirit. In fact, if we focus on the rates of worker disaffection, distressed companies, statistics on sick leave abuse, and the incidence of downright fraud, theft, and jaw-dropping court decisions, one might say that things are in chaos. But these are not simply problems with America's work force; they are indicators that something is wrong in the work world. They are glaring warnings that the remnant management models from the Industrial Revolution are being challenged in the twenty-first century.

Throughout this book, I'm going to be using terms like *quantum*, *spiritual*, *Newtonian*, *wave/particle*, *message/messenger* and *heart and soul*. All have relevance to productivity, your journey, and to a greater sense of meaning for your life and career. I believe leaders of the future must be familiar with these terms, and with their impact on the human spirit and the harmony of science and soul.

The Industrial Revolution was a powerful event. It has served as the foundation for how work should be done for the last one hundred-plus years. I believe, however, that future leaders must look at the work model of the Industrial Revolution and the twentieth century merely as an important transition time, not as an enduring structure. The Industrial Revolution shifted us from a world of self-employed farmers and tradesmen to a world where almost everybody works for somebody else. A structure had to fit the experience and socialization of the workers of those times.

Surely no one will argue that our work force is the same now as it was then. In terms of education, worldview, and experience, today's worker would not even be recognizable in the early 1900s. And yet, we try to evaluate production and set goals as though our workers are still forced to put in six twelve-hour days a week. We need a new model.

We have marched out an endless series of "change" books. We've tried in-house gymnasiums, and communication-style analysis workshops. We've experimented with skateboards in the hallways and letting dogs come to work, but we cram people into archaic company hierarchies and tether them to marginal, uninspired, old-school management styles. We talk about the "total person," invest in ergonomic furniture, and then pound on employee rankings that pit people against one another, instead of creating a feeling of organization with unified purpose and direction. Because we are playing with the edges and missing the core issues, it's no wonder that worker loyalty is fleeting and the mainstream perception among CEOs is that employees can't be trusted.

We put money into retirement packages that many organizations are failing to honor. We throw money at good employees when they threaten to leave bad employers—and the employers wonder why they can't keep good people! We throw money at short-sighted management so that the next quarterly report pleases the stockholders. This leaves someone else to worry about the long-term consequences after the immediate management has retired to their private corner of the world. We have a serious problem when a corporation has a pension plan debt that is five times the company net worth.

We're floundering. We have millions of dissatisfied employees who have subjugated their quality of life for success in the workplace. And the return on their investment leaves much in question. According to the Families and Work Institute, the total combined work hours for dual-career couples with children under 18 has increased from eighty-one hours per week in 1977, to ninety-one hours per week in 2002.[1] Many are merely putting in the required hours in some kind of emotional disconnect that ultimately shows up in bad customer relations and poor productivity. And yet, our numbers are going up.

What we're looking for is a new model for the twenty-first-century workplace, but the answer is not going to be found by reinventing old methodologies. As Stephen R. Covey said, "If we keep doing what we're doing, we're going to keep getting what we're getting."[2] I have looked at the problem from a different angle, and I believe that employees are looking for an ongoing sense of meaning in their lives and their workplaces. This is more than just a company or organization—it is nothing less than the heart-and-soul thinking of each employee.

If we start to look at the meaning of the workplace and how humans react to it, then we will begin to understand what twenty-first-century workers need in order to create success for their employers and for themselves. We need a deep understanding of the basic needs of the human spirit, and we need to recognize that both scientific and spiritual resources can be more helpful than a contemporary flavor-of-the-month strategy that is set up to fail. One must be direct here. I believe the twenty-first century must look at the fundamental definition of organization and what that really means.

I think that employees, especially front-line workers, and some leaders are beginning to understand this. The question has been how to quantify the search for meaning in a way that can be applied to the workplace. Over the years I have applied the ideas behind the Seven Needs for Personal Productivity ("Seven Needs") to employees' workplaces, to their job quests, and to their personal lives. I consistently hear about the changes they have made as a result.

I first presented the Seven Needs in my book, *Each Human Spirit: The Transformation of the American Workplace.* I developed this book for my workshop attendees and as a tool for my consulting clients. Soon after the book came out, I started hearing from people who had read it. I heard how it had helped them and how it "hit the nail right on the head." And then I heard that they wanted more—they wanted to go further to understand the spiritual and scientific foundations that make these needs so important.

I want to examine our quest for meaning and break it down (quantizing) into ideas and methodologies that we can use to gain insight into organizational behavior, and to find new meaning in our own relationships to the twenty-first-century workplace. By using my theories and principles, leaders and front-line employees will have an opportunity to improve both their work lives, and the health of their companies. They will gain the courage to be able to make a difference in the rest of their lives and have a more meaningful future.

Thank you for joining me on the journey.

—Art Bobrowitz

Chapter One

Something Is Going On

Every man owes a part of his time and money to the business or industry in which he is engaged. No man has a moral right to withhold his support from an organization that is striving to improve conditions within his sphere.

—Theodore Roosevelt[1]

Something Is Going On

Our universe, workplaces, and individual lives are governed by a series of laws. Two groups in particular—spiritual laws and scientific laws—are my focus. These laws have a profound effect in our places of work and an even more profound effect on the leaders and the employees who work there. Yet, few leaders have studied their principles and looked at some of the similarities and their application to leadership, workplace productivity, and the human spirit. We are losing our skills to listen, communicate, problem solve, and lead. Instead of leading, we are compromising and facilitating our organizations through crisis management.

Significant players in the business world are closing their doors, reneging on their pension obligations, and litigation is taking them into oblivion. The crisis also is taking hold in another arena—the public sector. State, county, and local governments across the country are faced with financial issues such as runaway spending, inflated monetary projections, and unstable budgets. Pension funds have reached critical mass after the market downturn.

Many private sector companies that are scrambling to become part of the new economy and emerging markets also have serious problems finding qualified personnel. Many complaints are valid, because employers are not getting the level of employee they need. Companies are inundated with employee applicants, many of whom lack necessary skills, even with four-year degrees. Schools are passing out inflated grades as if they are multivitamins, and employers are angry about the meaningless grade-point averages that are designed only to boost a student's self-esteem. Businesses are tired of having to pay to teach basic skills.

Front-line employees are losing their jobs and it is being recorded by C-SPAN as if it were something new. Why should this be on the news? Not to make light of the situation, but it has been happening for thousands of years. People used to lose their jobs when marginal organizations failed. One example is the darlings of the day traders, who have crumpled into the economic heap and off the cliff into oblivion. Yes, the business cycle should fluctuate and markets adjust, but big corporations, public sector organizations, and some educational systems are failing, not because of their products or markets, but because of the way they are being run.

Employers—some with thousands of employees—are downsizing with a vengeance to become lean and mean. They are rolling back employee benefit packages in an effort to stay competitive. Both public and private sector organizations have facilitated the mass exodus and will soon be wondering what happened to their knowledge bank.

Many governments on the state, county, and local level will face financial challenges because they, too, do not have the necessary, trained leaders who understand the value of the human spirit or who can make the connection between the science of organizational behavior and the spirit of employee commitment.

Governments also are finding themselves with an aging public work force approaching retirement. Many of these employees were given IOUs in the 70s and 80s instead of pay raises. Those early legislative bodies thought they had pulled a fast one and calmed the angry masses. What many legislatures underestimated is the power and tenacity of the human spirit. If Mr. Rogers were still alive he might say, "Can we say the word *commitment,* boys and girls?"

In the case of the public sector, agency directors and legislators have passed the buck of leadership responsibility. I believe many of these legislators entered their political chambers with attitudes riddled with political arrogance, and that they have spent term after term doing nothing but passing psychological sausage and calling it the will of the people. Public employees are to be seen and not heard. Again, we see the failure of leadership to make the connection between the scientific side of organizational behavior and the human spirit.

I had one twenty-eight-year public employee, close to retirement, tell me that he told a state legislator he was concerned with what the legislature was going to do about his pension fund. The legislator looked at the employee and said, "It's not your money."

Is the money in your 401K yours, or does it belong to the mutual fund that manages it? Does your IRA belong to the person who contributes or to the company where the person is employed?

Many legislators will struggle to stay afloat on a sea of red ink. Some will have to address issues to keep them from collapsing under their own weight. They have created bloated bureaucracies based on overly optimistic economic projections. States must face the reality that, in the twenty-first century, they may no longer be able to fulfill their economic mission. They say they need more money in order to fulfill the will of the people.

If this is true, then let's make an analogy we can understand. I am a pilot who loves to fly. Let's say that money for government is like fuel for an airplane. All I need to do to make the plane fly farther and do more is put in bigger fuel tanks. But, in reality, this doesn't work. More fuel means a heavier airplane. A heavier airplane flies differently, requires more training, and is more costly to operate. So, physically, the change is exponential.

Let's take a look at it from another perspective. You enter into a contract with a builder to build your house. Over the course of the project you notice small things that need to be done, and in the final days, you meet with the builder in your new home. You notice that none of the appliances or fixtures are there. The builder says, "I know we agreed on a figure to build the house, but I don't have any more money left to finish the job. You can accept the house as is or we can look at a different contract."

Your attorney would love this guy. Yet, this is exactly what many public and private sector organizations are doing with their employees and the citizens they serve. They agree on a contract to deliver a product, request services, and then grade the employees on their performances. The employees have lived through and adapted to shifting priorities, poorly-trained leaders, special interest groups, hostile attitudes, and management by committees.

It doesn't matter if the employee is a front-line employee, elected official or corporate executive—many of these people don't have the background to accomplish the task. So, while this is happening, tens of thousands of dedicated employees are leaving private and public service. This has a direct impact on the wellness of the private sector businesses.

Some organizations are starting to recover economically, not because of their attitudes, but because the economy is making a rebound. Even organizations with bad attitudes can make money when times are good. And, like flying an airplane, many of these manmade systems can no longer support their own weight. They, like other bodies in the universe, can collapse on themselves. We look to a spreadsheet for clues to our corporate financial problems.

The decisions leaders are making now will fuel a financial storm cloud. They may very well be dooming a financial generation over numbers they do not understand. We shot Enron in the face for its corporate antics, but public sector budgets are so complex it is almost impossible for legislative bodies to understand, let alone get their arms around, the issues.

We might have seen the symptoms we needed to see much earlier if we had looked at some unlikely partners: science and spirituality. Twenty-first-century leaders need to ask, "What are the scientific implications for organizational change and what might be the impact on the human spirit?" The human spirit is waiting for leadership to make the connection. Twenty-first-century leaders will need to understand the art of balancing the science of organizational behavior with the unlimited potential of the human spirit.

The public sector should not take all the blame. If we'd had the opportunity to walk into the abandoned offices the day after the employees left Global Crossings and ENRON, or if we were to look at the majority of companies that have failed since the bubble burst, I believe the pattern would be quite apparent. You wouldn't notice what is missing, such as the noise in the empty halls, cubicles, and conference rooms, and the smell of coffee, but you would notice the technological efficiency that remains behind. The latest techno-toys shout volumes as to what I believe is one of the major problems and where leadership fails to make the connection.

Technology Supports the Human Spirit

Technology has always had, and always will have, a connection to understanding, but it was never meant to replace the human spirit. Technology *supports* the human spirit. I cannot find what the source was or what institution taught that technology was more important than the interaction of the human spirit.

Employees who are still in the workplace are reporting less career satisfaction. A symptom is the loss of skills to listen and communicate. This is because technology is being given a higher priority than human endeavor and the human spirit. Many organizations and businesses are spending more money on techno-toys than training, and leaders have defaulted to technological advancement for answers rather than choosing to be ethical entrepreneurs.

Employees had the understanding and wisdom to know what was valid and what was not, but in many cases, they were never asked. Technology was never meant to replace the dynamics of communication or the human spirit. It failed management then, and will fail in the future, if not put in perspective.

By the way, if you walk down the halls and see the offices of the public employees who are just as dedicated as the private sector, you would see the same equipment, offices, and environmentally-correct cubicles. Many of those cubicles are now empty. I sometimes feel as if I am on the bridge of the Titanic. We will talk about the Titanic later.

I'll bet that the majority of those empty offices had the following:

- The latest computers, printers, software technology, copy machines, and ergonomically-correct chairs
- Cubicles that reflect the latest non-threatening hues that were supposed to boost self-esteem
- Framed slogans on the wall that were meant to inspire the populace to new levels of productivity
- Employees who, for the most part, were more educated, experienced, and had rather more impressive portfolios than their counterparts say, ten or fifteen years ago.
- Incentive programs and bonuses that made their way down the halls and into the portfolios on a monthly basis.

These companies and agencies had data, information, and the knowledge displayed on every hyperlinked screen, with real-time quotes and the latest in charts and graphs thrown in for good measure. It was pricey, it was flamboyant, it was the latest of technological everything—and it failed. The equipment didn't fail the company. The company used the equipment for something it wasn't designed to do; it used the latest in scientific technology to disconnect the human spirit. Science and the spirit were not connected—they were used against each other and the critical components of understanding and leadership, the spiritual sides of the workplace, probably were in short supply. I also think that many of those employees, who are now gone, did not truly understand what they were looking at every time they turned on their computers.

Many employees were never taught how, or bothered to interpret, what they were seeing, how it related to the larger picture, or understood that something sinister was going on. Their job descriptions didn't require it, so why should they have made the connection? I am sure they were paid adequately and did not have many complaints.

Some questions to ponder:

- How many employees found real meaning in their lives while working for these companies?
- How many had say-so and input into their destinies and were able to make the necessary changes to improve productivity, before these companies closed the doors?
- What was it costing them to stay in an uncomfortable environment?
- How many found their jobs as a continuing factor of quality of life?
- How many were true leaders who led the company with principles, values, and ethics?
- How many worked for a true learning organization? What were they really taught?
- How many believed what they did was really important to the organization?

Since these companies and legislative budgets crashed we have had two, maybe three generations of new desktop, laptop, and hand-held computers. And even more companies and public agencies are about to get flushed. Business websites are beginning to read like the obituary page of the local paper. We are beginning to face the reality that technology does not guarantee productivity in the private or public sector. The latest in electronic gadgetry looks good, fits in a smaller area, and is also tax deductible. But it doesn't guarantee productivity.

The Importance of the Human Spirit

Many organizations, both public and private, are not feeling well. A symptom of this illness is the isolation of front-line employees from management. Yet, we are reporting that the numbers are coming back. The spiritual laws are not even entering the picture. The numbers are coming, but they are in a different form and they may not be accurate.

The problems are the same. We are not teaching our people how to solve them. It is only the next round. Perhaps technology becomes a barrier to the needs for employees to interact with another human being. Fred Alan Wolf states in his book, *The Spiritual Universe, One Physicist's Vision of Spirit, Soul, Matter, and Self*, "Concepts like soul, spirit, self and God, are not fashionable among scientists. When they are used by scientists they are no more than metaphors for a human being's need to deal with the immensity of today's problems."[2]

On the other hand, concepts like universe, electron, quantum, and space-time are no more than powerful myths to the nonscientific mind. It knows they somehow exist, but they have little use in solving the real problems of humanity."[3] If you think those statements might be profound, think of what impact they would have if they were discussed by leaders in an organization. I am saddened that we are missing their purpose.

If I am ill and required to stay in the hospital, my recovery is essential and must also be practical. If all the dot boxes were the new way to communicate, hospital rooms would furnish the latest communications tools—cell phones, iPads, laptops, multifunction scanners, etc. Surely any patient would be glad to have these delivered.

But would their use quickly assist the patient in recovery? No.

When illness strikes, it is the human spirit that is the greatest healing tool—this essential contact with another human being, either by voice, interaction, listening, or just the sight of someone else. In many cases, someone may not be able to talk. The mere presence of another human being has critical healing qualities. This area alone is opening up exciting new fields in the dynamics of what we call healing. It is a scientific and spiritual process. We do this in the hospital and call it care giving. If it is done in the workplace, it's called managing your priorities.

The Role of Technology in the Workplace Today

We have created the illusion that technology is another word for communication. Technology supports communication. Again, it was never meant to replace it. I believe we are asking technology to do something we should be doing ourselves, and that is talking to each other.

We think we are communicating when we trade electronic information. What appears to be communication might actually be groping our way into some realm of productivity. We have relegated communication, problem solving, and leadership to voice mail, E-mail and handheld texting and feel a sense of HR or personal enlightenment. While all this is going on, we confine ourselves to a job description that is defined by an operations manual that challenges competitive thinking, let alone the laws of physics.

We are making decisions that impact the human spirit with the clinical efficiency of a spreadsheet. We pass off projects we don't want to do with a simple click from our workstation so it is automatically given to someone else or sent to a committee. Now we can create the same document or bright idea and receive a phone call and browse the Net while we sit in a latte line at the drive-thru.

We have change for a latte in our left hand and the control of someone else's destiny in the right. We call it success and the will of the people when we kill a project we don't want and send the debris to someone else's electronic calendar. This is not talking or communicating, leading, or problem solving. This is exchanging data and information for the purpose of trying to have less to do than someone else. This is not efficiency. This is substituting science for the sake of self-worth. It is an injustice to legitimate science and demeaning to human spirituality. This is denial and we are paying the price. We have given ourselves pats on the back and group hugs because all our computer programs talk to each other and share information. At the same time we are showing the human spirit the shortest route to the company parking lot.

Ed Oakley and Doug Krug, in their book *Enlightened Leadership: Getting to the Heart of Change*,[4] relate the story of Lester Thurow, the MIT economist, who uses the example of playing games and its relation to the world economy and applies it to today's workplace and organizations. In America, we pride ourselves with the game of football, a slow linear game with predictable actions, limited options, and lots of protection. The rules tell us so. We also have many time-outs and we can replace players at our discretion. This is much like our attitude in American companies and organizations.

The nineteenth century's dominant economic power was England. The English took their time, and their game, cricket, was slow, boring, and a gentlemen's game. They also were very composed. It wasn't thought proper to do it any other way. We look at this way of doing things as something from another era.

Today, many third-world countries are finding their economic feet. The game today is soccer. It is fast-paced action in different areas, has a larger playing field, few time-outs, and fewer replacements. This is an excellent example of what the new economy is like.

America finances its companies with a football mentality while trying to compete in a soccer economy. Thurow has it right: the global playing field is changing. Small groups of skilled laborers in third-world countries are becoming globally competitive. They don't care about EEOC and they care even less about family leave. All they know is they want to compete and produce for someone in another country and will do it with a work ethic that we may find startling. They deserve a chance.

The game plan is changing. Corporate America and many public sector elected bodies are dumping some of their best and brightest through retirements in order to stay lean. Many of those we are letting go are leaders and communicators. We are not letting employees who stay develop their potential to make the necessary changes in the workplace. Employees should have the ability to do open field running. I still subscribe to the philosophy that, if you have to ask permission in your company to be creative, then you are no longer competitive.

Read on and develop a deep understanding for the Seven Needs for Personal Productivity and move on to a heart-and-soul company. They are out there. We have become lethargic with our need to interact with someone of our own species for the sake of problem solving.

The Art of Listening

I used to meet with two close friends monthly until careers and true callings separated us. Both my friends have spiritually wonderful and organizational minds, and I saw my time with them as both prayer and productivity. Each month, one of us was given the task to prepare a couple of questions to ask the others at next month's meeting. The questions were always thought-provoking.

The point is, we had to communicate. We had to shut off our cell phones and other electronics so we could sit for an hour and a half and talk to each other. When one didn't understand a point that was made, we did not proceed until an explanation was given, challenged, and understood. It was a wonderful opportunity to just sit and enjoy professional company and walk away knowing I had just been challenged. And it was good!

Our conversations were business and spirituality. We all saw the deep connection between the two and were advocates for more spiritual identity through ethical business practices. From this relationship came the unthinkable—growth. We have grown in respect for each other and in our knowledge of our respective crafts. We have a deeper understanding about the power of communication and professional courage.

The greatest reward is the wisdom to see the incredible gift we have in the power of communication. Our playing field is big. We have limited rules and we are efficient. This also makes us competitive. All of us had strong backgrounds in public safety and community service. One friend is thinking about returning to school. The other is helping rebuild communities in the eastern European countries. I started my own company, published, and focused on a lifelong commitment to the development of the human spirit.

My wife and I have a cell phone in our car that we use only in an emergency or for a very critical call. We use our driving time to talk to each other. It is also my time for humility. I ask my wife about some issue I want to address in my work or writing. My wife, who is not even aware of what is in the manuscript, has the uncanny ability to listen to my complicated and somewhat obscure thoughts and proceeds to put things in perspective in what I call "easy speak." Her responses are dead on the money and delivered with a sense of brevity. To me, this is frustrating, exciting, and fresh! She has an ability to watch me swim around inside the shark-infested fish bowl of my mind while she sits on the outside developing her answer. The great part is—we communicate—and I wouldn't trade that for the world. Again, the playing field is big and a lot is going on. The rules, however, are clear and concise.

Each evening, my wife and I talk to each other. After dinner, we debrief our days and describe what went on. I enjoy hearing her voice and our conversations are more spiritual than scientific. When we talk, the TV, radios, and cell phones are off. We do not answer the phone when it rings. For over twenty-three years, we have made and kept a commitment to spend a part of each day just being with each other.

The art of listening has become a lost art. It seems we have become so fixated on doing that we have forsaken the most critical process in deciding what needs to be done—and that is listening to our organizations and our employees.

A Closet of Horrors Is Closer Than You Think

I remember that, as a child, I used to laugh at the old television comedy programs. One in particular was a scene where a man walks up to a closet. Unknown to him, the closet contained thousands of ping pong balls, arranged so that, were the door opened, a tsunami of ping pong balls would flood the room. The anticipation was worth it. After the man opened the door, he was up to his armpits in ping pong balls. I thought that was funny.

This scene can be compared to a nightmare where one is overrun by something that is seemingly harmless but becomes overwhelming. The man obviously has no control but a problem has been created—cleaning up something like that is no easy task. Can you imagine picking up thousands of ping pong balls?

Today I look on that scene in a different way. Twenty or thirty years ago, we laughed at the absurdity of that much of one thing entering our lives in such a short period of time. It seemed so impossible. And that is what makes something humorous—taking the possible and making it so absurd that you have to laugh at it. Well, fast forward to today and it isn't so funny anymore. Today, as we wade through the information age, it is quite real as we are bombarded daily with our own closet of horrors. Our worst fears materialize when we open the closet and thousands of information ping pong balls come out of our computers that we have to manage and clean up. The process is semi-scientific, but the reality is deadly to the human spirit. Today we call it "having all the information at hand."

The ping pong balls we face are all neatly sequestered in hard drives, laptops, voice mail, E-mail, texting, spreadsheets, cell phones, databases, balanced portfolios, early flights, E-tickets, lettered titles, career changes, keeping our homes, careers, and one-hundred-thirty-channel TVs, the Internet, satellite radio, the media, traffic, forty-eight buttons on the remote controls, and the variable rate mortgage. The problem really is quite overwhelming. What makes it even worse is, when we open the door, it is no longer a surprise. In fact, it is quite stressful. A person sitting in a cyber café with a laptop and cell phone has more computer power than many Fortune 500 companies had prior to 1970.

Think of what you would do if, each day, you had to manage such a situation. Yet, you do. What makes it even more stressful is, we now become the ones who put the balls back in the closet at the end of each day. Our version of productivity has now got us convinced that, if we put the balls in smaller packages and compartmentalize them and then put them back, we are being more efficient. In reality we are being just the opposite. It is here we have to be careful. What was funny yesterday can become reality today. What once was illusion now has a price tag.

So what has happened? It is at this point that we roll our eyes when someone, usually an adult, tells us that they remember when life was much simpler. It starts with the predictable, "I remember when..." The younger generation does not want to hear stories about a simpler life. Well, guess what? Life, though harder than today, *was* simpler in the past.

I am not making light of the problems of today. We are a much more complex society because we have chosen to make it that way. We have convinced ourselves that we are less efficient without our electronic ideology. We have defaulted the human spirit from a we:drive to c:drive. We have embraced the mythology that being digital is divine and if we can't deal with it, then we can simply create a file folder and store it. Let life's laptop store it for us. You see, the myth becomes reality because this methodology only stores problems if we let it. It does not solve them. And one more ping pong ball gets put in the closet at the end of the day. We are failing to listen to ourselves, let alone others.

How Productivity Can Come Back to Bite Us

How do we sort out what is important and what is not? One could easily say that we simply prioritize what is important. That does help. For years, many productivity programs have advocated governing values, principles-centered decision making, and many other very useful ideas. The principles they teach are timeless and critical. They also work. But they do take discipline and time to form the habit necessary to take them to fruition. But still, we must return to the starting point. How do we know what we need to consider and what is irrelevant? With the vast amount of information we are exposed to, something has to give. Is what we are putting in our computers valid? How do we know? Let's define the problem.

I am becoming convinced that everything communicates. If a butterfly flaps its wings in Florida can it affect a thunderstorm in the Far East? Let me phrase it a different way. Can an employee, failing to make a necessary system change in Florida, affect a production line in the Far East? When I say everything, I mean everything as in the universe type of everything. In other words, everything says something. Not everything, however, listens.

We live in a universe where we must listen if we wish to learn. I hope we can use the tools of technology to help us listen and discover the spiritual make-up of the universe. It will be these discoveries that will lead to a level of communication never before reached. Are you listening, leaders? We must cross the boundaries and use technology for our philosophical and theological questions and principles to see the parallels in the grand universe and the behavior of the human spirit. The universe is talking to us and I cannot believe that it is strictly in the language of science.

Right now, many of the demands of business are getting the focus of the new technology. This is the ultimate challenge to the leaders of the world. We need to see the relationship between what the universe is saying and see the parallels in the workplace and efforts of the human spirit. Communication then becomes an integral part of our faith and quest for truth. It is also critical to observation and experience. Finding the truth in our lives and our work is the challenge. Having faith in the process can be even more of a challenge.

The ideal situation would be for relationships to appear to have seamless associations. I believe the ties are there but it is up to us to discover them. If this is true then truth, productivity, science, and faith are not random occurrences but tangible entities wrapped in the garment of our life experiences. When it comes to the front-line employees it is called productivity. Unfortunately, they are still being separated by our professional biases. It is there for us to see if we choose to do so.

Saint Thomas Aquinas focused on this issue that it is seen with our free will and only if we choose to see. Truth then becomes a choice. If we choose to find truth in our lives then communicating those principles become an ethical responsibility. I believe that is called leadership. I have often heard someone say about a leader, "They told me the truth. They did not pull any punches." The irony, of course, is when we deal with the everyday life issues. We are told to seek compromise or consensus and to be careful not to offend. Is the conclusion we reach the truth or is it a PC platitude?

And then comes the ultimate time of truth, when communication is the most important concept in the world and we are in a doctor's office saying, "Tell me the truth, Doc." It is as if we must accept anything *but* the truth in our lives—yet, when we are in our last days, truth becomes the true priority.

Mickey Connolly and Richard Rianoshek, in their book *The Communication Catalyst: the Fast (but Not Stupid) Track to Value for Customers, Investors, and Employees,*[5] relate the following:

- We live and work in a web of conversations.
- Those conversations affect perceptions, priorities, and actions.
- For most leaders, conversational effect is accidental and slows achievement. (Remember observation and experience?)

- It is possible to converse by design and accelerate achievement. (This is why I believe the universe was designed—so that we, as humans, can achieve.)

These authors make a timeless connection about how leaders have major difficulties in the area of communication and almost stumble into achievement. They go on to say that: "...conversational skill is particularly important whenever we need to coordinate the efforts of different people to produce value." I find the word *value* important. Their statements make quite clear the connection between achievement, value, leadership, and communication, and most importantly, the goal of truth. Now I am also getting a little concerned. I want leaders to balance leadership, science, and spirituality.

These authors say that too many leaders don't even communicate. I half-suspected that principle, and that is why I will address what I feel is a HUGE disconnection in our leadership and work environments. For a clue, think of the word *technical*. What I believe is happening is that leaders are observing, but they are not taking themselves or their employees into the area of experience. We might be depriving our employees of the experience and discovery of truth.

If I am an observer, and witness events that have a profound change and sense of meaning, does that qualify as truth? Does one have to perform an overt act in order to experience a truthful event? Can I observe one who is wiser than I, and learn? Does this make truth a fact? Or is truth what I have learned from the fact? I believe we could go deeper and say that truth is one's sense of honesty about a condition or experience. Truth is something we must own. Ownership requires responsibility.

If we look at the word *honesty* we could say that truth has an implication of right and wrong. If this is true then, to the leader, the theological, philosophical, and ethical implications could be profound. Truth can give us spiritual comfort. Truth is direction. We find rest in our spiritual beliefs but truth can give us angst in what we must do with the knowledge we now have. I believe this is exactly what Moses went through with the Ten Commandments. His faith in God gave him strength and peace. His mission and what he had to do with those Commandments was the hard part. And truth gives us a sense of direction when we have a commitment to making ethical decisions. This means the knowledge of right and wrong. If a leader has to struggle with these issues, you have a challenge ahead of you.

Technology as a Tool

Employees are bombarded with tremendous amounts of data and information. We cannot turn around without having vast sums of data penetrating our very being. What part of that is truth? Fifteen years ago we left the office and got away from the phones and work. Today, we share more data and information with other people than ever before. Those numbers will more than double in the next seven to ten years. I also believe we are communicating less. Truth is becoming more elusive.

Today, the office walls are transparent as we leave at the end of the day with our cell phones with anytime minutes, laptops, and other techno toys. The lines between personal and professional are blurred. We call that productivity.

Our technology does give us real-time creativity. I am not convinced, however, that the new age is helping us make the right decisions. As we combine multiple sources of data and information, we make decisions by consensus. We have convinced ourselves that, if it works with data and information, why not do it with our companies and organizations?

Look how wonderful it is to meet and exchange data and information—but try to come up with an answer where nobody is offended. We end up walking out of the room having reached no conclusion.

If we do the same thing with a company, this could provide the same sense of bonding and accomplishment. We have now approached the altar of the god where merging companies (like a bad marriage) could give us even greater rewards. Not only does it *not* reward us but it costs us more in the long run to find the solution.

And that is exactly what the business sector has done. When a company has found itself in a communications void, it has found another company to get it out of its rut. The two companies have then merged their data, information, and knowledge bases because two companies can do it better than one. The expectations were and are there.

Some have found the results surprising, even though understanding and wisdom may never have entered the picture. What we are finding is that data, information, and knowledge are not enough—companies who merge also should have understanding, wisdom, and truth. This is supported by the research of Mickey Connolly and Richard Rianoshek, who found that companies that merged have a different tale to tell. They found that:

- 60 percent of merged companies have less net value five years after the merger than before.
- 30 percent have no increase in value.
- 10 percent met or exceeded their goals.[6]

"Toto, we're not in Kansas anymore."

If the research of Connolly and Rianoshek is correct, I believe the frontline employee is vulnerable to the same scenario. At what point are you no longer productive? Where is the line where all the new sources of data and information no longer provide the "edge" that is so necessary to compete in the business world? Where is the point of diminished return? Might there be a point where even training no longer provides a return for both the employee and the organization?

I wonder what employees would say if I asked them how much of what they do each day is adding meaning to their lives, the life of the company they serve, and how much of what they deal with is actually the truth. Does all the new technology really enhance their ability to be effective leaders in their lives and the workplace?

I do not have data but will speculate. I would bet that the majority of companies that burst under the economic bubble had technological hardware that was no more than one year old. I would bet that the majority were connected to some type of electronic communications system for productivity enhancement. I would also bet that, when the majority of them heard that their company was going down the tubes, many were not surprised. I wonder if it has changed today.

It is funny how communication between people increases in the bad times. Why isn't it so prevalent during the good? The competitive edge is an internal attitude, not an external environment of zeros and ones. It is our personal commitment to observation and experience. The competitive edge is sharpened by communication with other people and not by an in-house software program.

Leadership, through true scientific and spiritual communication, is a vehicle by which we can find meaning in our lives. I do believe that the line between science and spirituality is starting to soften. Paul Davies, in his book *God and the New Physics,* begins to state the case. "Indeed the rise of the new physics has been accompanied by a tremendous growth of interest concerning the deeper philosophical implications of science." [7] We communicate to relate our life experiences to one another. Communication is both a scientific process and spiritual event. It is not to be taken lightly.

And yet, we seem to be defaulting its magnificent opportunity. We communicate to give others hope so they have purpose in their own lives. And we communicate to voice and develop our attitude toward those things in life that cause us suffering. Communication helps us cope.

Effective corporate communication is not a wired or wireless technological infrastructure. It is the dedicated task of senior management and their staff to verbally communicate the goals of the organization and the state of their company and to lead the employees into action. What do they value and do they value truth? Communication is the voice of truth.

File servers and data storage units are not communication nor are they truth. Cell phones are not truth. Stock quotations are not truth and neither is employee of the month or a quote hanging on the wall on the way to the unisex restroom. Truth is the value-based verbal communication by company leadership to the ongoing health of their company and the people they employ. Truth is an honest conversation between people for the purpose of understanding and wisdom. It is more than data, information, and knowledge. It is the relationship with both scientific and the spiritual needs of employees, understanding someone else's point of view and using wisdom to find a better way. Truth is helping someone:

- Find meaning in his life
- Create the environment for communication
- Make the investment in themselves and be willing to pay the price
- Develop his quality of life
- Find meaningful relationships
- Learn and know that he is important.

So What Do We Do?

I want to look at the needs of employees, scientific applications, a decision-making model, and leadership styles that make a difference. I hope you seek and question further after you read this book. Leadership is a balance. We must seek assistance and guidance from our partners. I believe science and spirituality have much to teach us in a workplace that truly wants to learn. Leaders must have the courage to seek and understand their relationship. The new leaders must seek the application of both science and spirituality and of organizational productivity. Yes, the challenge will be greatest in our work environments. So now I offer you: a leadership observation, The Seven Needs for Personal Productivity: a Decision-Making Model, to help you implement those needs; a Leadership Triangle for guidance; and five positive leadership behaviors as a compass needle.

Am I against the electronic age and all that is going on? No. Am I concerned with how technology is being used by some leaders and managers? Yes, I question when leadership decisions are made by people who use electronic technology instead of listening and communicating. Managers are defaulting to E-cleansing of projects and messages and sadly, responsibility. I use my two computers and cell phone, and value what they can do and their ability to manage information. I will need them to succeed; they have purpose and merit. They should, however, never be used as substitutes.

The technology age has brought tremendous changes in our lives, and the data and information they give us is necessary. My concern is that we are saving more data and information than we really need, as though it were wealth. By doing this, we are limiting our playing field and are bound up with rules. Data, information, and knowledge must be managed and put in perspective; we are so inundated by data and information that they are being confused with understanding and wisdom.

I see people in leadership positions in the public and private sector who are making profound decisions that impact thousands of lives. They are doing it with incorrect numbers generated from high-tech tools, and their decisions are disasters.

We are in the age of hyper-technology. I fear we are also turning toward hyper-leadership. This is not a specific behavior but a general tendency to make impulsive decisions. This might be called management by malaise-of-the-moment. In today's professional climate, it is not surprising to make snap decisions simply because we are overwhelmed by the amount of data and information given to us.

Unfortunately, because we also are in the age of hyper-decisions, we need technology to understand and be productive. We need to manage globally but we also need to communicate and listen locally. While technology is critical to all we are as a culture and our responsibility to others in the world, it still needs to be put in perspective. I am afraid that leaders are letting technology manage us and they are not managing technology.

Thurow's soccer analogy is making more sense. It is dependent on players being responsible on different parts of the field. Their communication is constant and their roles varied. I default to the term message/messenger. Emerging nations will not wait for us. They have stood on the sidelines for decades trying to understand the rules of our game. They are fast on the track of finding a better way.

Communicating, decision making, and leading face-to-face need data, information, and knowledge. Understanding and wisdom means taking a much larger step toward understanding the other person or persons and doing so with our principles, values, and ethics. It is long-term responsibility. The understanding of right and wrong comes from the interaction of human beings, not from a formatted hard drive with an accumulation of data and information, or a back-up support system in IT, or a bookshelf full of policy manuals.

Technology has become a bureaucratic buffer zone for leadership responsibility. We are defaulting our leadership and communication styles to the personal computer and not to the personal relationship. We are not connecting the science of technology with the theology of the human spirit.

Just ask yourself the following questions:

- With all the new technology available to you, are you able to manage data and information more effectively today than ten years ago? Is the data and information really needed?
- If you are in a leadership position, are your employees given the opportunity, resources, and your ear in order to improve their jobs and your organization?

- Are you more content in your career with communication than you were ten years ago?
- Has your communication improved throughout your entire organization?
- If you have the latest in electronic information management, why would it not work?
- What is standing in your way?
- What are the human or electronic barriers?
- What change is needed in your organization that you are reluctant to discuss? Why?

We are a universe of similarities and mutual laws. It is time for leaders and educators to apply the beauty of these principles to organizational behavior and the workplace. Our faith in ourselves and the science of discovery are critical to the development of the human spirit. Let us look at some of the universal messages that can help the spirituality and science of leadership.

Chapter Two

On Listening to the Call of Leadership

"We must be the change we wish to see."
—M. K. Gandhi[1]

Leadership, Spirituality, and the Universe

If I ask someone to describe the term *leadership*, I do not believe I will get the same answer on any two occasions. I am coming to believe that a true definition of leadership is elusive. I could give a basic definition and say leadership is getting an idea, thought, or group of people from point A to point B with the minimum amount of weeping and gnashing of teeth.

I would like to explore a different perspective. Some say leadership is philosophy, ethical principles, a specific attitude, or a behavior. I believe that leadership has a kindred spirit with an unlikely ally; it has fundamental principles and related behaviors that have both deep spiritual and scientific roots. I do not believe they should be separated and twenty-first-century leaders need to pay attention.

I offer the following thoughts and observations from some unlikely sources. My interest was piqued when I started to see similarities between the spiritual beliefs of leaders and the laws covering some of the sciences. Religion and science have butted heads since the beginning of history and they still do. The thought of theology and human resources (HR) is oil and water to some. It is not the disciplines, but the leaders, that are at odds.

This is starting to change for some. I use the word *some* for a reason. Many thinkers stick to their respective disciplines with clinical efficiency. I am one of those who believe that it is time to look at the similarities and not the differences. If I read a poem, I gain insight in my own way, but every poem can be interpreted differently. Inspiration for those poems may be as varied as a palette of colors. It is time we think of religion, science, and the human spirit in a similar way. The human spirit is the vehicle that makes it happen.

I am not a scientist, nor am I a theologian—I am an observer. I look at the world, ask questions, and listen to what the world is asking of me. Many times that happens in the middle of the night. Just ask my wife.

I am intrigued when I can use an object, process, or condition in a new and creative way. One area in particular has caught my interest—the relationships between leadership, human behavior, some of the principles relating to physics and, an unlikely ally, subatomic particles.

Before your eyes glaze over, consider the following information. I, too, was raised in the minefields of the separation of theology and science. Never would I have put the two together—it was unthinkable. The two schools were never considered to complement each other.

Consider this: if leadership is a human condition, and we are physical and spiritual beings, then I believe they cannot be separated. No HR budget in the world has the time or resources to make a policy creating the separation. Best of all, I challenge you to enforce it. I believe we are doing ourselves a huge disservice if we continue the separation.

One only has to look at the great plethora of spiritual writings of the world and see the presence of natural laws studied by man. I would like to focus on the laws of quantum theory, which one might consider the new kid on the block, if you call the last century "new."

Quantum Physics and the Quality of Leadership

Up to the beginning of the last century, science dealt with the smallest particle known: the atom. One of the contributors was Albert Einstein, a twenty-six-year-old scientist working in a patent office, who challenged all that the scientific world had come to embrace. This led to the next level of scientific thought, called quantum theory.

Einstein not only challenged Newton's idea of the universe; he saw that same universe as a unique relationship where substances can act in different ways. Einstein, more reluctantly than others, recognized the essential dualism in nature, the coexistence of what scientists called particles and waves. He struggled to resolve his issues.

Many in the scientific community kicked and screamed. But other thinkers, such as Werner Heisenberg, Max Planck, and Neils Bohr, saw it differently and said we must go to the next level or, rather, down to the next level. In other words, our world got a lot smaller. Einstein peeked into the room of quantum theory; Heisenberg, Planck, and Bohr kicked open the door. Think of them as the Wilbur and Orville Wright of quantum mechanics.

Many agree that both Newtonian physics and quantum theory do not fully explain the universe. For example, when traditional laws of Newtonian physics are applied to subatomic particles, you do not always get the same result. That caused much angst in the scientific community.

A crash course in quantum theory would be impossible here. What I would like to relate are the conditions that I believe are key to my thinking. As I said earlier, I believe the principles that drive leadership behavior and the human spirit are some of the same principles that relate to spiritual teachings and the sciences, in particular, the behavior of subatomic particles. I wish to focus on two conditions in quantum theory, the actions of particles and waves.

Look at it this way. Let's call a particle a rock. A wave is created when that rock is dropped into a body of water, such as a pond or a lake. In the quantum world, this relationship is what scientists call "Wave-Particle Duality."

Scientists found out that when the laws of Newtonian physics were applied to subatomic particles, these particles did not respond in the same way. Something else was going on. But don't let this scare you.

Again, in the quantum world strange things start to happen in the realm of subatomic particles—the bottom line is, waves can act like particles and particles can act like waves. This means that, under certain conditions, particles adapt. We don't truly understand why this happens, but it does. Keep this behavior in mind throughout the rest of the book. It is critical that you focus on the word *adapt.* Picture it this way. A rock that is dropped in a body of water creates waves. The waves move. They are motion; nothing is carried.

Particles, on the other hand, have mass. Let's say that the Wright Brothers' airplane was a large boulder dropped into the lake of the Industrial Revolution and traditional thought at the turn of the last century. Their first flight caused a ripple effect of a new wave of thinking. The particle took another route but a by-product was the wave (the idea). In other words, the principles of waves and particles are present when we create a new idea and watch its adaptation to the world.

This duality does not support traditional scientific or Newtonian science. The Wright Brothers' thinking did not support the traditional industrial thought of the day. Even Einstein's theory of relativity does not necessarily agree with laws pertaining to subatomic particles.

So what does this have to do with leadership, our spiritual teachings, and organizational behavior? I believe quantum theory provides us with a glimpse into the governing principles of the spirituality of leadership and human behavior. Science is the mind and body, and theology is the heart and soul. I believe they are the essence of the universe and total leadership. Both principles have application to the human spirit and its scientific partners. The Industrial Revolution gave us new insight and it, too, has a seat at the table.

The Industrial Revolution

The Industrial Revolution and the great economic development at the turn of the twentieth century were direct products of Newtonian physics. Science gave us laws, actions, numbers, and formulas. It told us that time and energy will give a direct result. Repeat the process and you get the same result.

Leadership also was easy. It was direct, rigid, manageable, and gave predictable results. I think some leaders today still wish it were that easy. Have two thousand workers perform a process in a certain way, and any product can be mass-produced. Out of this thinking came Henry Ford, whose assembly line put a lot of Model T Fords in private driveways. It was the birth of the time/motion study, specific job descriptions, mass production, and that heart-stopping concept called outcome-based management.

This way of thinking held up for the majority of the last century. It works as long as the employee doing the work does what he or she is told, does not think too much, and performs the exact duties of the job description and what the system demands, day in and day out. Keeping one's mouth shut, and doing what one was told, doesn't hurt either.

The ideal situation would be to do so without any mistakes. When mistakes were made, new policies, rules, and regulations were introduced to stabilize the system. This was high modernism at its best. But what they were really doing was making the system worse, kind of like throwing new regulatory rocks in the waters of the workplace and causing more waves. Don't laugh—we are still doing it today.

This was Frederick Taylor at his best. Taylor was an American engineer and efficiency expert who conducted experiments around the late 1800s to early 1900s to determine the maximum possible efficiency of machines and people.[2] Taylor assumed one principle—that people will respond to a rule or regulation and their response will be the same in each condition. Taylor's theories would have worked if it weren't for one problem—people think, machines don't.

Let's go back to Newton. As long as we applied Newtonian principles and the traditional way of scientific thinking, we got predictable results. The organizational theory of the time espoused that the rules for the regulation of a process or desired result were the same for man and machine. It did not matter what internal processes were applied; the only thing that mattered was the desired, external result. The employee was simply a piece of machinery.

At the time, it was thought that it was better to make more precise machines and get less input from the human side. The worker was a component of a larger system, and the same sets of rules were applied to all. If the person or part did not respond, you changed the person or part until you got the desired result. 1 + 1= 2. Do it every day and the results were the same. Well, almost.

Traditional Management and Moses

Let's bring in someone else who can help me explain—Moses. I believe he had a lot in common with quantum theory thinkers such as Heisenberg, Bohr, Planck, and Einstein.

Following Newtonian physics, traditional management stresses that the real world is mechanical and consists of natural laws. Leaders must lead. They were not hired to motivate the employees; they were there to ensure that man and machine made as few mistakes as possible. If mistakes were made, you didn't change the machines, you changed the operator. It was like an equation: if you didn't like the number to the right of the equal sign, you changed one of the numbers on the left.

Now, if you deviate from this principle, you are in trouble. The law then becomes the tool of control. Most organizations only understand the movement of mass within its existing structure or form. For example, raw materials arrive at a plant and products are manufactured, then shipped from the loading dock.

So, according to Newton and Taylor, the manager is the *message* of the system, and the employee or follower only works according to this law. It is the traditional policy and procedure handbook. It is consistent, it is repetitive, and it has always worked, until now.

OK, where does Moses come in? Stay with me here.

Let us go back to the rules we observed earlier. In quantum

mechanics, the law adapts to the situation. Adaptive change may be needed to accomplish the task and afterward, the law might go back to its original state. Let us look at the duality model and apply it to something many live with each day—our spiritual beliefs.

I found some intriguing parallels when I took some of the principles of quantum mechanics and leadership principles and applied them to Judeo-Christian teachings and my spiritual values. What makes the quantum mechanics duality model so interesting is that, when applied to Judeo-Christian teachings, it adds not only meaning, but clarification.

Let us take the duality model and apply it to the Old Testament, Moses, and his experience. First we have to clarify the terms we will use. Let's take the term *message/particle* and apply it to Moses' job description.

Moses led the Chosen People from Egypt. He was both the messenger and the message (wave/particle.) In other words, his physical presence (particle) was critical but he was also the messenger (wave) when he spoke to his people and delivered both inspiration and words of encouragement; he also was a teacher. He then adapted to the role of messenger (wave).

Moses' role required him to become adaptive when he was given the Ten Commandments. Moses didn't know it, but God took him outside his job description and his comfort zone. His performance evaluation on the mountain when he got the Ten Commandments didn't go so well. Here is where Moses got into trouble. What Moses did next changed the course of not only his people and history, but his behavior also had an impact in the workplace. I believe Frederick Taylor would have been uncomfortable with Moses as a boss.

Scripture tells us God gave Moses (the message, particle) the Ten Commandments. When he saw his people worshiping false gods and idols, he did what any CEO would have done—he took action. (Frederick Taylor would have been thrilled at this point.) Moses reorganized the company, threw away the operations manual (message) by destroying the tablets with the Ten Commandments on them, and chastised the rank and file.

What Moses did not understand was the potential of being not only the message (particle) but also the messenger itself (wave). He did not understand the need to be adaptive. Moses was quite a CEO, but he doubted his role and confused being messenger with the message. To succeed, he needed to see that his new role was to lead, yet the message from God was also needed to inspire his people.

Now Moses was in real trouble. After destroying the policies, rules, and procedures for the chosen people, he ended up wandering around the desert. You would, too, if you had no direction. We will see later on how the desert experience has profound similarities with a principle developed by a botanist who looked through a microscope in the early 1800s, and with how excited Albert Einstein became at the turn of the last century when he looked at the same information in a different way.

I believe understanding this principle is critical today for any leader. Someone else now comes into the picture.

John the Baptist, Leadership, and Quantum Theory

Let's take a look at another relationship, this time in the New Testament. Scripture tells us about the important events in the life of John the Baptist, who baptized Jesus. From his life and teachings come fundamental beliefs that are still present in twenty-first-century Christianity.

What could possibly be the relationship between John the Baptist, Moses, Jesus' baptism, quantum theory, and twenty-first-century leadership?

John the Baptist baptized penitents in water as a symbol of the baptism of the Holy Spirit that was to come. According to the Bible, in Mark 1:9–11, John baptized Jesus at the beginning of his public ministry.[3] With the baptism of Jesus, John's ministry and work was accomplished, and his ministry came to a close soon afterward. Although it is uncertain that Jesus himself performed baptisms, the risen Christ commanded his disciples to preach to and baptize the nations as the sign of God's coming rule. Thus, from the outset, baptism became the Christian rite of initiation.[4]

And here is the connection. Remember how I used the symbol of a rock (particle) thrown into a lake and a wave was created? In the Scriptures and in the time of John the Baptist and even in some of today's religions, a person enters the water for baptism. A human being (particle) enters the water and as they submerge, waves emanate from this action. The motion of the water moves out in all directions, just as one's faith experience and ministry will radiate from a person during his walk in faith. In science, a new law or way of thinking has the same effect. A scientist (particle) brings in a new body of knowledge (wave) and the effects are felt on the shore of new knowledge.

Leadership, the Human Spirit, and the Waves of Change

In leadership, new managers and CEOs enter the pool of the organizational environment. Their presence (particle) is perceived in many different ways. Their impact on the pool of existing thinking and practices can have a ripple effect, or it can be a virtual tsunami of organizational change. This wave of new ideas is the result of their actions and plans for the future.

So we begin to see that the principles of organizational behavior and leadership are deeply rooted in the actions of Moses and John the Baptist. The Christian rite of baptism—a rite of passage—creates a new person when baptized. The symbolic immersion into the waters and the reemergence create a new person filled with the spirit of new hope, life, and dedication to God. The newly baptized are ministers of change.

I believe that what Albert Einstein was struggling to prove scientifically and mathematically at the turn of the century, John the Baptist was doing nineteen hundred years ago. I do not mean to make these statements for the purpose of "he did it first." What I am saying is, certain patterns and principles cross all forms of teaching and knowledge. What scientists are doing with particles, John the Baptist was doing with people. He took people (particles), submerged them in the symbolic waters of change, and the newly baptized entered the world with a new spiritual (wave) commitment. The message of baptism becomes the messenger of faith in the community.

The newly baptized then taught and lived the responsibility of Christian commitment. They lived the teachings of Scripture and also suffered the reactions of the communities and countries. Their fate was more severe. Pardon the pun, but they made waves that are still touching the shores of world and the culture of the workplace.

Each time we enter our workplace, we are immersing ourselves into the waters of creativity, both spiritual and scientific. We become the daily particle that collectively responds to our fellow employees and produces waves of change. Our ideas spread in all directions. We become the ultimate body of the universe. We can adapt, think, and most importantly, we can have faith in a better way. The human spirit cannot be separated from the mind and body. The human spirit is the repository for our principles, values, and ethics. They are the waves that emanate from our actions.

Those waves carry our commitment to produce change. And change is the birth of something new. When the wave reemerges, it washes up against new people (particles) with different and, hopefully, better ideas. And the cycle then continues.

We cannot separate our spirituality and leadership responsibilities. Nor can any organization expect, legislate, or litigate this universal condition. Each time we enter our homes, offices, or other buildings, it is as if we are stepping back in time and fulfilling our theological teachings and heritage.

The bar mitzvah and bat mitzvah also reflect the emergence of a person into adulthood. This emergence carries with it the new person and the responsibility for our actions and obligations to each other. It is the ultimate form of leadership training; it is a calling into a new life. It is an attitude toward our spirituality, leadership, and our daily journey into productivity.

Leadership can take many forms. I would like to focus on leadership in our own lives. When we begin to understand our spiritual connectedness, we begin to see how the Seven Needs for Personal Productivity (Seven Needs) in the following chapters can help us. We begin to see the importance of finding meaning in our lives and how say-so and input are critical. This means finding our voice and better communication.

We also look for what we need to sustain us, such as a fair wage. We search for a quality of life that may be spiritual, sociological, or both. Leadership also becomes an issue. We seek those who have a vision of what is right and just. Our principles, values, and ethics direct us there. As we progress, we see that we also find ourselves in need of learning. Growth is more than a physiological phenomenon.

We also know that what we say has value and that what we do is important and a contribution to the whole. If we understand the Seven Needs and know when we must be the message or the messenger, new patterns begin to emerge in our lives. It is a truly humbling process. I would like to relate a personal experience that describes the message and the messenger. I was oblivious to the principles at the time, but looking back on it today, the message was quite clear.

A Personal Experience about Message and Messenger

In 1967, I was in the United States Air Force and stationed in Alaska. I had recently been promoted to Sergeant and was assigned to flight line duties. Shortly thereafter, my supervisor assigned me to a project on the flight line and told me I would be responsible for seven people.

The flight line can be a very tense and sometimes dangerous environment. I was soon to learn the difference between the message and the messenger, but never understood its true meaning for many years. During one of our assignments, two of the airmen were working on a project and they asked for my help. All seven of the men were in the area so I didn't see anything wrong with lending a hand to the two airmen.

What happened next was a lesson in life. By my consenting to help the two airmen, I became the messenger of assistance. What I did not realize was that the time it would take to help the two people was more than I had anticipated. In doing so, I also sent a message to the other airmen.

It was about that time that my supervisor drove up. He called me aside and proceeded to verbally enlighten me as only can be done in the military. He asked me if I was able to see what I had done. I related that I was helping two of the people with a task. He then told me that he commended me for my dedication, but that in doing so, I was focusing all my attention on the two airmen and then could no longer focus on the other five I was also responsible for.

"You are responsible for the safety of seven men in a potentially dangerous area. If you focus on two, the other five are no longer getting your attention. You are sending them a message. What is it?"

I realized that, as a supervisor, I was responsible for everyone and everything they did, including their safety on a very active flight line. I now look back on it and realize I wanted to be a message of assistance. It took many years to see that my behavior was a messenger to the other people in my charge. I wanted to be a messenger when the situation called for me to be the message, one where my men needed to know that I was taking care of them in a potentially hazardous environment by looking out for them. I didn't look at it as a new way of thinking. No, I am not like Moses but, on that day, I learned something new. I never forgot the lesson.

The paradox again arises because the theory of wave-particle duality is relatively new. One hundred years is pretty new. The only reason it happened is because a small group of scientists chose to take traditional scientific thinking and look at it in a new way. I believe both the Old and New Testaments have been teaching the principles of quantum mechanics, traditional laws of physics, and wave/particle duality for thousands of years.

To me, wave/particle duality is a fundamental part of theological, sociological, and philosophical teachings. One could argue that wave/particle duality has deeper and earlier roots in theological principles before its adaptation to quantum theory. It is critical to business, management and, in particular, our spiritual selves. The principles of effective leadership are spiritual events. We are finally getting around to the spiritual teaching and the quantum principles that describe them.

In the New Testament, Jesus' suffering is beyond comprehension—far beyond the agony that could be experienced by mere mortals. At his crucifixion, he cried to his father, "Father, why have you forsaken me?" I often wonder if Jesus, the man, thought He had failed as the message...but what a powerful messenger! I wonder if, during his crucifixion, He thought He had failed at both when He had failed at neither. His human experience and spiritual message are still making waves! This relates how a leader must assume the role as messenger but situations will arise when she must also be the message. It is the human side of waves and particles. One is *what* we are, and the other is *why* we are.

Enter Saint Thomas Aquinas and Free Will

Saint Thomas Aquinas made an important step with his timeless contribution, *Summa Theologica*.[5] Thomas Aquinas thought of a system that was intellectually consistent, uniting the Bible and Aristotle (i.e., the affirmation of natural reality as a whole including the body and the mind[6]). He said that the free will of man was a critical component.

You will see later why Wilbur and Orville Wright would have really liked him. What Aquinas said next would not be consistent with some present day thinkers. He said that free will is indifferent to good and evil and is a choice, therefore, it is impossible for free will to be a habit—it is a power. Aquinas was a philosopher whose thoughts attracted a lot of attention.

It is interesting when we look at the Greek language for an interpretation of the word *philosopher.* The word *philosophy* (*philosophia* from *philein,* to love, and *sophia,* wisdom) means the love of wisdom. Once again, I think we must look to the term *leadership* in the same sense. True leaders love something we do not know. In its proper acceptation, *philosophy* does not mean the aggregate of the human sciences, but "the general science of things in the universe by their ultimate determinations and reasons," or again, "the intimate knowledge of the causes and reasons of things, the profound knowledge of the universal order."[7]

I believe a true leader must have kindred feelings rooted in philosophy. *A leader must be a lover of reason, order, and wisdom.* I believe someone with that type of thinking is someone who would love the science of Thomas Aquinas, who saw the relationship between philosophy and theology. Aquinas understood that the two couldn't be separated when it comes to man. Just for laughs, ask some of your friends who are in leadership positions how much of an influence Thomas Aquinas had on their careers. We are spiritual beings whether or not we are leading our own lives or the lives of others. Our adaptation and free will cannot be suppressed. Frederick Taylor would have fits.

Again, we have another example of wave/particle. I can't help but believe that some of the fundamental thinking of Thomas Aquinas flew that special day with the Wright Brothers, only they didn't know it.

We have the power to change but we must be open to it. Our actions (free will) in the workplace are choices that have results. Those results take the form of a degree of power. For example, we exercise choice to seek a position we desire. From that position we establish and implement our agenda. What we choose to produce, learn, acquire, conserve, or steward is our legacy. This is leadership in our lives.

Thomas Aquinas laid the foundation for Gandhi, you, and me. Gandhi stated, "We must be the change we wish to see." As Aquinas states, free will is indifferent to good and evil. However, we still are accountable. If we have a fundamental grounding in principles, values, and ethics, our decisions will reflect that teaching. We have now exercised leadership in our lives.

Free Will and Freedom

The responsibility of free will carries the dual edge that evil can be just as strong a product. We have relegated the evil side of leadership to a forum of different applications and agendas. This "stamping" of applications causes me concern. We must not overlook the application of the evil side of free will.

I do not think there is any better example in our recent history than Adolph Hitler. The record books speak for themselves. It is here that I wish to look at its business application. The power of evil in a business environment will not make the evening news or talk show circuit. This minimizing is just as destructive as any international or political exposé.

Evil is not equal. Its purpose is the destruction and elimination of the human spirit. The key to the freedom of free will is accountability. And true accountability is a form of restriction. This paradox moves us forward. Freedom is not a form of expression. Pure freedom is a true form of restriction.

Voltaire said, "If God did not exist then everything would be allowed."[8] Freedom is not the right to do anything we want. It is the obligation on our part to do it with wisdom but also be accountable for our actions. It means we have the opportunity to discover.

Ask any great scientist or theologian: one word—freedom—is at the heart and soul of what they do. They have the opportunity to discover. Freedom is not a manmade law that is written in a political document. Freedom is a fundamental condition of the human spirit. That is why freedom is critical to being a true leader. The discipline of freedom is also critical to productivity.

Business/Management/Spirituality

(Apostle: Disciple, Follower, Missionary, Messenger)

When I was in the final publication stages of my first book, *Each Human Spirit,* my editor, Kristi Negri, asked me how I wanted my book referenced in the Library of Congress. It was a question that I had not thought about. She gave me a suggestion that I later found both insightful and profound: she suggested I reference it under business/management/spirituality. It seemed like the right thing to do.

I now look at those elements as inseparable. I believe that the three most important words in *Each Human Spirit* are on the bottom of the back cover—business, management, spirituality. Those three inseparable words link the entire concept of leadership, theology, science, and organizational behavior. I believe they will be the three most critical elements in the twenty-first-century workplace. Each of the three words has its own meaning, but takes on a greater sense of purpose when linked with the others. I address this issue later on in the area dealing with *quality of life* in the Seven Needs for Personal Productivity.

The Role of the Leader

I love this quote from the book of Wisdom 9:3: "To govern the world in holiness and justice, and to render judgment in integrity of heart."[9]

I believe the leader must know when he must be the carrier of the message (wave) and, at times, when his actions must become the message (particle). He must be adaptive and do so with integrity of heart. I believe that true productivity and leadership is business, management, and spiritual in nature. It is a clear application of free will and integrity of heart.

This lays the foundation for twenty-first-century quantum careers. It is the conscious effort on our part as leaders to seek a better way and, more importantly, improve the process to do it. Unfortunately this could be good or evil.

The essence of leadership is in knowing that something needs to be done; the leader must be the message and/or messenger. Add to this the importance of the word *character* and ethics becomes important. I choose to focus on the good application of free will. A problem arises when the manager defaults to the message when the task may require a messenger.

Another word for *message* could be job description or possible team application. A leader may be assigned to a position with a designated job description. If he sets the team responsibilities and stops there, he is sending the message, "I am in charge and you will do as I say." This could be a mixed message. Is the team there to act as a team or should they simply do what the manager says? This is no longer a team; it is a committee tasked with validation. This could have been a stable working environment or, as reflected in what happened in the 1900s, it could also be a disaster.

In other words, the team's role may be to validate what management has already concluded. The messenger made it clear. In my personal beliefs, any team that is assigned to a project with a manager who is forcing a predetermined outcome no longer constitutes a team—it is a committee or a group of people. The roles, process, and purpose have changed.

Validation is not necessarily improvement. True improvement, like leadership, involves an ethical application seeking the common good. In this way, the messengers create the message. The messengers are both the leader and the team.

Gandhi and Wisdom

We are not using our wisdom to do the right thing. Again, Gandhi addresses the issue: "All your scholarship would be in vain if at the same time you do not build your character and attain mastery over your thoughts and your actions."[10]

If, however, the leader assumes the position and takes Gandhi's point of view and lives the message, she now becomes the messenger. What a wonderful statement on leadership and our ethical responsibility. This is the art of taking internal values, spiritual beliefs, and the company philosophy and making it live outside of the job description. Isn't that a concept in this day and age? It is the true meaning of the word *organization*; the company becomes alive with not only the mind and body but the heart and soul of the workers. It is the manifestation of the free will. It is the opportunity and environment for the employee to aspire to greater things.

The manager now becomes a messenger of behavior and change. Ethical productivity is the spiritual manifestation of a free will. Science and spirituality now become partners. It is the perfect example of the duality of wave and particle, message and messenger, mind, body and the human spirit. I believe that is the platform for change. It is disturbing the way change is made in the workplace. Now it is often done with clinical efficiency and sometimes with all the subtlety of a train wreck. There is a better way.

I would advise leaders to learn from Hernando De Soto's book, *The Mystery of Capital: Why Capitalism Triumphs in the West and Fails Everywhere Else.*[11] De Soto uses an analogy that refers to political change in a country. I believe that any leader who is trying to advocate change in his organization could use his example.

De Soto says that change, like capitalism, "should not be as simple as running a bulldozer through garbage. It is more like rearranging the thousands of branches and twigs of a huge eagle's nest—without irritating the eagle."[12]

Invisible Obstacles and Employee Dynamics

In 1827, British botanist Robert Brown observed through a microscope the behavior of pollen grains floating in water. His interest was piqued by their random behavior of bumping into one another. What is interesting is that his study went unnoticed for over seventy-five years. No one paid attention to it until the turn of the century when a young physicist, Albert Einstein, looked at Brown's work and used this information in a completely different way.

What Brown saw is now called *Brownian motion*. It is the constant movement of tiny particles suspended in a fluid or gas. These particles had no apparent organization or direction; you could say they lacked leadership, much like Moses' challenge in leading his people. The motion of the molecules of fluid strikes the suspended particles, similar to bumper cars, only in three dimensions. When something runs into something else, they move.

Although Brown didn't know why this was happening, in 1905 Einstein looked at it in a different way and said the movement was caused by the random bombardment of molecules in whatever the suspension medium was. Einstein also came up with a mathematical formula for kinetic theory. His predictions about the motion of particles that are randomly distributed in a fluid were later confirmed by experiment.[13] Keep this thought. It does come back soon!

Let's look at another example. We can safely say that the universe is mostly a vacuum. If you realize that the universe is expanding, it means that more nothing is being created. If we have a large percent of nothing, then all the stars and planets make up very small percent of the universe. What we have to understand is, quantum mechanics probably is the governing body for that large percent in which we have cosmic seas of subatomic particles moving at the speed of light through this vacuum.[14]

How then do you merge Einstein's theory of relativity with quantum theory and tie them into leadership? Enter Paul A. M. Dirac, the first person to consolidate relativity and quantum physics in dealing with all the electrons and subatomic particles whizzing through the vacuum of space. We will also show how important and relevant Dirac is in the Five-Step Decision-Making Model in the next chapter.

Here again it gets interesting. You have to keep one thing in mind. Just because something merges, it doesn't mean it always gets along. Dirac was specifically interested in the electron in the late 1920s. What surprised Dirac was that electrons, when observed in a vacuum such as space, didn't travel in a straight line—they took a jagged course through space while still traveling at the speed of light. It was referred to as "jitterbugging" through space. These electrons appeared to move more slowly because of the many oblique movements—they did not take the shortest path.

Does this sound familiar? Success in life is never a straight line. It, too, is a series of variations. Have you ever had to run down a concourse to try to catch an airplane when you were late? What did you do? You had to jitterbug around people and obstacles. If all was not in your favor, you missed the plane. This is exactly what Dirac encountered.

What was happening in Dirac's case is that the electrons were running into potential electrons with negative energy. Negative electrons, which are smaller than positive electrons, don't exist on their own and only come into being when they are run into by an electron with a positive charge! So, the vacuum of space holds certain electrons as *potential (wave)*, not real matter. Stay with me here! Dirac discovered that, when these negative electrons were bumped into, they came into existence (particle). The result of these collisions was eventually called a *positron* or *antimatter*.

So what does this have to do with leadership and the company you work for? Have you ever been in a situation where your project has lost direction and someone asks, "Why did that happen?" Let me ask about the antimatter in your organization, in other words, those invisible obstacles that your plans, projects, and employee productivity run into in the vacuum of negative leadership. Have you ever had a project veer off course?

The following are my examples of organizational antimatter or those invisible obstacles that employee and organizational energy run into and that cause them to veer off course. A project will veer off course when:

- Fear is an invisible obstacle.
- Bad attitude is an obstacle.
- Procrastination is an invisible obstacle.
- Poor management training is an invisible obstacle.
- Poor planning is an invisible obstacle.
- Shifting priorities are invisible obstacles.
- Poorly-written policies are invisible obstacles.
- Inaccurate data and information are invisible obstacles.
- Unrealistic performance measures are invisible obstacles.
- Lack of funding is an invisible obstacle.
- Your project is run through more people to give it more energy.
- It is subjected to the maze of your organization.

Who are the positrons in your organization? Every project in your organization is like a charged particle in the vacuum of space. When that project is developed, it runs into many types of invisible obstacles, rarely going in a straight line. In other words, it jitterbugs around the collision and may never get finished, or it fails! A project or product in the workplace has the same behavior of a subatomic electron in the vacuum of space.

Let's look at it in a productive scenario. How about an ethical and purpose-driven leader who lets creative people in a company team up and work on a project, and out of the relationship comes a collision of creativity? And then something totally unplanned but surprising takes place and spins off in another direction. In Newtonian thinking the shortest distance between two points may appear to be a straight line, but in the quantum reality, it may not be the most creative or productive.

If Paul A. M. Dirac were alive today he would be proud of his equation. His discovery is directly related to organizational behavior and the workplace. However, I bet you won't find Dirac's name in any operations manual or management training handbook. I wonder how many HR managers have ever heard of him. I also wonder if his discoveries are taught at any graduate business school as related to human behavior.

Leadership and the Team Concept

So how do molecules or particles in suspended fluid that randomly bump into each other (the Einstein-Brownian theory) tie in with leadership and organizational behavior? Let's switch from science into the leadership arena and substitute the word *information* for particle. Let us also change the medium from fluid to the workplace, an organizational culture with poor, little, or no communication. Let's take that same workplace and subject it to little, poorly trained, or marginal leadership. The employees are looking for direction but it is elusive and ideas just sort of swim and bounce off each other in a random fashion. What we're simply saying is that information, ideas, and communication in an organization are no different from the Einstein-Brownian motion principle.

The theory is, unless particles or ideas are given specific direction, they will randomly bounce off each other with no set direction. The principle is the same whether it is in a laboratory or in a company or organization without a purpose. I believe this is one of the main reasons for the sense of disillusion that is felt with teams.

So, while many organizations have abdicated leadership and replaced it with the team concept, many of these teams also have failed because people got together, swam around, and became nothing more than people bumping into each other in a sea of consensus or indecision. No matter what type of organization is involved, whether it is spiritual or scientific, success comes from ethical and value-driven leadership. The great scientific achievements of the world were never made by consensus. Thank goodness the Scriptures don't preach that heaven is governed by a committee!

The Need for Direction

I believe the Einstein-Brownian Motion principle also has spiritual applications. Let me give you an example. In the Old Testament, Moses broke the Ten Commandments which were the policies, rules, and regulations given him. So afterward, the Chosen people wandered in the desert. It was as if they were aimlessly running into each other, accomplishing nothing. This also is reflected in Isaiah: "These are the shepherds who know no discretion; each of them goes his own way, every one of them to his own gain."[15] Get the idea?

What would you see if you examined your own organization under the microscope of human behavior with both a scientific and spiritual perspective? What behaviors would you observe? This, of course, relates not only to your entire organization, but to individual employees. Are people working for their own gain? Do they care if they bump into their employees? If employees do not have a sense of direction in their own lives and this behavior is present in their work ethic and the organization, what happens?

Ask yourself the following questions. What are the highest priorities in my life? Will I see my life as one full of balance and harmony, or will I go through life *bumping* into things? Do I have a plan for what I want to do, or does my life seem like nothing more than a series of random events? Why is it some people, like organizations, seem to go from one accident scene to another?

Take another look at your own organization. Does it have a plan?

What direction is it pointed? Are your values and expectations in harmony with your work and your company direction? Have you ever been in a situation where employees seem to be wandering around and making comments like, "We have no leadership or direction"? Are ideas and endless meetings taking place with nothing coming out of them? Maybe your company lacks an Attitude Statement and basic goals. Where are you going? How do you know?

Picture the employees in your company and how they relate to what Robert Brown saw in a microscope seventy-five years before Einstein identified its significance. Scripture gave us an example of these thousands of years ago. Human behavior, science, and Scripture have more in common than many want to admit. It is time we acknowledged their significance and interrelationship.

The Importance of Ethics in Leadership

Let's take a closer look at the ethical side of leadership. One of the most influential writings dealing with our responsibilities as leaders is from the Bible's book of Wisdom. Written over a hundred years before the birth of Christ, the book of Wisdom lays a strong foundation for the role of leaders.

Wisdom 1:1 says: "Love justice you who judge the earth; think of the Lord in goodness, and seek him in integrity of heart."[16] What I find interesting is the use of the words *justice* and *integrity*. What this is saying is, if you are a leader, you must use wisdom and moral conduct if you are to lead. So, to be the message and the messenger, you must have integrity.

A wonderful definition for ethical behavior is "the application of wisdom to moral conduct." One could write volumes on the issue of moral decision making and its application to the American workplace. It is the true application of business, management, and spirituality. And that has a direct effect on employee dynamics. After all, as goes the leader, so the employee is told to follow.

Employee Dynamics

Employees must be considered a dynamic. The human spirit is energy that is both dynamic and spiritual. It is the most efficient product in the world. Organizations must understand and communicate with employees to tap the greatest resource they have—the human spirit. When tapped, this ethical energy, which is a renewable resource, can be directed at organizational goals and objectives.

The flow of productivity is always accompanied by the flow of knowledge. Knowledge is fluid and can only be managed by the adaptive nature of the human spirit. If we do not provide an environment that ignites knowledge in the workplace, then our employees will go nowhere and neither will our products. New products are created by the relationship between old and new knowledge.

Information flow in an organization must be expressed in a language that reflects volume. Language is not only the spoken word—in corporate America, it can be the product that is being delivered or adapted to meet customer needs. The process is again, seamless.

An organization is like a strainer. And each opening is an employee. Knowledge does not discriminate as to where it enters or passes through an organization; it doesn't just pass through the employees.

Management is responsible for teaching the employees how to listen to and understand what the organization is saying. Therefore, at all times leaders must be asking questions like, "What is the dynamic of our organization telling us?" or "What are the needs of not only my organization but the people working there?" Information related by employees and the dynamics of human behavior are but one of many sources of organizational information.

Processes are the stepping-stones to productivity. What are our products telling us? Do we see productivity only as the result of the effort? Or do we look to a different level where true productivity is a state of spiritual commitment, constant movement, and a range of potentials? Do I see the duality in their purpose? As a leader, am I teaching it?

We must train our twenty-first-century leaders and employees to understand the spiritual dynamics of leadership, organizational behavior, and the relationship with the human spirit. Our challenge in life is to know when we are to be the message or the messenger. But first, we must lay the foundation, knowing our direction is important. The decision-making process in choosing that direction is critical. The Five-Step Decision-Making Model, which I present next, is the foundation for implementing the Seven Needs for Personal Productivity, seven fundamental needs leaders can use for employees' commitment and productivity. These are presented in next chapters.

Chapter Three

The Five-Step Decision-Making Model

"One fallacy in managerial reasoning is that if you analyze the data carefully and thoughtfully enough, you will get the right answer. They look to the data, not to the people."
—Thomas Moore[1]

I wonder how many different decision-making models there are in the world. We are in desperate need for more education and the application of basic decision-making skills.

I wish I could say that I was the author of this brilliant model but I was unable to find the author to give credit, despite months of searching. I include this decision-making model as a testimonial to its author. The model is both insightful and timeless. I have used it in countless examples and recommend it to anyone who must make an ethical decision. This model reinforces my belief that all decisions should be value-based.

I found this model because I was attempting to resolve an issue with a client and became aware of the vast amount of information that was on the table. During the conversation, I made a mental note to myself that it would be nice if I had some way to assist my clients to prioritize and assist them with decisions. My answer did not come immediately, but I became sensitive to the idea that I had to look for a better way. I think what I enjoyed most was the process of looking for the answer.

Over the course of several years I have had my nose in volumes of books, articles, newsletters, and documents. The problem is, I get so excited about reading something new that I forget where I read it. Again, just ask my wife. She is always stumbling over books, or discovering magazine articles and reports all over the house.

Whenever I look for something, it validates the concept of chaos theory. Quantum theory is right at home in my search process; I believe it is called "having a moment" when you completely zone on where or when something happened.

The Shortest Distance between Two Points Is a Curved Line

To shift gears, at the turn of the century, Einstein argued convincingly that gravity stretches and distorts space and time, and this is confirmed when star beams are influenced by the sun's gravity as they graze their surface. In other words, light bends. As Paul Davies says in his book *God and the New Physics,* Einstein carries the same weight in the scientific community that St. Paul does in the Christian community.[2] Einstein said convincingly what other physicists have long thought about curved space-time as an explanation for gravity.

In the workplace we know that, once we identify a goal, we then work toward it. What we fail to plan for is what we will run into along the way. Goals, like light from a distant star, can get diverted along the way. In other words, our course to reach our goal may be distorted and take us in different directions. An example is those organizations that have a penchant for benchmarking and that fail to take this into consideration. Too many organizations see their internal processes as linear in nature. If a set of criteria is implemented, the result should be the same every time. And if something does go wrong, they usually look to the human element as the defect. The people are held accountable for a process that has physical limitations. Einstein would never have made it as a supervisor in HR.

Again, in the early part of the twentieth century, Paul A. M. Dirac studied electrons moving at the speed of light through the vacuum of space. He was looking for a single equation that would explain relativity and quantum theory and found that electrons do move at the speed of light through the vacuum of space—but not in a straight line. Obstacles "pop up" and cause the electrons to move through space on a jagged path.[3]

Don't we have similar problems? Wouldn't it be wonderful if our career, families, educations, and relationships all moved in straight lines? They don't. Why then do we teach problem solving as if it were a linear process? It is not. Problem solving and decision making are physical, jagged processes. We run into many unknown things because life does not proceed in a straight line. In fact nothing really does, especially in space. I also believe that, if we took the concept of a straight line and applied the principles of quantum physics, we would find that the term *straight line* is an oxymoron. It is a difficult concept to grasp but a straight line is actually an illusion. If we are to solve a problem, we must also address what we will do if we run into something along the way.

In our fast-paced world, as we are bombarded with vast amounts of data, information, and an ever-expanding knowledge base, we have frequent episodes of data and information overload. I believe it is important for a creative process to have so much information that groups almost vapor lock. It is out of that process that many ideas and concepts poke their noses into the minds of the work group. It is a form of self-organization. I love the term *chaos*.

As I said, overwhelming someone with information must be used selectively and with a dedicated end. I would like to give some words of caution: any such group must have strong and dedicated leadership in the group. This is not the time for facilitation.

Be Careful of Some Leadership Models

The leader, by the way, may not necessarily be present. Let me give a very troubling example. We are facing a problem with terrorism. Terrorists train with a dedicated group of people, then return to their target country to become sleepers. They assimilate to the lifestyle of the country and later activate to perform a terrorist act. The leader is not physically present; however, the ideology becomes the leader. The terrorist cell is the team. We can learn much from their behavior.

First, we must understand that this type of action and decision making does not follow many of the mainstream models. Their goal uses a decision-making model that has an evil end. Do not look to this group as one grounded in principles, values, and ethics. Their mission is clear. Picture it as a focus group with AK-47s. Keep one thing in mind: both good and evil require making decisions. The model I wish you to have requires value-based decisions and ethical principles. It requires you to prioritize and decide what is relevant to making your decision. Your daily experiences may still overwhelm you. But you will have the tools to make the difference.

Types of Information

If you are bombarded by an overwhelming amount of information daily, you may be headed for trouble. I have found that most of the trouble comes from the notion that all information is the same. It is not. In fact, the following model has been so helpful because it helps you discover what is relevant and what is not. I like to call this the signal-to-noise syndrome. This is another bit of science. Basically it means that not all the data, information, and knowledge are relevant or even valid.

Signals have value; they tell us something. Noise, maybe an irritating sound that is a by-product of the signal, does not have value. It can be catastrophic when your company follows the noise, thinking it's a signal. Many organizations are doing just that—and they don't even know it. One example of this happening might be shifting priorities, and managers who pull their employees in different directions with the latest fads in fool-proof philosophies.

I spent some quiet time thinking about how much data and information I am exposed to each day. I cannot help but feel that this age of overload, this bombardment of information, might be having an opposite effect in that it is actually acting like an anesthetic. I believe we are "dumbing down" a couple of generations with massive amounts of nonsense. Let me make one thing clear: I am an advocate of massive amounts of data and information if you are in a structured and directed decision-making process. I am concerned with the amount of daily noise we are exposed to that is irrelevant for any form of structured decisions.

Some say we are more individualistic than ever. Isolated, yes, more individualistic, I don't think so—the opposite is true. I believe we have entered an age of conformity. Maybe we could call it media malaise. One cannot turn on any radio, television, computer, or cell phone without some group, cause, or database telling us to sell, trade, buy, or embrace something. This has led to an environment one could almost call an "information fetish." It is as if we have lulled ourselves into thinking we are more important if we are surrounded by more information.

What is happening instead is that we are being desensitized. Our hard drives, cell phones, and laptop computers have vast amounts of storage space. And we are beginning to believe we are more important if we fill up that space. Then and only then, does it seem to validate our self-worth.

Yes, new ideas and thoughts are what make us grow. We grow when we embrace something because others think we should and we do it out of a negative thought process or conflict of values. I made that last statement because it begs the question: is all the information I have around me supporting my values so I can make wise decisions? If it is not, then why do we embrace it? We don't have trouble with enough data, information, and knowledge in our lives— we have trouble finding the truth they hide.

Never Be Shamed into a Decision

One only has to see some form of media to have some organization or group assault our value system by trying to shame us into compliance.

It is as if they want us to feel guilty. We then start putting our arms around issues because someone says we have to and not because we want to. That does not enhance our faith or value system. We cannot be all things to all people on all issues. This can be a barrier to our calling to be a message or messenger.

As someone once said, "Our faith then becomes a mile wide and an inch deep." So where is this leading? I believe we have defaulted our values to compromise. We have deferred making decisions and we are losing decision-making skills in the process. We have taken the approach of the injured. I believe we have to ideologically crawl under the front porch of our intellectual house to heal and lick our digital wounds.

We have been so inundated with data and information that we have prostituted conscience and choice processes for conformity. Some think all the data, information, and knowledge points in that direction. We only move on to a higher level of understanding and wisdom when we begin to understand ourselves and what we value.

Teams Are NEVER a Substitute for Leadership

As you'll see throughout this book, the model will describe that data, information, and knowledge alone will not necessarily help us make better decisions. In fact, the quality will not improve even if we make more. Here is where there is injustice in the workplace. In the 70s, 80s, and 90s, we expected employees to find answers as a group, as a team. I believe the expectation is still there—but something has happened that isn't healthy.

The idea of teams started out with the best of intentions. In order for any team concept to work, it must have strong leadership. Based on the identified data, information, and knowledge, the team was given the project and parameters. The leader delivered the message and then became the messenger and led the group through the process. When the process was finished and recommendations were presented, the leader made the decision.

What evolved was just the opposite. Some leaders saw this as an out and defaulted, letting the team make the final decision. But what if the team had made its decision based on inadequate or poorly developed data and information and, maybe, a knowledge base that was not complete? Poor leadership is what happens when a team leads—that was never the purpose or objective of teams. I believe Dr. W. Edwards Deming, who pioneered the quality management movement, would give us one of his thundering orations and chastise us until the sun went down.

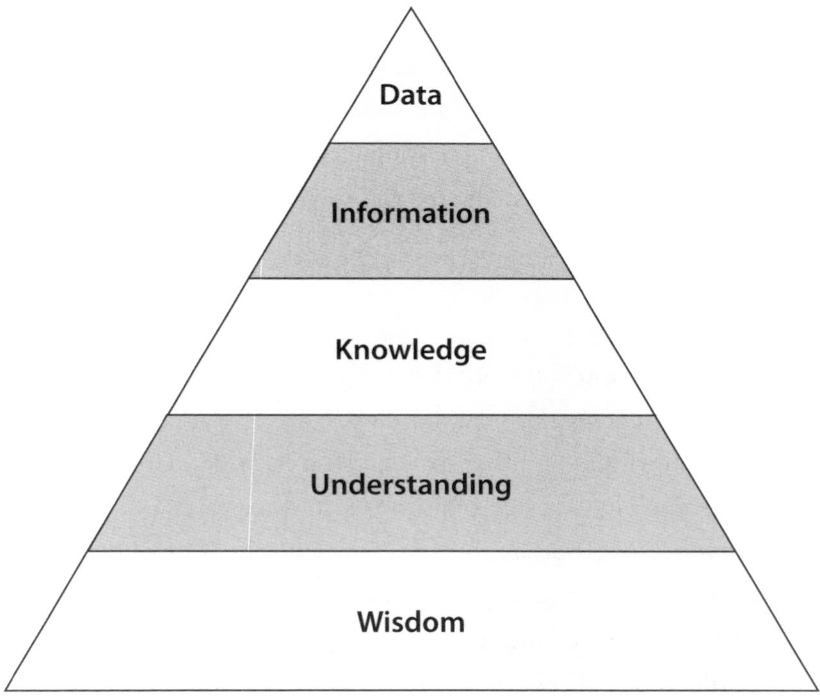

Figure 1. The Five-Step Decision-Making Model

The Five-Step Decision-Making Model

Let's look at the model. I have added my own thoughts as the model became more clear and meaningful. The model is divided into five parts: Data, Information, Knowledge, Understanding, and Wisdom.

One can make a decision from any of the areas. The interesting part is that the decision you make may get you different results from those you would achieve using another area. Our biggest mistake is that we make our decisions way too early! You will see the value of following each step to its conclusion, and that making wise decisions is the goal.

I would like to start by sharing the thoughts behind the five areas for decision making. These steps will help you clarify your own decision-making process. The decisions we make every day are made from the foundation of each of these words. You will see that the quality of each decision depends upon on which word we stand. Let's start by looking at data. You will also notice that most decision making comes from the top down. Note here: Wisdom, our goal, is at the bottom and rightfully so. Wisdom, in decision making, is a physical process. The "weight" of the process and implication is truly realized. Wise decisions are not necessarily easy to make and the weight of their importance can even be life-changing.

Data

Let's start at the top and work down. Data is the voice of any system or process. Your company, small business, college, relationship, or family is a system with a voice that speaks to you every day. Unfortunately, we usually don't look at our company or, in some cases, our family as having a voice. We associate the term *voice* with the voice of the people who work at a company. This is not necessarily true. Your system has another voice and that language is data.

William Scherkenbach says in his book, *Deming's Road to Continual Improvement,* "We hope that the data supports our current level of knowledge. If the data is faulty then so is the knowledge. If this is true, then the product of our system can no longer be considered valid. What happens then is our belief in the system also comes into question."[4] So, if you understand data in its truest form, you will never look at your system or business in the same way again. We have asked data to do something it is not designed to do because we have confused the term *data* with information. Data performs a specific function. It is a language and anyone who truly studies data is bilingual.

The problem occurs when we ask data to communicate something it was not designed to do. I offer the following clarification. In *The Deming Dimension,* Henry R. Neave quotes Dr. Deming: "Data is only useful if we know how to use them; they are no use on their own."[5] And "Wherever there is fear, we get the wrong numbers."[6] Dr. Deming also had other thoughts about productivity in his book, *Out of the Crisis*: "Measures of productivity are like statistics on accidents: they tell you about the number of accidents in the home, on the road, and at the workplace, but they do not tell you how to reduce the frequency of the accidents."[7]

In order to understand data, we must first meet the rest of the players. You see, data becomes clear and understood when viewed through the lens of a system. No system, no data. W. Edwards Deming in his book, *The New Economics for Industry, Government and Education*[8], gives an excellent description of a system. He says that:

- A system is a network of interdependent components that work together to try to accomplish the aims of the system.
- A system must have an aim. Without an aim there is no system.
- The aim must be clear to everyone and include plans for the future.
- A system must be managed. It cannot do it itself.

Take a moment here and substitute the name of your company or organization for the word *system* and see if your organization meets the criteria as a true system. Are you a network of interdependent components? Do you have an aim? Is it clear to everyone? What are your plans for the future? Remember, employees can only be as successful as the system lets them be. And that means leadership.

Data requires caution. It is a snapshot of that moment and speaks the current status, or state of an event. Data does not necessarily tell the truth. As stated, it tells the state of the system or process. If the system or design process is flawed, the value, integrity, and accuracy of the data will follow suit. Data does not tell you how you got where you are and it does not tell you where you are going. It only tells you where you are now. Data has no conscience. It is an independent statement of a single condition. Data has no meaning unless it is associated or becomes relative to another number or set of circumstances.

Example: If I am on a road and my car speedometer says sixty-five miles an hour, I could assume from the data given to me by the speedometer that the vehicle I am in is traveling sixty-five miles an hour. I then can assume that, in approximately one hour, I will be about sixty-five miles from where my journey began. This is given the assumption that my speedometer is working correctly. Other independent sources of data are from my observations—the feeling that the wheels are turning, hearing the engine running at a higher speed, and seeing things getting smaller in my rear view mirror.

Let us take the same scenario, except this time; the vehicle is on an icy road. I step on the accelerator, the wheels spin, the engine noise rises, and the speedometer goes up to sixty-five miles an hour but I am standing still. The speedometer is telling me the status of the same system. It has no conscience or allegiance to any other data source. Both systems are accurate. One scenario will take me down the road at sixty-five miles an hour and the other will have me stand still. Both numbers, however, are the same and they reflect the system in its current state. So, data is relative and must be validated with other sources. Data gains meaning over time. As described in the previous examples, the outcome of both examples can be drastically different, even catastrophic.

Let us say we look at our community as the highway and our local police agency as the vehicle. Our monthly report (speedometer) tells us that based on monthly statistics; officers are efficient in targeting speeders in a certain area. The more tickets that are written, the more the speed drops. So less speed means a safer highway. Is the data changing? Yes. Does it improve the system? You don't know. All you have is one source of data and it may not be telling you the truth. You have not seen a pattern over time or other outside sources that tell you there is a direct relationship between writing tickets and reduced speed. If this is true, then the more tickets you write, the slower people will drive. If this is the case, then you could say the true outcome would be that, if everyone got a ticket, traffic would stand still. Is this true? Not necessarily so. City leaders may like the revenue, but your public image will be in need of damage control.

Many public safety agencies still operate on the premise that stricter enforcement and presence will produce the desired result. It may, to a certain degree. What does happen is that the system you are addressing eventually leads to a stable state. In other words, enforcement works to a point. After the system is stable, additional enforcement will not change the result, no matter how many resources you direct to it. Many public systems, too, become victims. If you provide funding for a problem, it eventually may reach a state of stability. We believe providing more money should solve the problem. We know this is not so.

Some agencies do not understand this principle because they are making decisions based on data alone. They assume past events are a true indication of future behavior. This may be true in some cases, well, almost true. Past behavior is not an *exact* indication of what may occur next month—it can be an indicator within an area of variation. This is critical. What we have to avoid is making life-changing decisions based only on data. If I apply that thinking to the human spirit, then I must conclude that no one has the possibility of change in her life or behavior. If this is true, then if I change numbers, I can change behavior. That is why I believe the behavior of the human spirit is more in harmony with the principles of quantum physics. The duality and range of possibilities of both the human spirit and quantum principles are profound.

Here is another example. Last month's numbers do not necessarily indicate next month's results. If this is true, then the only information I can use is from what happened in the past. That would be like driving down the road with the windshield of my car covered and making all decisions on the data I see in my rear view mirror. Some might call this the legislative process. Of major concern is that, in many organizations today, this is considered contemporary thinking. When it comes to corporate America, it can be devastating.

Have you ever heard the expression, "Everyone jump, the numbers are in?" The latest, poll, survey, questionnaire, or other data-gathering devices have just been formulated by the newest computer with its turbo intergalactic software. Surely now we can make wise and empowering decisions! Besides, you are not being paid to sit still. It is interesting to watch the broadcast media "jump" on the latest opinion poll numbers and deliver the results as fact. Don't EVER make a decision based on an opinion poll. Don't just sit there, do something! Woe be unto those who sit in high places and operate under this premise!

It is interesting to note all the states with budget problems in the past few years. They wait for the data to come in so they can balance their budgets but the numbers are always worse. The numbers tell the state agencies to do something. In many cases, legislatures make it worse by tampering with a stable system where the numbers (data) simply were incorrect in the first place. Many states base their numbers on a projected date in the future. Changing the system or trying to increase the numbers may actually be doing more harm than good.

OK, it is important to remember that it is unwise to make decisions based only on data. Data is important but you must remember that its purpose is to support other documented information and data sources over time. The relativity of data plays an important role in our decision-making process.

The greatest task you will have in using this model is holding yourself back from jumping to any conclusions. Our culture wants us to make quick and speedy decisions. I am asking you to be sure the data you are using reflects the true picture of the system with which you are dealing.

We are free to choose what we wish to do with the vast amount of data in our lives. Again, please do not make any life-changing decisions based on data alone! If you don't believe me, just ask Enron.

Information

Information is multiple sources of data. It gives a broader picture of where you are but it does not necessarily tell you how you got there. Information does not represent a true picture of a system or its status. It is in the best interest of the user to take information at face value. Do not rely on information as truth. If I were to give a definition of information I would say information is data supported by opinion.

A good example of a source of information is the media and the evening news. One must use extreme caution in making life decisions based on the evening news. In far too many cases, the evening news is data from multiple sources, glued together by opinion and practiced personality. The news is designed to do just that—inform. It also edits.

Information is a larger picture of various data sources that assist in decision making. Information should rarely be the root cause for the decision. Information comes to us in many forms and in just as many agendas. It is not uncommon for different people to reach different conclusions based on the same data and information. Information can be and often is personal opinion. It is useful. Information can be used in conjunction with other information, personal knowledge, and experience to form an opinion.

Let's look at an example. The evening news has the local weather report with temperatures (data) and a three-day forecast (information). You decide to look on the Internet (more data and information). You decide that your car does not have snow tires and your driving skills aren't so good on snowy roads (knowledge). You wait a couple of days and see if you would like to wait for better weather (wisdom).

How about another example? A public safety agency employee relies on numbers (data.) He gets a set of traffic numbers over time (information) and draws a conclusion based on his training (knowledge). If the same numbers were given to someone of a different discipline, such as a traffic engineer, a different conclusion could be drawn. Again, each discipline could be making a different observation if the system generating the numbers is incorrect. Information is data that, over time, can support a larger body of knowledge. Information can be far from the truth.

Public safety agencies operating under traditional policing models will often use data and information to formulate projects such as highway saturation patrols. These patrols are created to attack say, the DUII, or driving under the influence, problem. The problem is perceived from data generated from previous arrests and the percentage of people who are driving and may have been drinking. While the data and information generated to address the problem may reflect the state of a given situation, increasing patrols and arrests may not be the true answer. Removing an impaired driver from the highway will save a life. It may not, however, show statistically that it had an impact on the number of drinking drivers, people who choose to drink, or other situations that may also cause loss of life.

For example, if I have a fire and I put water on the fire, eventually the fire will go out. How much water is enough? If there are hazardous drivers or drinking drivers in a given area, how many patrols does it take to impact the situation? If there are too many patrols, there actually may be a negative impact on the system or problem. I can put too much water on a fire and create a whole new set of problems. After the situation is stable, no amount of resources can improve it. Today, this is a huge challenge to public service organizations.

The goal is to change or improve the system. If the saturation patrol did neither, all the arrests in the world will not have an impact. Remember, this is a two-way street. Increasing patrols may be something the system will not respond to. Statistically, the same number of people will be arrested and a similar number of fatalities will occur. An unlimited number of new laws will not make a difference. A police agency using the same methods with new laws may not statistically make a difference. Basically, nothing has changed. The system is statistically stable. Improvement can only come from changing the system.

Information is essential to a decision-making process. Like data, it is a piece of the equation that must be considered. The challenge is knowing the difference between data and information. Data is specific numbers. Information is those same numbers over time. Again, data and information alone should not be the criteria for making decisions. Unfortunately, many people make their decisions based only on those two things.

Radio Stations and Information—Understanding Signal to Noise

Get in your car and turn on your local radio station. Adjust the dial so you can hear a clear broadcast. What you're hearing is the electronic signal coming from a source of information—a transmitter.

Now let's take it to step two. Put your car in gear, head for the end of town, and then keep driving. But something starts to happen. The farther we get from town, the more we hear something else on the radio. It is subtle at first, but then becomes more obvious. What is that hissing sound? It is as if something is starting to interrupt the signal. The clarity of the initial signal seems to fade and seems to become distorted.

What is happening is called *signal to noise*. The closer we are to the source of the signal, the clearer the reception, and vice versa. The signal is only as strong as the transmitter or system lets it be. Signals from radio stations are like the mission, goals, and communication in our organizations and communities. The clearer the signal sent from leadership or the source, the stronger the employee reception.

But let's return to our car ride and see what happens. The farther we are from the transmitter or source, the more noise develops. In fact, the noise eventually takes over and eliminates the signal. Remember, as the signal decreases, the volume doesn't. The noise can become so overwhelming that we turn down the volume. In our company, that is like tuning out the organization and the message of the company. This is a physical process that has nothing to do with HR. It has everything to do with the physical make-up of the organization. Here is a case where the wave/particle duality can have a profound effect on the human spirit.

If organizational leaders take it for granted that employees understand the company issues and direction, they are sadly mistaken. In other words, communication stops. Again, it is like our own personal principles and values. The farther our behavior wanders from the source of our values, the more fragmented it is. The same situation happens with any company or public agency. The farther we get from the source of communication, like the true company direction, the more noise or interruptions develop. Signal and noise is stored in our computers and databases in the form of inaccurate and overwhelming amounts of data and information. The real implication can be a heart-and-soul issue.

Does your company or organization teach or even know the difference? It can also be the personal and professional interruption, signal to noise, of the multiple layers of management, policies, and procedures that no longer are as effective as specific goals and objectives. Now that we have that down, here is where it really gets interesting.

Let's go back to the signal-to-noise issue. Remember, the signal is the message and the noise is the interruption. Both are messages from the same source. The signal sends one message and the noise sends another. The noise tries to cover up the signal and, if we are in the right location, the noise will cover it all together. It is up to us to understand the difference.

This understanding does not come from wandering the halls and cubicles of the workplace. It must be taught, and management has the responsibility to be the instructor. Here is a critical example of management moving from being the message to becoming the messenger of accurate information. Again, the application duality is paramount. Both signal and noise are a language. Signal and noise speak to us and say different things. Our goal is to understand and improve the signal. And here is where we are challenged.

What about Our Businesses?

We have already talked about how our businesses talk to us. What are they really saying? Out of the data, information, and knowledge we receiving each day, how much is signal and how much is noise? What is interfering with the processes and necessary changes? This may be reflected in what it is you may need to alter, discontinue, or implement. Remember, both signal and noise are reflected in data and information. Does your organization have leaders who are just making noise?

Ponder for a moment the amount of information you have to process in the workplace. It requires us to ask, "How much time do I spend each day just managing information." If you get an answer to that question you will begin to grasp the problem. Now the second question is, "Of the information I have to manage, how much is truly a signal of the company speaking to me and how much is noise that has no relevance whatsoever?" If the second question doesn't cause you some problems, then the third one may: "Do I know the difference between the two?"

If we say that we want to capture the essence of employee productivity, then would we not want to understand what our organization is really saying?

What about Our Communities?

One of the greatest challenges we face is the delivery of quality services within our communities. We can look back on the 1990s with fond memories of stable financial streams and services eagerly awaiting their share. The model has changed. Many communities now find themselves with limited finances, conditioned service organizations, and a questionable cash flow. Let us go back and ask the questions. *How much of what our community is saying to us is signal, and what is noise?*

Communities are facing a crisis of epic proportions. What are the most important issues? Most communities have focus groups or form a task force to study a problem. They hold open meetings at council sessions and focus on getting the pulse of a community. While the desired outcome is getting the pulse of public opinion, that may not be the actual outcome. Filling a council chamber or meeting room with two hundred advocates who are passionate about their subject does not necessarily represent the opinion of a community of twenty thousand.

We may take the number attending as a signal when what they are saying is passionate and delivered with conviction. Their information, however, may not reflect the real issues. Of course they are sincere about what they are saying, but is what they are saying truly a representation of the community? Not necessarily.

Community meetings can be a representation of the issue if the subject has polarized the entire community, such as in a natural disaster or safety issue. If the issue is a cause or subject that a group of people feel passionate about, then what is presented in the meeting may not be the necessary data and information needed for community leaders to make a decision. While the information presented by a special interest group merits consideration, if we look at it from the view of signal to noise, it requires community decision makers to consider what part of the information was signal and what part is noise.

The part that becomes challenging is understanding that the information given must also be rational in order to represent a true signal. This is what makes many community meetings appear fruitful on the surface, while rendering minimal results. Dedication and zeal may shape data and information, but they may not truly represent the issue under question or the problem within the given system. Passion for a product or idea does not mean that it would be practical. Again, data and information only tell you where you are at any given moment.

Let's make it relative. The data and information gained at a community meeting is no different from what we get when our car is traveling down the highway or on a pond of ice. All you're getting as the result is a piece of the system. The actual result of your perception can be completely different.

Community meetings, for example, gather data and information and may provide some new pieces of knowledge. Planned with the best of intentions, they actually may be doing more harm than good. They look to data and information as the message when, in reality, it may be the messenger of a bigger issue or problem. This is why signal to noise also is relevant to data and information. In many community meetings, interested parties tell officials what they want them to hear and not necessarily what they need to hear. Community meetings are not necessarily the conscience of the community. They are a piece of data and information with signal to noise as their voices, and they must be kept in perspective.

Technology Can Be a Double Agent

"But wait a moment, Art. We are in the digital age! That means we can make a very clear copy from one master and make an infinite number of copies with no noise or distortion. That means we can eliminate all the noise. It is called satellite technology. Everything will be clear."

This may be true. That theory, however, is dependent on one small but critically important point. And that point is, we have a clear understanding between signal and noise. In other words, when it comes to our company, the data and information may be noise and not a signal because it may be built into the master document, proposal, or policy. This means all you have is a very high-quality, digitally-mastered product that may be telling you nothing!

The mission, values, principles, goals, and customers are all part of the signal. As I said earlier, multiple layers of management, poor or few communication policies and procedures, unrealistic goals, poor leadership, and performance measures are also part of the voice of our organizations and communities. They are considered noise.

Our goal is to understand the difference between the signal and noise. It is not uncommon for us to react to the noise of our company and communities with the best of intentions, but we may be, in fact, doing more harm than good. Our goal is to understand what our organizational system is really saying.

What is the voice of your company? Have you been working hard and trying to improve your numbers when you may have been reacting to noise and not the true signal of your organization? Signal and noise are two forms of communication. They are your company speaking to you. Addressing them in the wrong way can have a devastating effect on your company.

Remember, the latest technology delivers both the signal and the noise. It does not discriminate. It is up to us to understand what is being said. From that we develop our knowledge base. Bad data and information means bad knowledge. If not done correctly, the result could be terminal!

You should ask yourself the following questions:

- How do you listen to what is going on in your organization or company?
- What signals are coming from your company?
- What noise is coming from your company?
- Were you given the necessary education to identify and know the difference between signal and noise?
- Can you give examples where noise coming from your organization was addressed as a signal?
- Can you give examples when signals were thought to be noise? (Both signals and noise cost money.)

Remember that noise is information, processes, and strategies that are no longer relevant and performance measures, benchmarks, and goals that have no documented purpose. It is really too bad.

Moses would have been better off if he had not smashed the Ten Commandments. He would have understood the principle of signal to noise. He broke the message or the signal. He led his followers into the desert, and the farther away they got from the Ten Commandments, the more noise entered their lives. They had no connection between science and spirituality when both were relevant and working in harmony. Their governing values were on broken pieces of tablet. All they heard was the noise of each other.

Knowledge

Knowledge is information with theory. This means knowledge is data and information that stands up to natural laws until someone comes along and proves it different. Even Plato made this distinction. He said the creed of the soul is "knowledge is more important than opinion."[9]

When we use the term *theory*, we operate under the premise that a certain application of data and information over time will produce a consistent result. In the science world, that is what made Newton the rock star of his time. The problem is, traditional decision making usually stops about here. Data, information, and knowledge seem like three sound areas on which to base decisions. Can you? Yes. Should you? I wouldn't make it a habit.

Thomas Aquinas believed that all knowledge originates in sensation, but data related to sense can be made intelligible only by the action of our intellect. Aquinas also believed that to understand the highest truths, the aid of revelation is needed. He was stating that intellect and faith are components that complement each other. I call that the harmony of science and the soul. We need both.

Revelation is the basis for the doctrines and practices of most of the world's major religions. Revelation may be in the form of a vision, is often accompanied by words, or it may consist only of words.[10] I believe Aquinas is telling us that the knowledge of the world, an integral part of our faith experience like us, evolves.

If data, information, and knowledge are enough to make lifelong decisions, then why are so many people unhappy? Why are we so quick to blame others for our unrest? Thomas Merton relates in *New Seeds of Contemplation*, "It is not that someone else is preventing you from living happily; you yourself do not know what you want." (Remember signal to noise?) "Rather than admit this, you pretend that someone is keeping you from exercising your liberty. Who is this? It is you yourself."[11]

The following is an example of knowledge with theory, and how a new application changed both the system and the theory that supported it.

Galileo, a fifteenth-century astronomer and thinker, built a telescope. He did not build it with the intention of going into the telescope business; he was not into market economy. What he did next with his telescope, however, changed the traditional basis for knowledge, science, and theology. Galileo's first mistake was to look through the telescope. Up to that time, much of the collective knowledge and those in authority told Galileo, "Do anything you want with your telescope. Just don't look up." He made an even bigger mistake when he looked at the sky through the telescope and said that the sun was the center of our solar system. It may have been a mistake then, but it changed our lives forever.

Up to that point, the knowledge base and the current theory was that the earth was the center of the universe. This was taught as fact because much of the data, information, and knowledge base of the time was driven by the church. No one had proved or said anything different. You see, back then information was validated not necessarily by what was said, but by who said it. So the world believed the church and politicians and, in many cases, no one dared to challenge them. It turns out both were wrong.

Galileo upset the theological apple cart. The theory changed, as well as the attitude of the church toward Galileo. I think Galileo believed he had a responsibility to look through that telescope. Being right does not mean your life will be easy. That hasn't changed, even today.

We are also confronted with the idea that knowledge is all that is needed for effective thinking and decision making. This idea does have followers who look at knowledge as finite, a stationary state of being.

Knowledge is fluid and has to change. If knowledge didn't change, it would simply be data and information. We cannot dwell in one area of knowledge alone; otherwise it becomes a psychological cyst where we look for a certain level or point of intellectual comfort.

Werner Heisenberg said that if we measure location, then we cannot measure or understand momentum. His principle is critical to the twenty-first-century workplace, but that comes later. We can measure one or the other, but not both at the same time. His principle definitely applies to knowledge. The fact that we become comfortable with a certain volume of knowledge means we will miss that very same body of knowledge as it adapts and changes when someone simply asks why. It is then that we must be accountable for our thinking and what we do and teach others.

It would be nice to believe that a body of knowledge has a conscience. Another book could be written on that statement alone. What gets us into trouble is not the body of knowledge, but the people who happen to be in possession or in control of that knowledge. It is here we have made some serious mistakes. I would like to give you an example of a group of people who were in possession of a body of knowledge. What they did with it speaks for itself. This group had a meeting and the result of that meeting was one of the most significant events of the twentieth century.

A conference was held where fourteen leaders from business and government were called together to address a pressing issue. They possessed a body of knowledge and the purpose of the meeting was to make a decision. The conference was chaired by a government official and dealt with an issue of national importance, a program to create a system for the management of soon-to-be homeless and indigent citizens. Eight of the fourteen leaders who attended this important meeting held PhDs. This conference, called the Wannsee Conference, was held in Berlin, Germany, in January 1942.

The meeting was chaired by Reinhard Heydrich, Gestapo Chief appointed by Adolph Hitler. At issue was the "Final Solution of the Jewish Question." European Jews were the soon-to-be homeless citizens. After discussing the topic, the meeting was closed and it was decided that the matters in question no longer permitted any further delay. During this eighty-five-minute meeting, which was followed by breakfast, they decided the fate of over six million people. These were educated but ignorant people who possessed the knowledge necessary to deal with the issue. All the data and information and pseudo-knowledge they chose at the time told them so.

Many managers and leaders do not have the knowledge of theory of management and leadership. They do not understand the implication of the human spirit and the role of the individual in the workplace. They suffer under the illusion that bringing in technology and staying on the cutting-edge will make the difference. It will not! These are not separate issues. I believe if these eighteen delegates had understood the balance and harmony of science and soul, they would have reached a different conclusion.

We have embraced the latest in technology, automation, and state-of-the-art machinery. Unless the leader understands the theory of management, then all these tools do is take the leader's organization up against a greater source of noise. New machinery only creates the same problems faster. New tools, such as computers, are designed to perform certain functions but they do not solve problems. Only the people using the tools can solve the problems. Only the people understand the soul of the company.

We have created the illusion that knowledge and tools alone increase productivity. This can create a greater problem because the latest in technology or efficiency does not guarantee success. In fact, we may be making a product our customers do not want or no longer need, but we do so with as much enthusiasm, fanfare, lower cost, and lots of high-techno-toys as needed to make it happen.

Computers are necessary. Be sure that the data and information inside them is valid. If it is not, then you will get very efficient, timely, and faster errors. Computers are an invaluable link to assist leaders and managers. Leaders must make sure that the data and information they contain will help them make the decisions they need. In the same vein, management must be aware of this if their organizational system does not produce the desired result.

Leadership must look to the system for changes and not to the people who probably will be held responsible. Sadly, reality tells us that most managers go directly to employees. Surely, additional training or counseling will make the difference. The employee was working as hard as the system would let them work and to no avail. If the products are below quality and the market begins to erode, then cutting costs is the only alternative. And the first place to look to change the line on the spreadsheet is the reduction of employees.

I wonder how many employees have been laid off from organizations when it was the employee—not the machines—who had the answer management needed to make the necessary changes? I wonder how many employees who have these answers walk out the front door of organizations and take them to a competitor. How ironic that this is when we think of the issue of true productivity.

The answers needed by managers in a time of down markets and tight budgets are not located on an assembly line; chances are, they are standing in an unemployment line. The interesting thing is that management systems put them there. How interesting it is when an organization throws out people because they don't understand the machine, and the problem all along is the system that supports the machine.

We fail to understand one of the fundamental principles of leadership: that, for the most part, most people want to learn and do their best. It is not only one of the intrinsic values of the human condition, but it is a fundamental obligation of management to create an environment for learning. This is another example of science and the human spirit. I believe the human spirit wants to adapt and express itself by being both message and messenger. Sadly, I believe we are not training our leaders for this important duality. If we look at one of the most challenging aspects of leadership, it deals with facts. Facts conjure up the notion that certain things are true and never change. Wouldn't that be nice? If life were a series of facts, then leadership and free will would be a walk in the park.

But a leader depends on knowledge and, hopefully, possesses understanding and wisdom. This means that any decision a leader makes must be supported by the data, information, and knowledge at hand. Knowledge, of course, is only as valid as the theory that supports it. In other words—and here comes the paradox—a leader must be more comfortable with what he doesn't know than with what he does know. Again, if the theory is no longer valid, then that segment of knowledge no longer exists. Leadership is being comfortable with theory—the unknown.

I believe we have two facts and five situations in our lives:

Fact One:	All of us were born.
Fact Two:	All of us are going to die.
Situation One:	Everything in between are events and all events have variation.
Situation Two:	Some events (our attitude) we have control of and some we do not.

Situation Three: It is our task in life to figure out which events we can control and act on.

Situation Four: We all have a free will and are obligated to do something with it. That means knowing when to be the message or messenger.

Situation Five: We are accountable for our actions and the results.

Remember, knowledge in the hands of people without a conscience can be devastating. Knowledgeable decisions do not always equate to ethical decisions. It is here that we make a significant decision. Do I decide on knowledge alone or do I choose a deeper understanding and take responsibility for the outcome and move to a higher level?

Understanding

It is here that the human spirit is different from any creature on this planet. It is here that we decide the implications of right and wrong. It is in this stage of the Decision-Making Model that Darwin doesn't fare so well. Free will and accountability now play crucial roles.

Isaiah 6:9 gives us insight into the purpose and importance of understanding. "Listen carefully, but you shall not understand! Look intently, but you shall know nothing!"[12] Isaiah's prophecy is again mentioned in Matthew 13:14–15 where Jesus was asked why he spoke in parables. "Because they look but do not see and hear but do not listen or understand."[13] Many of the great leaders of the world and even ones in our companies and organizations are frustrated because they have visions no one sees or understands. In some cases, it may be the leaders who do not understand.

Isaiah 6 says at the end of verse 10 to "understand with your heart."[14] Understanding is applying our value system. Understanding is the front door to ethics and wisdom; it is the taking of knowledge and putting it in the presence of our heart and soul. It is instrumental in laying the foundation for wisdom and finding out who we are. It is taking knowledge and passing it through our value and belief system and then making a wise decision. If this true, then do I accept this? Do I choose to be the message or the messenger?

Again, we see the importance of signal to noise in our lives. Do I understand the difference? If I am not able to have my personal values filter out what is of true value to me, then I will be bombarded with much "interference" in my life, much like driving away from that radio station with the volume turned up!

This is when we must be careful of the effects of conditioning. We are warned by an external, political, or other type of value system to be careful. Each one of us must listen with our heart, even though our value system may offend someone else. Our thinking (wave) means we must listen with our hearts and souls (another wave), and our behavior then causes us to act differently (particle). Wisdom *knows* the difference.

Again, quantum theory supports the Scriptural context. If you take all the actions of thought, heart-and-soul decisions, and behavior, you have the total person. The principles of wave/particle duality are all in one and, like the human spirit, are adaptable. Here we have freedom of choice and our ethical responsibility for free will. Our decision is to use wisdom in knowing when we are to be the message or the messenger. Again, Scripture has assumed the responsibility to teach scientific principles.

We see the world as we experience it. Understanding is a clear vision of our principles, values, ethics, and obligation to follow those principles. For some, this stage in the process can be disconcerting. I look at understanding as the pointing of the compass needle, taking data, information, and knowledge, and applying that to how we see the world.

Understanding is why we do something. It is the realization that a course must be set and followed. It is the ethical application of who we are. Understanding goes beyond the teaching of theory. It means we must look at the essence of what we believe. This goes beyond mind and body. It means we look to and pursue a journey where heart and soul are present. Understanding can be put into perspective through our defined spiritual beliefs. It is as if we are called to make a decision with our whole being. It means a picture of what we must do is taking shape. In order for the final step to be taken, this step is critical.

For eight years I had the privilege of teaching Franklin Covey's programs *TimeQuest* and *What Matters Most*. The importance of those two programs required participants to develop, identify, and set goals by their governing values and an Attitude Statement. Some call it a Mission Statement.

I highly encourage people to develop a personal Attitude Statement, a statement of purpose. If you own accompany or are a CEO, develop an attitude statement for your organization. Attitude Statements say what you believe and where you are pointed. Attitude Statements are more focused than traditional Mission Statements. From an Attitude Statement you can develop your long-term, short-term, and ongoing goals. All of those are driven by your principles, values, and ethics.

Picture your Attitude Statement as your way of thinking and behaving. Your governing values are the quantized particles of your life. They are the single elements that make up who you are and let you adapt to life. If you develop these principles and have an Attitude Statement, they can assist you in making better decisions. Must you have an Attitude Statement? It would not hurt. I teach Attitude Statements to my clients, and not mission statements. Attitude is where the compass needle points in relation to the horizon!

One of the basic principles I taught was the importance of value-based decision making. What I have found since starting my own company is that a number of people have no idea what I am talking about. What value-based decision making teaches is your ability to define what the most important issues in your life are and what your plan is for implementing them. It helps people define what is important to them, not what others want them to do, or think they should do.

What I observed when teaching is that, as time went on, many students saw the defining of the values as a compass needle. Spiritual essence played a significant role here. Many people then began to see what truly mattered in their lives and how much they had been reacting to others and putting out brush fires.

What impressed me the most was their growing sense of personal direction. For some, it was the first time in their lives when they found a direction and it felt right. Their attitudes and values acted like compass needles that started to point their lives in a physical direction. They were deciding their future based on what they believed in and not on what others thought they should believe. They began to *understand* and put in perspective all the data, information, and knowledge they had been exposed to. It was time for them to set priorities and take external knowledge and turn it inward. They were preparing themselves for the next step.

Wisdom

"Love justice, you who judge the earth; think of the Lord in goodness, and seek him in integrity of heart."[15]

—Wisdom 1:1

Wisdom is the final connection, our goal. It is here where personal and organizational leadership lives. It is also here that I believe most decisions should be made but too few actually are. Leaders understand that we find the connection between leadership, science, and spirituality in wisdom. We look at the data, information, and knowledge given to us, internally process it for the final connection, and find truth. I believe this is not just the cardinal virtue of that name, but the universal moral quality. This addresses the fundamental principle for value-based decision making which defines our goal, the application of wisdom to moral conduct.

Making wise decisions means we have formulated a belief system where we understand the theory of knowledge and the impact data and information have on our actions. It is here that we are able to complete the circle that started with Thomas Aquinas. He comments in *Summa Theologica* that we have free will and free will does not know right from wrong. In other words, that part is up to us. Doing so makes us accountable for our decisions.

If this is true, then I don't know about anyone else but I would like to make decisions with as much going for me as possible. So what we have goes beyond making knowledgeable decisions. What Thomas Aquinas is saying is, we must strive to make wise ones. That is our goal.

Remember, he also stated free will is power. I believe Aquinas was attempting to make the connection between the philosophy of Aristotle and the theology of the human spirit. His document would only have been read by a small percentage of the population in his time and yet, today, it has profound implications. Aquinas' efforts were a solid step in the belief that mind, body, heart, and soul are related and cannot be separated. His premise is that we are spiritual beings and that decision making, though relegated to our human side, has profound spiritual applications. We have an obligation as business leaders to strive for wise decisions. To me, it is quantum thinking at its best.

This idea goes way beyond making a knowledge-based decision. Aristotle, too, poured this foundation in his teachings. He related that notions (data), when isolated, do not in themselves express either truth or falsehood; it is only with the combination of ideas (information) in a proposition that truth and falsity are possible (knowledge). What our goal becomes, is grounded in the belief that knowledge is formed with theory and changes.

Knowledge is only as valid as the next person who finds a better way. Understanding and wisdom hold us accountable to gather together all the pieces and base our decisions on an ethical model and governing values. Again, Aristotle relates the connection between body and soul. Aristotle says *soul* is defined as the perfect expression or realization of a natural body, and that there is a close connection between psychological states and physiological processes[16]. Body and soul are unified in the same way that wax and an impression stamped on it are unified. It is seamless and they rely on each other.

I believe this reinforces our responsibility to seek the truth when making wise decisions. We must decide right from wrong in our lives. Wisdom means that we may do the opposite of data decisions such as, "Don't just sit there, do something!" We may now be in the position that, when we look at the same situation, we realize there is nothing we could do to produce significant change. What now becomes evident is the statement, "Don't just do something, sit there!" It is necessary to understand that the closer we come to making wise decisions, the closer we come to the spiritual beings within us. We know that life does not present its events in the order we would like—life is events under pressure. This pressure knocks us off course and we make decisions that we ourselves, or others, may challenge later. Again, we see that the shortest distance between two points is a curved or irregular line.

I look for challenges in the application of the Five-Step Decision-Making Model. Our goal is to know the validity of making wise decisions. If you are under extreme pressure, under which of the five areas would you feel the most comfortable making a decision?

A famous quote that is profound in its simplicity with an application that applies to the decision-making model is the Serenity Prayer: "God grant me the serenity to accept the things I cannot change, the courage to change the things I can, and the *wisdom* to know the difference." This prayer, which is commonly attributed to theologian Reinhold Niebuhr[17], became a regular part of Alcoholics Anonymous (AA) after founder Bill Wilson used it in early meetings and published it in the *AA Grapevine*, AA's journal[18].

Making wise decisions has profound theological implications. It again presents to us the beauty of the paradox. If I work to make ethical and value-based decisions, I'd better have a degree of comfort in knowing myself. And yet, the decisions we make using that criteria may take us into areas we have never been before. Wisdom means being comfortable with being uncomfortable. Wisdom means we must adapt. This could bring a true duality in our lives, one where we must be able to understand when we must be the message and/or the messenger for change. Knowing more of ourselves is a critical process. It requires us to see a sense of right and wrong in what we do.

This is not a cold analysis or doses of data. It is seeing the ethical implications of our actions and acting in the best interest of the situation. It was the teachings of twentieth-century theologians such as Reinhold Neibuhr and Dietrich Bonhoeffer that emphasized that theological consideration of right and wrong could not just be made in an intellectual vacuum. It had to take into effect culture and the context of actual human lives. It also had to honor the human spirit.

The Book of Sirach 4:24 gives us a clear message about where we need knowledge, but it does not preclude wisdom. "Where the pupil of the eye is missing, there is no light, and where there is no knowledge, there is no wisdom."[19] This tells us that, if we are not open to others and the possibility of new knowledge or possibly looking at old knowledge in a different way, then we have no light.

The Book of Sirach says if we have no light then we have no possibility of wisdom. Knowledge is like a rest area, not a destination. We stop in at a body of knowledge and rest. We gain our strength, become energized, and move on.

The thought that knowledge is transitory and serves our immediate needs is foreign to our Western thinking where we are taught that knowledge is the goal and learning is the process. The appreciation of knowledge means we can never own it. We must understand that we can love learning but we cannot love knowledge.

Knowledge is a wave, a self-replicating thought that questions who and why we are. Our love must be for wisdom through understanding. In wisdom we have the paradox—to love what we do not know. Our own experiences can be knowledge, but if we do not have vision, we cannot have wisdom. I believe wisdom is more than just knowing; it is living and understanding with ethical convictions.

Wisdom can be a faith experience with our actions based in scientific reality. Faith means that we must find comfort in the questions and not the answers of life. Once we become aware of something and know it, we can no longer rest in the answer. Faith requires us to move on and continue the journey. Faith means we can only believe what we do not yet know.

Wisdom is the understanding that life is two planes of thinking, the comfort of asking questions and questioning the answers. Victor Frankl said that it is life that asks us the questions, and the answer we give life makes us responsible. And Neibuhr responds with the process to make it happen by asking us to accept the things we cannot change, the courage to change the things you can, and the *wisdom* to know the difference.

True leaders understand that they never relinquish free will to knowledge. They understand that free will can only be fulfilled through wisdom, and wisdom is knowing the difference between being the message and being the messenger. This duality of understanding is *quantum leadership thinking.*

Summary

"The greatest obstacle to discovering the
shape of the earth, the continents,
and the oceans was not ignorance
but the illusion of knowledge."
—Daniel J. Boorstin[20]

To summarize, the components of the Five-Step Decision-Making Model are:

Data: Data is the voice of the system. It has no conscience, does not tell you where you are going or how you got where you are. Data is a moment in time.

Information: Information is multiple sources of data. It reflects sources of data over time. Information is not necessarily accurate. Do not make life-changing decisions based on data and information alone.

Knowledge: Knowledge is information with theory. Knowledge is a given set of statements that lend themselves to be true until proven otherwise. The majority of decisions we make in our lives are based on data, information, and knowledge. (Eighty percent of all decisions are made here.)

Understanding: Understanding is the ethical inclusion of data, information, and knowledge. Picture it as a compass needle pointing us in the direction we should seek. This is the application of signal to noise. It calls us to consider our principles and values to the table of our decisions.

Wisdom: This is the formulation of the rightful application of data, information, knowledge, and understanding. Wisdom in decision making calls us to have a dedication to the application of right from wrong in our principles, values, and ethics. (Twenty percent of all decisions are made here.)

Questions

- What are my governing values and goals?
- Do I have an Attitude Statement for focus?
- What in my life might be signals and what might be noise?
- Do I know the difference?
- Do I advocate and make decisions based on data, information,

and knowledge, or do I move to the higher level of understanding and wisdom?

- If I had to make a decision under pressure, would I like it to be driven by knowledge or driven by wisdom?
- Am I working in a mind-and-body company or do I have a heart-and-soul organization with *quantum leadership thinking*?
- What significant decision have I put off?
- Do I have the data, information, and knowledge to understand and make a wise decision?
- What would I change to make a positive difference in my life?

CHAPTER FOUR

The Seven Needs for Personal Productivity: Meaning Is the Core Need

"Ultimately, man should not ask what the meaning of his life is, but rather must recognize that it is he who is asked. In a word, each man is questioned by life; and he can only answer to life by answering for his own life; to life he can only respond by being responsible."
—Viktor Frankl[1]

The Seven Needs: An Overview

It is with a deep sense of commitment that I dedicate these next seven chapters to each of the Seven Needs for Personal Productivity ("Seven Needs"). Fulfilling these needs is the core issue; it is instrumental in finding meaning in our lives and our choice of careers. We are then challenged to make wise decisions and accept the obstacles presented in our path.

I believe the Five-Step Decision-Making Model helps us understand and make wise decisions to add meaning in our lives. Finding meaning is at the heart and soul of the Seven Needs. Viktor Frankl dedicated his life to helping others find meaning. He explained that it is a certainty that happiness can be attained by furious pursuit and a consequent rage at the unsatisfying results. His useful word for this is *hyperintention*, a tendency that only inflames what is usually the real problem: our own self-centeredness. "Everything can be taken away from man but one thing—to choose one's attitude in a given set of circumstances, to choose one's own way."

The sane are those who accept this charge and do not expect happiness by right. Thus, Frankl's own logotherapy, which views suffering not as an obstacle to happiness but often the necessary means to it, is less a pathology than a path. In other words, we must find happiness in our own lives and address those needs with more than an action plan. Frankl states that attitude is a critical component[2].

In the time of Frederick Taylor and the Industrial Revolution, this would have been viewed as nonsense. Yet, we are now in a time when employees can expect multiple careers, extended life spans, and a lifelong learning requirement. I believe Frankl was describing our need to understand when we must be the message or the messenger in our lives, and the same for leaders in the workplace. He spent his adult life letting us know that we must be adaptive to a given set of circumstances.

This is yet another example of the wave/particle duality of the human spirit. Our Newtonian world works in many cases but, when it comes to the human spirit, we do not respond in the same way. This relationship is amplified when the duality of human spirit confronts the rigidity of the organizational chart. In plain language we call it job stress or career crisis. It is here that the Seven Needs will help you adapt and make quality decisions for both personal and career choices. We are quantum beings in a Newtonian workplace.

Developing the Seven Needs

Developing the Seven Needs has been a journey for me. Many writers, theologians, philosophers, and front-line employees have inspired me and made a significant impact on my thinking. I use words, phrases, and meaning to express my view of the world. It is the same in my journey for the Seven Needs.

In my reading I found that most writers had pieces of the puzzle but I didn't think anyone had the answer I was looking for. I had gnawing questions about everything that was unanswered—just like in life. Some of the pieces came together during continued talks with my students and working professionals; my love for reading gave me the rest.

What eluded me was an alternative to thinking of the Seven Needs as only a list. I struggled with the idea that productivity was a linear process. Success, like light, bends and is not a straight line. Einstein had it right. I also believe it is a spiritual, organizational, and organic system. Life, like the universe, never runs in a straight line. I am beginning to believe that the term *straight line* is an oxymoron.

Productivity is alive; it adapts and it evolves. Again, Paul Davies addresses the issue in *God and the New Physics:* "Scientists also are searching for meaning; by finding out more about the way the universe is put together and how it works, about the nature of life and consciousness, they can supply the raw material from which religious beliefs may be fashioned."[3] All of them work in this wonderful harmony with huge pieces we do not and probably never will understand. I believe that approach came both from conditioning and traditional problem-solving models. It is adaptation in its most elegant form.

Workplace leaders need to understand that the Seven Needs can go a long way in helping them to understand and develop a communication and productivity format. Our culture emphasizes linear thinking, problem solving, formulas, and looking for answers. We are taught that we begin the process, go to the end, celebrate success, maybe accept failure, and then start over. We get our reward at the end. I did lose many a night's sleep over thinking about that.

So what I did is write, explain, and teach the Seven Needs as equal entities. Initially, I did not see that any one need was more important than another. The deep insight that the Seven Needs is actually a process came over time. They are not an action plan; I came to the conclusion that they are a *listening device.*

We have taken *listening* away from our culture because we do not listen or herald listening as an attribute. We do not spend enough time keeping our mouths shut and eyes and ears open, listening to people, processes, organizations, and systems and, most importantly, our businesses. We have not accepted the fact that our organizations and systems speak to us.

Listening is a *Circle of Needs*, an instrument for gathering crucial signals to meet life's challenges. It is a continuous action that lets us examine our mission, goals, and journey.

Figure 2. The Seven Needs for Personal Productivity—Meaning Is the Core Need

How the Seven Needs Relate to Each Other

Listing the Seven Needs was one thing, living them was something else. So another form had to be created. What becomes clearer to me each day is the connectedness of the Needs. Each relates to the other with *Meaning* being the core.

In constructing the Seven Needs Model, I had to decide which of the needs was the key to the other six. I found that, once I put *Meaning* in the center as though it were the core of a molecule, the remaining needs seemed to revolve around it in harmony with our sense of free will. This model empowered me to gain control of not only key life skills, but I was able to apply them to a chosen way of life. I believe the Seven Needs Model has given me a sense of understanding and wisdom.

I now think of the Seven Needs as being more structured. If one were to picture them as a stethoscope placed against the pulse points of one's life, listening for a beat, then they might be thought of as helping one to listen to life itself. If I explore each of the Seven Needs, I may enhance the core and find meaning in my life.

The Importance of Free Will

If the Seven Needs can help us listen to life, then free will is the on-off switch for life's radio. The Trappist monk Thomas Merton said, "We must not imagine that we only discover this destiny by a game of hide-and-seek with Divine Providence. A man who fears to settle his future by a good act of his own free will does not understand the love of God."[4]

Free will can be seen in science, culture, and community by looking at our actions and deeds; it is our spiritual reality check. If principles, values, and ethics are the genetics that help us define meaning in our lives and who we are, then free will is the DNA that helps us get there.

The Seven Needs tell me that life direction is a choice; our free will is the medium by which we listen to The Seven Needs. It is up to us to decide what we want to hear and do with it. In that sense, both Thomas Merton and Victor Frankl were saying the same thing: that life is asking us. Ultimately, what is our plan?

The next step is the question, "Do we choose to listen?" We have an obligation to ourselves and our lives. At what point do we listen to what life and maybe our career really are asking us? The Seven Needs model only listens for questions. It is free will that helps us find the answers.

Finding Meaning in One's Life

I want to change gears now and complete this chapter with a discussion about the core issue: *Meaning.*

A deeper description and discovery of the word *Meaning* requires the examination of a personal journey. I would explore terms such as *wave/particle, message/messenger,* and responsibility. This would quantify who I am as a person and what I have chosen as my principles, values, and ethics in order to get me there.

I am not just asking *who* I am, but *why* I am. Remember, Frankl said that we do not ask life, life asks us. It is not easy to find an answer. I won't feel guilty about not finding one, because Aristotle didn't either. If we have a sense of meaning and purpose in our lives, we are making a statement to the world. That statement is reflected in our lives and career choices. While the declaration appears to be one of direction and destiny, it also makes one vulnerable to those who are not as centered.

Meaning in one's life means you are listening; it doesn't state that you are not necessarily equipped for life's journey. Free will lets us decide whether or not we choose to act on life's calling. If we are called to leadership, then we are required to take the risk. The decision to do so is supported both scientifically and spiritually. This is dedication and looking for a deep sense of purpose and direction in our lives and careers. This spiritual moment in our lives is one that we often do not listen to.

This is why many people find that prayer is such a powerful tool. Prayer is a form of listening, although many fail to understand this. Prayer is listening to the deep convictions of why we are and it can be the message or messenger. Prayer has strong duality and quantum implications. St. Benedict said that work is prayer and prayer is work. So prayer can be an action/particle, listening/wave and the message/

messenger of what God is saying to us, and it can help us prepare for life's obstacles.

How to Deal with Tough Times

If your calling puts you in a leadership situation, your challenge will be more than setting goals—it will be overcoming obstacles. Dr. Robert H. Schuller, best-selling author and minister, relates a story about tough times. It is a great example of what one has to understand about career and life success, and looking for a different way.

Schuller relates how people are like potatoes. After the potatoes are harvested, they have to be spread out and sorted by size in order to get the maximum market dollar. In the potato industry, this has always been done using people and machines. After the potatoes are sorted and bagged, they are loaded onto trucks. Again, we look at an industry that wants to deliver the best product possible.

One farmer never bothered to sort the potatoes but he seemed to be making the most money. One puzzled neighbor finally asked, "What is your secret?"

The farmer said, "It's simple. I load up the wagon with the potatoes and take the roughest road to town. During the eight-mile trip, the little potatoes always fall to the bottom, the medium potatoes land in the middle, while the big potatoes rise to the top."

Incidentally, that's not only true of potatoes—it is a law of life. Just as big potatoes rise to the top on rough roads, the tough people rise to the top in rough times. Remember, life is not a direct route. (Remember Dirac's equation where electrons bounce off other obstacles in the vacuum of space and yet form an organization?) Think of Dirac's experiment as a high-tech potato truck!

We face many challenges in the workplace. We are bounced around and may even feel we'll never find our niche. We never seem to fit in and feel as if we are in a time/space vacuum with each day being a random event. We let life just happen. We may see this as part of the struggle to find our calling, which may be our current job or our ability to lead others. Whatever our situations, we must accept that we will get bounced around, taken over some rough psychological roads, and constantly sorted and compared to others.

We often hear people who have deep spiritual beliefs talk about being in the desert. Jesus often went to the desert to pray and to be alone. These symbolic references remind us that we often need to make a decision, and feel we are alone. We are pretty much predestined to enter a period of void in our careers and lives. Like the electron that passes through the universe and collides with other obstacles, I can imagine the lone scientist who looks at data and information and sees it in a completely different way from her colleagues. That, to me, is a desert experience.

At times, we want someone to listen to what we have to say. We struggle to have the world listen to our message, and plead for society to also listen to the answers we've discovered so that we may help others. But the opposite may be true. We need to ask questions in order to get answers. Again, we have the challenge: are we trying to answer the questions we ask, or are we listening to the questions life may be asking us?

We see ourselves and our career choices as a message to the world, but we, in fact, may be suffering the same fate as Moses. The world may instead be asking us to be a messenger for some other thought, purpose, or voice. There is a conflict over the duality of one's true self. We must understand our complete spiritual purpose and sort our difficulties into their relevant sizes. By doing this, we are then able to listen to life and the obstacles we find in the road.

Dedication and direction are viewed by our culture as having a narrow and restricted focus. We are becoming too consumed with the idea that success is a right. We are not preparing for the possibility that the scientific rules of organizational behavior can go south on us. If they do, along with them go your attitude and ability to risk and have faith in the unknown.

We are constantly reminded that we do not see the big picture. I think it is more important to listen for, rather than see the big picture. This is an example of signal to noise. Is what I am now doing with my life a true signal or is it just random noise? Do I know the difference? If life had no meaning, how would you know what you are hearing? A person with a statement of purpose and meaning also has a clearer sense of awareness. It is the realization that one is making a statement to life, "I can be adaptive to the world but I will do it with a sense of principles, values, and ethics to accomplish that purpose." This is the true manifestation of the message and the messenger. It is the adaptive duality of life.

Life may not be asking us—it may be shouting at us through our daily noise! Will we respond? This does not mean the experience we encounter will be a pleasant one. Nor does it mean that the response will hold an answer. I can almost assure you that what life or career may be asking of you is not what you may want to hear! It means that we will experience a series of events that will reinforce our commitment to life and see the good in all we do.

And that, to me, is the fundamental issue in a meaningful life and career: to see the good in all we do and those we meet. This means when the times are really tough! This is not easy. It cannot be legislated, litigated, mediated, or reached by consensus. It means we must act and take responsibility for our own free will by listening. I believe this is what Viktor Frankl meant when he said happiness is not a right. It is up to us to find the good in an adverse situation. We are free to look for specific results. We are not entitled to it. We only have the right to try. To me, this is Personal Leadership 101.

Is Having a Job a Right?

Let us look at some of the issues we face today as they relate to Meaning. Much discussion is being voiced regarding livable wage. Communities are now setting standards where they are telling businesses within their boundaries that they must pay a livable wage. Their hope is to provide an environment for working people to find a sense of meaning. It is an honorable move but it may not get them there.

The focus is, of course, on the term *livable*. Livable for one person may be completely different for someone else. Livable wage is like saying we will pass the law before we design the environment or problem. I, however, must ask, "Before we have a livable wage, does having the right to a job add meaning to our lives?" *Is working and gainful employment a constitutional right?*

The Declaration of Independence tells us we have the right to life, liberty, and the pursuit of happiness. I believe we are guaranteed the freedom to look for a job and develop our skills and the right to try. The rest is up to us. If Aquinas, Aristotle, Frankl, and Merton are all correct, then I believe we are not entitled to a livable wage, but we do have the right to try for it and are obligated to do so!

In the early 1990s, I was asked to speak to college seniors in a government class. I found the students both entertaining and engaging. As part of my presentation, I had them do an exercise where they identified some of their governing values and linked them to career goals they wanted to achieve to add meaning to their lives. I was somewhat surprised when it became apparent that many students were challenged by this exercise.

As the seminar went on, I asked them to link what they stood for with what life was going to present them after they left the institution. I wanted them to know that their education would give them more employment opportunities in life, but along with that was the supporting principle that they were also responsible for those decisions. I could see that this statement was not sitting too well with the some of the students.

During this entire process, the professor sat in the back of the room closely watching. It was at this point that I began to realize further clarification was necessary and I asked the following question: "How many in this room believe the Declaration of Independence guarantees you the right to be happy?" What happened next was unexpected.

Well over half the students in the room raised a hand signifying yes and, in particular, so did the professor.

I then said, "The founding documents of the United States of America only guarantee that in this country you have the right to try."

I certainly got the debate that I wanted. These dedicated students were under the belief that finding meaning or happiness in their lives was not only an expectation but a right. I told them that the right that was guaranteed by law was the right to try to be anything they want to be in this country. I couldn't help but think that they believed the laws of life and successes were absolute. The message is that they were responsible for their decisions, that they must exercise free will to achieve their goals, and the right of the individual to make those decisions is a fundamental core value of this country.

I left the classroom that day with the knowledge that many of those students truly believe that success was a provision guaranteed them. I am still amazed at the number of people I talk to, spanning demographics from high-school educated to the working world, who believe happiness is a right. Happiness is not a right and never has been. If we take a right for granted, it has no meaning.

In America We Have the Right to Try

While I admired the zeal and conviction of the students, I also mourned for their apathy and minimization of the word *meaning* and what it truly meant. That is the price of freedom. It also lends credibility to those who try to succeed. Here in the United States at least, you can try. You have the opportunity to let life challenge you and, in doing so, you challenge the obstacles of life. Again, a particle can act like a wave and a wave can act like a particle.

Life asks you. I see that the greatest challenge is in the workplace, and that when we are given the opportunity, we fail to listen. We can make choices with our free will; accept the consequences, even sadness, to achieve our life goals. This again is where Viktor Frankl says it is choosing our own path to find meaning.

We can also say that success and achievement are rights that are owed us. We can even litigate for it if we feel the perceived wrong is great enough and we are owed the right. This is the opposite of *meaning*; it is the external manifestation of choices. This, Frankl says, is not a path but pathology.

In the June 2001 newsletter of Mount Angel Abbey in St. Benedict, Oregon, then Abbot Joseph Wood related information that is enlightening and relevant to our journey to understand meaning. Abbot Wood cites the research of Tom Beaudoin, who presented this information at the American Benedictine Abbots Conference in Oceanside, California.

In his research, Mr. Beaudoin related some characteristics about Generation X, which he defined as early 30-year-olds. These were:

1. Pluralism or the acceptance of many beliefs ("Who am I to judge?")
2. Ambiguity or uncertainty over issues
3. A lack of consensus on truth. They have difficulty agreeing on what is the truth and what it represents.
4. The triumph of consumer capitalism—why some make more money than others
5. The divorce culture, in which 45 percent are children of divorced parents and products of the day-care experience. Many of this generation appear to have lived an early adulthood, while others have lived an extended adolescence.[5]

Beaudoin's article also talks about Generation X's attitude that the political process doesn't change anything. They find spirituality is an individual journey rather than a formal association with a structured religion or facility. I have observed that many people make the same choice in the workplace. They do not readily associate with a structure or organization. They do identify with specific projects, ideas, and their personal direction.

This article emphasizes how Generation X is looking for a value system but is not able to find the foundation—they are in a desperate search for meaning. And here is where I believe they are making a mistake: they are asking questions from their experience, but not listening to what questions are being asked of them.

Based on Tom Beaudoin's information, I believe they are asking the following questions:

- Who am I to judge? What is the right thing to do?
- What is the truth and where do I find it?
- If we are all supposed to be equal, why isn't life economically fair for everyone?
- What is the correct definition of the word *family*?"

They have set sail on an ocean called life. Their ocean is supposed to be smooth and level, everyone is equal, and their destination is a straight line with no obstacles. And if it is not, then someone is at fault but they don't want to be the first to put the blame on anyone. Maybe litigation will find the answer for them. The particle of their lives is adrift on an endless sea of waves.

The Greek Immigrant's Lesson: Time and Love Know No Boundaries

Here is a story about a messenger, an elderly man who found the meaning of life and taught me a lesson. As I look back on his profound message, I often wish he could have been a guest at some of my seminars. This man had a quantum sense of Understanding and Wisdom.

It was the late 1960s and I had been home in Wisconsin on military leave. I was on my way back to my Air Force assignment and was trying to catch an early morning flight from Milwaukee, Wisconsin. I had gotten to the airport around 7:00 a.m., was checked in, and had about an hour-and-a-half wait.

I always enjoyed walking the concourses and seeing the different aircraft and their destinations. I liked to imagine myself on each plane and wonder about the places they were going. I always made it a point to walk all the way to the end of the concourse and, if possible, find an empty seat at a deserted gate. It was a good time to just collect my thoughts and rest.

Memories are funny things. I am amazed how we can remember the most insignificant details, yet completely blank out on something that may have happened last week. On this day, I made my way over to a deserted gate. I remember the sun coming through the window and, as I began to relax, I gradually became aware of the presence of someone else. An elderly gentleman was sitting about ten seats off to my left and staring out the window.

He looked to be in his late 60s, with a face and hands that said hard work. If I passed him in a crowd I probably would not have even noticed him. He looked as though he was deep in thought.

As I am always the one to initiate a conversation, I went ahead and introduced myself. After initial small talk, we came to the question everyone asks at an airport: Where are you going and where are you from?

The gentleman told me in an accented voice that he was Greek and had been in the United States about four years. He was living in Milwaukee with his daughter and son-in-law. I asked him where he was going and he said he was waiting for a plane to arrive. I asked him what gate he was looking for. He said, "This one." I looked over at the boarding area desk and kiosk that handled the gate. No flight announcement, time, or destination was posted. Even the lights were off.

The man went on to tell me that it had been a lifelong dream to bring his family here for a better life. His children had come earlier and now were citizens. He and his wife stayed in Greece to work and save money. It took him sixty-plus years to realize his childhood dream to come to America. But he did not have the money for both himself and his wife. So they decided that she would stay in Greece until he could send for her. He was now at the airport to meet her after four years of waiting.

As I look back on this story, I am aware of the profound sense of suffering his family had experienced. He said he had been back to Greece once in the last four years to see his wife. The cost of plane fare back and forth delayed their goal of having her come to America.

All his hard work had led to this day. It was 7:00 a.m., and he was waiting for the love of his life. He said he had many setbacks along the way but her flight had left Athens and was due at this gate.

"When does she arrive?" I asked.

He stared straight ahead and said, "Eight o'clock tonight."

Looking back on that day I now realize that, once we understand the why of life, we then will find the how. To this man, the work or wait did not matter. All he knew was that he did not want to miss her plane and he had arrived twelve hours early to be sure he wouldn't miss it. He had listened to life and his family would now be whole. Einstein was right. The relativity of time made no difference. Even though they were twelve hours and still thousands of miles apart, I believe the man and his wife were talking to each other. That is love, commitment, and listening—that is attitude. The principles of Einstein, Frankl, Newton, Dirac, Moses, and Thomas Aquinas were all present in this very simple but wise man.

I wished him well and left. I went on with my life. I wonder how many people looked at this man, thinking he had nothing to do but waste time at the airport. Of the hundreds of people who walked by him, most probably never gave him a second look or the time of day.

When I formulated my ideas for the Seven Needs and thought about how Meaning is the core issue, I immediately remembered the elderly Greek gentleman at the Milwaukee airport as if it were yesterday, not over forty years ago.

This man was committed to his family (message, particle) and also lived a portfolio of values (messenger, wave). His sense of spirituality was completely focused on the woman and family he loved. Time, distance, and obstacles were not issues. He had found meaning in his life and knew that quality of life meant having his wife by his side. This man was living on pure faith, attitude, and a deep and simple sense of what the meaning of life was all about.

His story had an element of Einstein's time/space. He heard life's calling described by Frankl and listened to the questions life was asking him. And then he lived out what Thomas Aquinas had related: we have free will, we are obligated to do something with it, and we will be held accountable.

I would like to add a footnote. In the fall of 2003, my wife Roseann and I were back in Milwaukee to visit family. I had just written the piece on the Greek gentleman and had read it to my wife the week before. As we were waiting for our airplane I said to her, "This is it."

"This is what?" she asked.

"This is the concourse and the windows where I had the conversation with the Greek gentleman waiting for his wife. It was right here."

We both stood for a moment and just looked. Much had changed but the windows still looked out to the same area. For a moment I stepped back to that day so long ago and remembered that wonderful Greek gentleman waiting for his wife. I hope her airplane was on time.

You don't have to be profound to deliver a profound message. There is nothing more enlightening and wholesome than a message from the human spirit and its ability to overcome adversity. My Greek gentleman's experience was a profound lesson in love and leadership. He never would run a Fortune 100 company or manage an international operation. He did, however, have heart and soul and commitment to the woman of his life. That was attitude and leadership. It is needed in the workplace today.

I believe the most important messages in our lives and careers come from those who have the message we need to hear but we never take the time to ask. It is those tens of thousands of employees who are sitting in corporate cubicles somewhere, and we either fail to take the opportunity or have just relegated them to being an interruption in our lives and organizations. Faith knows no institution but the human spirit. We never ask for our own personal reasons. And it is our loss.

Profound Incidents Happen When You Least Expect Them

In 2000, I was working under contract for a regional community safety organization. It was wonderful work. It gave me the opportunity to travel and spend time with communities in the western United States, including Alaska and Hawaii. To this day I take great satisfaction in spending time with people who tell me all about their neighborhoods and communities. It is also interesting that, no matter the geographical location, many of the problems are the same.

If you have never been to Alaska it is one of the places everyone must experience. And when you do, you know you will never be the same. Alaska is more than a way of life—it is a calling. On this occasion I was asked to work with a small group and present some community programs. This was not my first time in Alaska. I have always loved the state and never passed up an opportunity to return. This time, however, I would experience something that had a profound effect on my life; it would also help me define my life and what purpose I was to serve. It definitely gave me meaning.

I was going to Bethel. For anyone who does not know, Bethel is close to the Bering Sea, about three hundred miles west of Anchorage. The community is small, with less than twelve thousand people, and you can't drive there. Everything, and I mean *everything,* is flown in by one airline. When you fly in from Anchorage, they put you in the back of the plane because the front of the plane is filled with cargo.

My significant incident happened after I completed my presentations and was flying out of Bethel in the late afternoon. I was in the middle seat in the last row on the left-hand side of the Boeing 737 (in the back of the plane, of course). Riding in the back of the older 737s is a lot like sitting on a high-frequency tuning fork. It is a true aviation experience. As I sat down and buckled my seatbelt, I began to make small talk with the woman who appeared to be in her seventies sitting by the window. Her gaze was fixed and she did not make much eye contact, in fact, she spent most of the time looking out the window. It became obvious that she was concerned about the bad weather. There was low visibility, rain, scattered snowflakes, and winds to about twenty-five miles per hour, typical weather for Bethel.

As we taxied to the end of the runway, I asked the woman where she was going and she said she was going to Florida to see her daughter and her grandchildren. Our conversation turned to the differences in the weather between Alaska and Florida. After remarking that her trip was going to be a long one, she became very quiet.

As the pilot turned onto the runway and spooled up the engines, she turned, looked me in the eye, and said, "Would you please hold my hand?"

Without saying a word I took hold of her right hand. She continued to look out the window and held my hand as if her life depended on it. I could sense her nervousness each time the airplane hit any little bump in the runway. During take-off, sitting in the last row of an older 737 is not the most pleasant experience—think of it as riding in a covered wagon on the Oregon Trail doing one hundred thirty miles an hour.

It didn't take long for the pilot to get the wheels up. As we went into the clouds, I felt her grip tighten. I remember telling her that the cloud layer wasn't very thick and that we should be in sunshine in a couple of minutes. Sure enough, after a few more minutes we were in clear skies and the ride was smoother. She began to relax and finally let go of my hand.

"I hope you didn't mind holding my hand," she said.

I told her I hoped it helped her. She said it did and then she explained, "Several years ago I was in a plane crash. Only half of the passengers survived. Since that time I have been deathly afraid of flying. We crashed right after take-off and it was in bad weather. Once we get airborne I am OK."

This woman has left a lifelong impression on me. Here was an excellent opportunity to let fear rule her life, yet she refused to bow to her fears out of love for her family. She had taken an incident of unavoidable suffering and found meaning. She also taught me that, even if we have a situation in our past, it does not mean that we cease to be human or stop living. I wonder how often we choose not to make a career change because of fear. How often, maybe, we even lost an opportunity for finding a sense of meaning in our lives because of fear.

I did not have anything to say that would have made a difference to this woman. I was the message and my role was simply to be there for her, to hold her hand when she felt fear, vulnerability, and a deep love for her family; it was not a role of expectation, knowledge, deep message, messenger, wave, particle—all these terms applied to one vulnerable human spirit who had a deep love and commitment to see her daughter and grandchildren.

The rest of our flight was spent in idle conversation. We went our separate ways in Anchorage. I did not ask her name and probably will never see her again. I look back on that incident as a clear instance of my role as a message and as a human being who had the opportunity to help another.

As I was remembering this story and thinking of the Seven Needs and the search for Meaning, I had a profound sense of the survival of the human spirit. I think her grandchildren are truly lucky and would agree with me.

Ask yourself the following questions:

- When was the last time someone just needed your physical presence?
- Did you know what it was about? Was it work related?
- Did you feel awkward and had the feeling that you needed to be saying something?
- Was it someone you knew or was it a stranger?
- How did you handle it?
- Did you question yourself later on and ask why you were chosen?

Meaning Can Help to Clarify Values

I would like to share with you another incident that not only added meaning to my life but changed it in more ways than I can imagine. In 1966, I enlisted in the United States Air Force and was sent to Alaska. It was not uncommon for troops to fly through Alaska on their way to Vietnam.

My job involved working with the aircraft on the flight line. I remember looking in a transport aircraft coming back from Vietnam that stopped to refuel and seeing that it carried the remains of US soldiers being taken home. I often wondered if any of those remains were those young, scared faces I had seen in the previous months going in-country.

It was there in Alaska that I met one of my best friends, Mike Radford from Snow Hill, North Carolina. Mike was a southern gentleman through and through. He loved to play bridge, pinochle, and was a pretty good poker player. We were together in late 1966 and 1967, and then in early 1968, I was transferred to Ellsworth Air Force Base (AFB) in Rapid City, South Dakota.

After my transfer, I got the notice that Mike not only was scheduled to return to the lower forty-eight but he was also assigned to Ellsworth AFB and would arrive several months after me. We had two more years and planned to travel together.

Mike, stubborn one minute, sympathetic the next, but always a southern gentleman, especially wanted me to meet his family in North Carolina. One of our favorite topics was BBQ. I used to kid Mike because he used to tell me how important BBQ was, how his Dad made the best BBQ in the world, and about the deep tradition of BBQ in North Carolina. I used to tell him hot dogs and hamburgers were BBQ, and the debate was on!

Mike also was anxious to show me his alma mater, the University of North Carolina at Chapel Hill. He was a Tar Heel to the bone. As time went on, we talked more and more about our North Carolina trip. I was really looking forward to what Mike called southern hospitality.

Mike and I shared a room at Ellsworth. We were more like brothers than friends and it seemed like we knew what the other person was thinking. We were young, proud to be serving our country, and we were good at what we did. We were so young and so alive!

All that would change one morning in July of 1968. Both of us were assigned to the flight line. We both talked about going to breakfast after and then going to work. Mike was making his bed and complained that he had a really bad headache. I was going to ask him if he wanted an aspirin. He didn't answer me and I turned around to ask him again. He had this stare in his eyes. I started to say something and he just opened his mouth and collapsed.

I yelled to the guys across the hall and someone called the ambulance. Mike did not say a word nor did he respond to any voices. Even the medics could not get a response. My First Sergeant wanted to know if I wanted to follow the ambulance. At the time, I thought that was the dumbest question he could have asked. Hell, yes, I wanted to follow the ambulance! We were about five minutes behind.

In the hospital, a doctor came into the hall where I was sitting and told me that Mike had passed away. On the way back to our room, I told the First Sergeant that I wanted to be the military escort who would take Mike's body home. He told me that he would check with the commander. All I remember next is going to my room, crawling in my bed with my uniform on, and crying so hard it hurt. Hours later, the First Sergeant knocked on my door and said, "Bobrowitz, you're going to North Carolina."

The only thing I could think of was that this was a hell of a way to meet Mike's parents.

The experience of taking your best friend's body home to his family is a life-changing experience. As Frankl says, we can find meaning in our attitude toward unavoidable suffering.

The Air Force cut my orders, made all the arrangements, and called me in for a briefing. Mike and I would fly on commercial air service. It seemed strange that I would be in the cabin and Mike's casket would be in the baggage compartment. My commander told me that I was responsible for Mike from the moment of our departure until the time I arrived in North Carolina and met the funeral director at the airport. This meant that I was to be in sight of the casket at all times, except on the airplane.

At the time, Rapid City airport was under construction so commercial airlines were landing at Ellsworth. After checking in, I went through the military checkpoint and walked to the airplane. I thought how strange it was for Mike to be loaded in the baggage area from a hearse. After the hearse left, I walked up the stairs into the DC-9. I looked for an empty seat on the baggage loading side so I could see the baggage operating area.

As I took my seat toward the rear of the aircraft I noticed that a couple of passengers were involved in an agitated discussion with the flight attendants. Eventually they got up and left the plane. I really didn't take notice until we were in the air and I heard one flight attendant say that the couple was distressed because they had seen the casket being loaded onto the airplane. They said it was a bad omen and wanted a different flight.

I had spent my share of time traveling the commercial airlines during my service. One got used to the stares from people who didn't like the military during the Vietnam era and our position in Vietnam. I know I became more proud of the uniform I wore. I still believe it is one of the most honorable services you can give.

Taking your best friend's remains home to his family was another challenge. I did not bargain for this when I raised my right hand. I had to transfer flights and airlines with a four-hour layover at O'Hare in Chicago. When we arrived at O'Hare, I walked down the stairs of the aircraft and immediately went to the aircraft baggage door to wait for the casket to come out. It was a strange feeling to be riding in the right seat of a vehicle towing the baggage trailers and knowing one of them carried your best friend. The ground personnel pulled a canvas curtain around the cart that carried Mike. As we drove by the concourses, I wondered how many people waiting had a similar attitude to the couple who'd gotten off at Ellsworth.

I waited in the office of a warehouse-size freight building with aisles of stacked boxes and parcels—and stored next to all the stacks of boxes and freight was Mike's casket. As I looked out an office window, I watched the employees making sure packages and boxes made their way to their destinations. It would have been interesting to hear what they thought as they passed Mike's casket.

About an hour before the next flight, I got a folding chair and went into the warehouse and sat by Mike's casket. It probably looked a little strange but I didn't care. Small vehicles with tandem trailers passed me—this guy in an Air Force uniform sitting on a folding chair next to a casket. I really didn't care. I couldn't think of any other place in the world I wanted to be at that moment. In a few hours, I would be giving Mike to his parents and I just needed to let him know that I was there. It was the most logical place to be.

At eight in the evening we landed in North Carolina. As I looked out the window, I saw the hearse parked by the baggage cart and immediately recognized Mike's dad from the photos Mike had often showed me. When I got off the airplane, I went directly to the aircraft baggage door. The hearse was backing up to the door as I approached.

Mike's dad was there and I introduced myself to him and told him how sorry I was. He kept looking over his shoulder at the conveyor unloading the bags from the cargo bay. As I look back now, his expression seemed to show both fear and denial: fear of seeing his son and the denial that this was really happening and the unfairness of unavoidable suffering. Mike's casket was the last article that was placed on the conveyor. Mike was home.

We took Mike directly to the funeral home. It was there that his dad saw his son for the first time since his death. I think the opening of that casket was the hardest moment of his life. It was very difficult for me. His dad had to acknowledge that it was his son in that casket. How I admire that man to this day. I so clearly recall seeing the weight of the world slowly settling on his sagging shoulders. Mike was not on leave; he had come home to stay.

My job was to have Mike's dad identify his son, then the funeral director could accept possession of his remains. While this was happening, I was still processing what my commander had told me: as a representative of the United States Air Force, I had to be professional and make sure the needs of the family were met. The hardest part was yet to come.

I spent a few days with Mike's family. Because it was a small town, everyone knew about the tragedy. To this day, what I had to do at that funeral was one of the most memorable tasks I will ever do in my life.

On the day of the funeral I sat in full dress uniform by the family. At the end of the service, the funeral director and I removed the American flag that was draped over Mike's casket and folded it in the military manner next to the casket. The funeral director walked up to me, I assumed the position of attention, saluted, and he gave me the flag. Still at attention, I then walked to a position in front of the Radford family to present the flag.

I remember the words to this day, "...Mr. and Mrs. Radford on behalf of the United States Air Force, a very proud and grateful nation, I present to you this flag." I then bent over and presented the flag to Mike's mom. My duty was done: I had brought Mike home. I was both the message and the messenger. Mike now rests near the family property in North Carolina. His mom and dad said they wanted him close to them.

Meaning: encountering someone or something, doing a good deed or act, and our attitude toward unavoidable suffering. On the day of Mike's funeral, I did all three (and I had not yet heard of Viktor Frankl).

I look back on that time and realize that it was a changing moment in my life. I did an inventory of what had happened. I had left my family, enlisted in the Air Force, was sent to Alaska, froze my butt off, was assigned to Strategic Air Command in South Dakota, sweated my butt off on a flight line that could reach 120 degrees, felt the looks of disdain and had people move away from me at airports because they didn't like uniforms, and delivered my best friend home to his parents in a casket.

Life was asking me. I sure as hell wasn't asking it. I was fooling myself if I thought I was asking life. I think if I had to describe the word *meaning* I would say it is a clarifying of values. I believe I did more growing in those years than I could have imagined. I was twenty-two years old.

Life had changed for me. I had seen death, decision, despair, and responsibility. I was responsible for these lives and I had the life of a friend taken from me. If someone had asked me about life's values at the time, I probably would have looked at them as if they were nuts. I would have had a problem describing what *value*, *meaning*, *message*, and *messenger* meant. I did, however, know that I was rapidly developing an acute sense of what I stood for.

I lived through other significant events in my career. Years later, I felt public safety was calling, and I listened. Why I chose law enforcement is still somewhat of a mystery. I did know that I knew I could do the job. I also felt that it was important to stand for something.

As I look back on those events and the thirty-five-plus years that have passed, I am acutely aware of what my military experience did for me. I did not know until years later what a profound experience it was. It was not a career of notoriety or any type of fame. I was just one of the many thousands who served their country. When I left the Air Force in 1970, some of the new recruits called me the "old man." I was twenty-three.

I do know that my experiences changed my life in ways I discover each day. I know I have a deep love for my country and our flag. I get the same lump in my throat when I hear the Air Force theme and I miss Mike. He's with me to this day.

New Generations Will Face Tough Choices

If my assumptions are correct, Generations X and Y are facing real issues about choices and the lifelong implications of those choices and a search for meaning. If this is true, then my heart aches for them. I also believe they are not asking questions that have not been asked before. I do believe their careers will have some significant but not insurmountable challenges.

If we look at Viktor Frankl's approach to the importance of meaning in one's life, then these generations are facing strong challenges. The gift of free will challenges us to listen to what life has to say and make choices about us, our lives, and our careers. We have the choice to decide how we are going to think and how we are going to feel.

Prior to 1970, we taught students the importance of being good by teaching value-based decision making. What we have done since then is to default to teaching the importance of feeling good. This second focus will profoundly impact our work environment over the next thirty years. Value-based decision making puts the responsibility on our shoulders—it is not a group process or something that is reached by consensus. The world is not flat, and everyone is not standing on a level, even surface with a comfortable climate and a pocket full of money. Life is mountains, valleys, and deserts, lakes, and listening and holding someone's hand because we must be challenged to traverse these obstacles.

Two things are certain: life is not fair—it was not designed to be that way, and no two people go through life the same way. It is not a consensus issue—individual decisions choose the path and set off on the journey that lasts a lifetime. Life is not linear; it is a series of continuous events and each one is a connected learning process, like a jigsaw puzzle. The shortest distance is a *curved* line. Each day we are required to look for pieces that connect. Each day may, in fact, lead us in a different direction. They are all connected but more of a design than a single line. The Seven Needs and the core need of Meaning, if developed and given the opportunity, will all listen silently for the questions being asked.

The Seven Needs Are Interactive

Let us go back to the productivity cycle. What we choose to do adds meaning to our lives. The other six needs for productivity add to the meaning in our lives and vice versa; they support each other. As Abbot Joseph Woods related, the issues Generation X is dealing with are pluralism, ambiguity, lack of consensus, triumph of capitalism, and divorce.

It becomes clear that the Seven Needs (finding meaning, say-so and input into their destiny, a fair wage, quality of life, meaningful relationships, educational and learning experience, and knowing that what they do in life is important) can help them with their concerns and their journey.

I have become aware that the discovery of meaning in one's life is not something that is gone one day and then, presto, meaning has arrived and your career direction is assured. It is more like a garden or a field as it grows. Life is like all the plants, vegetables, weeds, and stones. You spend your time planning and thinking about how your garden will grow. But times occur when the weeds of experience seem to take command.

We get frustrated and angry because the stones in the earth also get in our way. It is like the electron passing through the universe. The journey never stops and all we do is run into new obstacles and turn in the bend.

When I was a child, our backyard garden always had stones which were barriers when I would weed with my dad. I had to pick the stones out because the garden wouldn't grow unless we got rid of them. As I look back, those weeds, stones, and barriers now seem like a door; when I removed them from the garden I was actually opening up the earth for more light, nutrients, and growth. I was the messenger and the garden was the message. Wave and particle were acting with balance and harmony.

I have learned now that listening to the "why" of life and career was the key—that the rocks and weeds of life are an important part of life's message and that I am the messenger. Again the paradox becomes the truth. It is time to move on.

Life Questions

- Do you ask life or do you listen to what life may be asking of you?
- What has been the most meaningful event in your life or career?
- What have you bumped into along the way?
- Who has been the most meaningful person you have encountered?
- What event in your life or career caused you the most suffering?

- What attitude and path did you take to see yourself through?
- What life event was your most significant change in attitude?
- Is your current attitude causing you concern?
- What positive change would you bring into your life to make a difference?

I believe in the harmony of science and soul. Both are a gift from God. God tells us the "how" of the universe through science and the "why" through our soul.

Chapter Five

Does My Work Give Me Say-So and Input into My Destiny?

"Now God grant I speak suitably and value these endowments at their worth; for He is the guide of Wisdom and the director of the wise...
For He gave me sound knowledge of existing things, that I might know the organization of the universe and the force of the elements."
—Wisdom 7:15, 17–18[1]

One of life's great pleasures is to be able to sit in a concert hall and listen to the beauty of a stringed symphony. We do not have to read music to be able to listen and be deeply moved by a stringed instrument and its ability to capture attention.

What we hear and do has mathematical implications. One can go back to the Greeks who understood that numbers had relationships, just as notes from a stringed instrument do. Early Greeks knew that, if all the strings on an instrument were of the same length and thickness, they would get the same sound. They quickly learned that, if you had one string twice as long but the same thickness, you got a different sound but it was still in harmony with the others. The Greeks taught us that numbers are relative and, if one squared a number or multiplied a number by itself, it would result in another number that was larger but still related to the original number.

Fred Alan Wolf in *The Spiritual Universe* tells how the early Greeks saw the harmony and relationships between numbers and the organic world[2]. To some Greek thinkers, numbers were contained in matter. The beauty of their thinking was their observation of the relativity of mathematics and the organic world. It was as if numbers were speaking their voice to the world, yet they were related in nature and in music.

Today, we see the relationship and harmony of the Greeks' thinking and enjoy it in a concert hall. We experience the relationship of strings, wood, metal, and the human spirit that combine to produce harmonic sound. It is most appropriate to think of it as a spiritual experience. These principles, unfortunately, are falling on deaf ears in the workplace.

The Greeks' thinking set the stage for man's realization of the harmony of the universe. What we have lost in our thinking is that we have not brought the lessons of the concert hall to the company cubicle. Our company leaders have lost the sense—or maybe they never understood—that each human spirit is a stringed instrument and that people will orbit around sounds, ideas, teachers, and relationships. Employees are systematically plucked like musical strings, but what is lost is the manager's ability to understand that each sound in an organization is looking for harmony within the grander scheme of things. We are evaluated by our ability to compete with one another when the opposite may be true. There is a need to be in harmony with one another.

I know it is a cliché in the English language but few realize the true depth of the statement, "We all must read from the same sheet of music." What we must understand is that employees need to know where they fit symbolically on the scale and, more importantly, what song is being sung by the organization and if the employee behavior is in harmony with that plan. Remember, management writes the music, the CEO is the conductor, and the employees are the instruments. Each human instrument wants a voice in the grand scheme of the things. I wish leaders would understand the elegance of such a relationship.

In continuing the thought, in the workplace, let's say that each employee is a string on an instrument called the organizational culture. It, too, creates a sound. The goal of the leader is to understand what song needs to be played and whether it is in harmony. Does your workplace provide that opportunity? I wrote a statement back in 1982 that speaks to this issue, "The individual song held inside each human spirit is beautiful beyond words, unequalled in lyrics, and most likely never to be played."

My heart aches for many organizations. I believe leaders, in addition to laws of science and spirituality, should also be taught the principles of music and its relationship to management. The harmony and organization should complement each other. I believe they need to see how the universe and the spiritual elegance of their employees is a daily symphony of design and worth. What is most troubling is, leaders implement clinical policies to design a listening organization but default their leadership style to the false god of a laptop, iPad, and a leather chair.

I cannot count the number of times I have heard employees say they did not have a voice in their organization. Their frustration was quite real and open and spoken with a sense of frustration. To me, this means they had experienced this over time. Bottom line: it was nothing new.

It is interesting how the issue of say-so and input seems to transcend time and technology. In this era of voice mail, group meetings, data transfers, and the pseudo-communicating work force, say-so and input of employees is still an issue of critical importance.

We have asked scientific principles (technology) to accomplish something they were not designed to do. In other words, we have used technology instead of interpersonal communications to solve the problem of lack of communication. The following is a small example with big implications.

The Two-Edged Sword Called Voice Mail

When voice mail came to the workplace, everyone touted its usefulness and efficiency. Many organizations even eliminated staff because now they could just ring into a mega-communications system and all would be well. It didn't, it isn't, and it won't but it is here to stay. Customers were lost, put on hold, or parked somewhere in cyberspace. Many still are.

We even have businesses that tell us to have a credit card ready just so we can talk to product assistance. I believe it is a relational reach to say that these companies are designed to listen to the human spirit. If they are, then more importance has been placed on one's ability to pay, and one's value to these types of companies is now based on the expiration date on a piece of plastic. There is no difference between a credit card expiration date and the percentile rating on a performance evaluation. Numbers have become the god of good ideas, replacing the human song. Numbers have no conscience. The numbers of music can carry a beautiful melody. The numbers of misdirected management can have catastrophic consequences and bring an ear-splitting noise to the bottom line of the corporate ledger.

It is here we see the true agony of employees and customers sending a message and attempting to enter an orbit called communication, only to understand no one is listening. There are no strings, there is no tone, there is no system, and there is no symphony.

The employees and customers didn't like that the personal touch was removed. Why should they? Think about the last time you were parked on hold. If you had to call back for some reason, would you know how you got to where you were? Every time you call a business, they give you a menu of choices that is one level of the organizational food chain. If you goof up and you enter the wrong information, you must go to the end of the cyber line and start over. Now, think for a moment. If this is the system the company uses to assist its external customers, you can imagine the communication procedure the regular employee must experience inside the company.

I always enjoy working my way through some voice mail gerbil trail and when I get about seven or eight steps in, I get a recording that says, "For quality control purposes, your conversation may be monitored." What could you possibly improve? This is not having say-so and input. You have to have empathy for the employees taking care of you on the other end. They didn't create this system. Again, this is holding employees accountable for a system over which they have no control.

So, on the surface the new system may handle the mechanical process of moving information and data within the company, but is the company really improving the system and solidifying its internal and external customer relationships by using this method?

Remember Gandhi's words: "We must become the change we wish to see." Is this the system we really want to see? Is this the way management wants to be seen by their employees and customers? Are we a listening organization or have we become a recording one? Voice mail has become a location for us to park our problems. Where is the elegant design? Are we an organization that replicates good ideas or just numbers? Which method requires true communication?

Unfortunately, many companies still haven't gotten the message. What technology has failed to do and will never overcome is the need for interpersonal communication. People need to talk to people.

Now, ask yourself: Is your company an organizational symphony? Who is conducting? Who has not been practicing? This is not a mechanical process that is relegated to staff meetings and interoffice memos. As I stated in my book, *Each Human Spirit,* it is more than mind and body; it is the heart and soul of the human condition. It is a nurturing and learning process. Leaders need to understand that employees are symphonic instruments in the orchestra called organization.

Most musicians in an orchestra don't have the talent for a solo career. When playing together with other members of the orchestra, however, we may have a world-class symphony. It is the same in the workplace. Each employee may not stand out but together in a system of communication and listening, wonderful things can happen. W. Edwards Deming often used the analogy of the symphony in his writings.

We are in a global economy with barriers being torn down and others built by the day. We embrace the words *seamless*, *ergonomic*, *cyber*, and *gigabyte*. All these words are meaningless without the influence of leadership, science, duality, spirituality, and timeless communication. It is not about time. It is about being timeless.

If this were not true, then I could be the conductor of a Beethoven concerto and be in Chicago, but with each of my stringed instruments in a different city around the world and in a different time zone. Each musician must have a clock in front of him because the musicians must all start playing the first note precisely at eight o'clock in the evening my time. And no one will be playing together.

Sound Is Important in Our Lives

I recently read a magazine article where the writer was describing conditions in an orphanage in one of the former eastern European countries. The in-depth article gave a tragic account of the number of unwanted babies. What made an impression on the author and on me was his description of the sound of the babies in their cribs. There wasn't any. The author was struck by the lack of verbal response of the babies. These babies were not being taught or exposed to the sounds, noises, and words of the nurturing voice of another human being. They were not developing those communication skills. Their voice was one of silence.

I must ask myself: Why wouldn't that same series of events continue to happen when we are adults? I don't believe it does change when we become adults. For that matter, is that same scenario also happening in the workplace? Why would we not assume a greater role of silence, stagnated skills, and communication barriers in the workplace? The tragic scenario is that most employees come into a company wanting to communicate. I wonder how many employee interview and evaluation sheets have an area marked "strong communications skills." If the person is hired, he often learns when to keep his mouth shut and do what he is told. Again, this is another paradox: we use corporate communication to teach silence.

If we are relegated to our environmental and ergonomic cubicle with a restrictive job description and annual percentage evaluation system, then I think critical skills will suffer retribution somewhere. It is as if leaders have used technology to insulate themselves from each other. It is unfortunate that the necessary communication required between management and employees will take a very hard hit.

Communication skills should never be an elective in the University of the Workplace. Leaders who understand the scientific applications of communications tools also understand the human spirit needs to hear the human voice—the real human voice. If you are not teaching corporate communications, then why would a digital substitute like an iPad or cell phone spur the front-line employees on to new levels of productivity and communication? Say-so and input are critical components to each of us finding *Meaning* in our lives.

We Want Say-So and Input into Our Destinies

It is interesting that we have more people than ever in the world and the population is growing. And yet, we see technological barriers that keep people from communicating with each other and solving mutual problems. Environmentally, we are physically growing closer together but when it comes to communication and say-so and input, we appear to growing farther apart. Say-so and input support *Meaning*. It is a link to the human spirit. I sense a frustration with tools for communication, but employees are expressing frustration that their supervisors and organizations are not listening to them. I am coming to believe that many supervisors are not listening to employees because they don't know how!

Figure 3. The Seven Needs for Personal Productivity—Say-So and Input

What is even more intriguing is that we call this productivity. One, of course, must be realistic and state that the technological age is critical to the volume of information that must be managed and communicated. But somewhere we have crossed the intellectual line and defaulted to a hard drive as the answer to our problems.

I sense an ever-growing problem with the human spirit's not being able to communicate with like kind. We have defaulted the fundamental voice of say-so and input into issues of selected menus and the created importance of the star, pound sign, flat screens, headphones, file servers, texting, and control, alt, and delete.

One day, I was slowly surfing through the TV channels with the remote control. This boring process became even more of a conflict when I began to realize that nothing was on. What I did become sensitive to was the remote control itself. The number of remote controls and the number of buttons has increased over the past twenty years. We now have remote controls that can be combined so we only need one. It is amazing.

In one of my seminars I use an old TV remote control as a teaching aid. I inform the participants to pay close attention to the remote control in their houses. I ask them to keep one thing in mind the next time they watch TV with a group of people: whoever has possession of the remote control controls the room. Yes, we do have choices. We can say something, which probably will call for a vote. We could say nothing and let the remote control and person holding it take us where they may. Our third option is to leave the room. Think about how often we complain about how we do not have say-so and input in the workplace, yet we relinquish the very thing we need at home, in conference rooms, or in our cars, and find ways for other things to do it for us.

I would like you to take some time and follow this process. In a quiet place, take your TV remote control with you. Do not do this in the same room as the TV. What I would like you to do is relax and study all the buttons on the control. My remote control has over forty-eight different buttons. I can do any number of combinations with my TV. But that is not our purpose.

I would like you to now focus on all the problems and negative issues in your life and your workplace. I'm talking about issues, such as anger with a relative, denial about a problem you have to face, or work issues, such as a person at work who is causing you stress.

What may come to mind is the lack of interpersonal communication and things over which you have no control. It might even be that you want to make a change in your life but fear is in the way. What I want you to do next is rename some of the buttons on the remote control. Give them names such as anger, guilt, fear, frustration, and denial.

It may even be the name of another person. Name a button after them anyway!

Now I would like you to ask the following questions:

- At work, am I in charge of this remote control or am I giving control to someone else? What about my personal life?
- Who am I giving control to?
- Who am I giving the power to "punch" my buttons? Why?
- Why am I deferring my ability to communicate to someone else? Is it someone who has positive or negative influence in my life?
- Why am I letting this happen?
- If it is happening, what am I getting out of it?
- What is the message and who becomes the messenger?

Beware of Too Much Control in Your Day

I am not an advocate of one maintaining total control for twenty-four hours a day; in fact, that is the opposite of my intention. I think we can see how we can have both positive and negative external influences in our lives. I refer mostly to people.

For example, our spiritual beliefs can be a dynamic influence on who we are and what we do. These can be quite positive and they can and should help us design our relationships, values, goals, and objectives and assist us in the workplace. Others, too, like mentors, close friends, or relatives can likewise influence our remote controls.

It is clear that we can have both positive and negative influences regarding say-so and input. We get into trouble, however, when the negative side, such as negative behaviors and people, manipulate and use control for negative purposes. It is then that we lose our ability to communicate. This type of behavior should be a red flag and you should ask yourself who is in charge of your remote control.

Our goal is to make the connection between Say-So and Input and Meaning in our lives. If we truly are on a journey of discovery and sense of purpose, we need to be acutely aware of what influences us and why. As I stated, influence, like communication, can be good and bad. It is something that one must appreciate and use with caution. If we are going to understand who or what influences our individual remote controls, we must use extreme caution in letting someone push our buttons.

The remote control is a great example of a particle. Think of how a remote control, when handed to someone else, can cause a wave of unrealistic life events and loss of personal control. Think of how often we do this at work. Isaiah 56:11 speaks directly to a person who hands over her personal remote controls to someone else. "These are the shepherds who know no discretion; each of them goes his own way, every one of them to his own gain."[3]

Think of all the other remote controls we have in our lives such as cell phones, laptop computers, microwaves, home security systems, and even our hot tubs and the GPS in our autos. All have control panels that have conditioned us to believe we are in total control. In reality, we have relinquished our feeling at the moment for a control panel of external choices. We have created the illusion that giving others more access to our lives makes us more efficient, more important, and needed.

I believe we have relinquished far too great a percentage of who we are to the remote control called compromise. This creates an interesting communication scenario. We want to be in control but we turn over that very control when someone asks for it or, in a dysfunctional sense, when someone demands or forcibly takes it. We actually relinquish our ability to have say-so and input.

Say-So, Input, and Performance Appraisals

I wrote about performance appraisals in my last book and will write about them in this one. I will continue to write about them until they go away. I would like to turn the scientific community loose on performance appraisals. If ever there was something that can stifle communication and turn creativity into a company compost pile, it is a performance appraisal. For many, it is the only time the employee really is asked for her opinion. What would your input be? It would almost take on the character of a "caustic court," one where speaking one's voice would be a moot point because the sentence is already on paper. I feel so strongly that these appraisals have become a system and process that, in the hands of the incompetent manager and, for the most part, are nothing more than junk science.

Performance appraisals should provide say-so and input into our destiny. I am coming to the conclusion that the voice of the employee is taking a back seat to the voice of the data being generated by the company system. What really concerns me is that far too many managers see this as more important than the employees themselves. The company system, minus the employee, is winning out. We are using appraisals to justify dysfunctional systems and skewed data, and not to improve employees.

Again, the weapon of choice is the performance appraisal. It is management's version of the remote control. Remember, whoever has the remote control has control of the room. Being in control is one thing but using that control for one source, or limited sources is something else. I must ask this question, has anyone EVER come out of a performance appraisal spiritually fulfilled?

Tom Coens, an attorney and organizational trainer in East Lansing, Michigan, knows from first-hand experience that the fixes often fall short. He says, "I had fifteen years under my belt of actually designing appraisals, adding new bells and whistles. And each time, we ran into the same problems." He found that no matter how well intentioned the process was, employees still came away demoralized and the ratings were subject to bias and error.

I must ask now: Is anybody listening? What IS the song being played in those companies?

Coens questioned the whole appraisal system. In the book he coauthored with Mary Jenkins, an HR consultant, *Abolishing Perfor-*

mance Appraisals: Why They Backfire and What to Do Instead, they contend that the appraisal system reflects an outdated patriarchal procedure that is inherently flawed.[4] Ratings are biased and subjective and often discourage people instead of motivating them. This sounds very destructive for any employee who wants input into his destiny.

Coens and Jenkins' research shows that employees often think they would be ranked higher than what eventually shows up in the performance review. Now picture this: if what Coens and Jenkins say is true, employees are handing over the remote control to the appraiser before the evaluation and symbolically saying, "I will be whatever channel you want me to be. Just point and click and I will respond."

Coens and Jenkins found that up to 80 percent of employees think they're in the top quarter of performers, and 90 percent believe they're in the top half.[5] This is an obvious gap between how employees view themselves and how managers appraise them. Why do employees believe one thing when something else may be true? Employees who think they are outstanding performers are demoralized when they're rated as average. Under many of the new appraisal systems, they would have to be average or below or the system does not work. What causes such a disparity in opinions? More important, do the numbers actually mean anything? Performance appraisals are data and information. Far too many do not tell the truth.

What school or institution teaches that self-worth has more value if you are in the top half of a subjective scale? The word *elegant* does not apply here. This is an insult to managed data and information in the hands of a knowledgeable observer.

All appraisal systems are designed for a purpose. What is it? Is it designed to show who is above average, average, or below average? I believe any appraisal system that has an average will give you only one number. Fifty percent of the employees will be above average and 50 percent will be below average. Substitute chimpanzees for employees and you will get the same result. The key issues are: What will management do with the information once they have it? What training do they have or what training will they receive in order to interpret the data? Will the results improve the system and the willingness of the employee to speak her mind? Will management want to improve anything? Are they making decisions based on data, information, and knowledge alone, or are they understanding the true duality and making decisions based on wisdom?

Coens and Jenkins also contend that appraisals try to do too much. Companies use appraisals to coach and develop employees, give feedback, document performance for legal reasons, drive merit pay raises and promotions, and improve company performance.

The authors say that abolishing appraisals doesn't mean giving up all those goals. Rather, they advocate pursuing those goals by finding alternatives that aren't based on the faulty assumptions of appraisals. Those assumptions include the belief that one coaching and development system works for every employee and manager and that a forced process can produce commitment.[6] This is like the conductor who understands that it is important for the musician to read music and have the opportunity to learn. This works under the system where supervisors are responsible for employees' development and appraisal can be done objectively.

Employees are not focusing on work if they have to think about their appraisals. I do not advocate the statement, "If it gets measured, it gets done." A better statement would be, "If it gets measured, it's easy to get manipulated." An interesting principle associated with this is the relationship between performance appraisals and a law relative to quantum theory—the Heisenberg Uncertainty Principle. I will discuss Heisenberg in detail in another chapter but a brief explanation now is that this law has to do with measurement. Heisenberg said the more precisely the position is determined, the less precisely the momentum is known and vice versa.

When you measure your employees, are the numbers based on them moving or are the numbers based on a specific number or grade at a given moment, such as percentile? If the employee is measured at a given point, this also means the company has to slow down. After all, the employee is the company. That's why we call them position descriptions, remember? Neither number can describe an accurate measurement. What management is actually doing is causing the organization to "shudder." Accuracy cannot be obtained. The bottom line is, you cannot have it both ways. We will talk about this later. For now, think about the Newtonian implications. They are huge!

Coens and Jenkins argue that employees need to be responsible for seeking their own feedback, that employees' and managers' needs for coaching and development vary, and that ratings aren't reliable, even when people try to do their best to be fair. I believe this must include frequent and direct communication between management and employees. I'm sorry, but e-mail and voice mail and texting don't cut it.

Coens and Jenkins don't suggest throwing out the system all at once. Abolishing performance appraisals requires a cultural shift, they say.[7] Companies can't do it unless they start trusting their employees and gain a working knowledge of quality-management theory.

Let me give you an example where a senior executive got caught up in a hopeless situation.

How Not to Do It

A senior manager was hired to perform specific management tasks. During the hiring process, the new executive was told what the performance appraisal would consist of: criteria, expectations, and goals. This executive had a very hands-on and direct management style, no frills and based on results. To some, it was described as abrasive.

What evolved next was the beginning of a long and troubling process. The senior managers who hired this person informed the executive that performance appraisal time was approaching. What happened next was anyone's worst nightmare.

Because this person had made some enemies during his employment, it was decided by senior management that a better view of the situation was necessary. The senior executive team came up with a new plan for evaluating this person's job performance. In other words, they moved the industrial goal line. They informed this person that they were going to hire an outside facilitator and decided it was in the best interest of the organization to get additional feedback from a wider range of people, lengthening the appraisal process.

I like to describe this method as the Pontius Pilate method of performance appraisals. By hiring an outside facilitator, all the bad news came from him. This allowed the senior executive team to wash its hands of the process and still be seen as having everyone's best interest in mind.

The new executive had been on the job less than a year and was stunned, surprised, and disappointed by the eleventh-hour changing of the ground rules. This senior executive had spent several months designing the review process with the executive team. The evaluation was designed to include communications, budget process, strategic planning, and self-directed teams. The new form was signed and dated with specific tasks for each of the areas to be addressed. Each task was given a percentage.

You can almost see the train wreck coming. Newton, Einstein, and Heisenberg would have covered their eyes over this scenario. The executive team not only changed the process at the eleventh hour but they did not stop there. They crafted a new document with new roles and responsibilities. This addition created a highly subjective document and process and this type of evaluation could be fair to no one. It would almost be impossible to evaluate this executive. Can you imagine the devastating results that were now being foisted on the rest of this organization?

What was interesting was that, when some of the managers cried foul, some members of the executive team were surprised at the reaction to their changes. They stated that it was simply a way to get a wider range of feedback. Senior management claimed the new, eleventh-hour process was more open, collaborative, and inclusive. How would you like to work for an organization like this? By the way, when all was said and done, this scenario did result in litigation.

This organization should have listened to Coens and Jenkins. As of this writing, this organization still doesn't get it. Heisenberg would have shaken his head. W. Edwards Deming would have made all the managers attend one of his infamous four-day seminars. Their employees have the "hunker in the bunker" mentality. Say-so and input make one open and responsible to change or the possibility thereof. Policies, rules, and regulations cannot be a substitute for an employee needing to speak and her organization being willing to listen.

For someone to speak and another person to listen is a fundamental dynamic of the human spirit. It is the speaker (message) and the listener (messenger) who sends the message back to the speaker. Out of a true conversation, a rock of a new idea gets thrown into the pond of creativity. And the wave of new thinking has a chance to make a difference.

Say-So and Input Should Be a Process

Coens and Jenkins recommend something called *debundling* to address the various functions of performance appraisals. They say that companies should assign teams to design new alternatives and introduce them on a pilot basis to be reviewed after six to twelve months. Companies should look for unintended consequences and address those before rolling out any new initiative company-wide.

Meanwhile, companies can maintain simpler performance appraisals to handle the other objectives until the team gets around to designing new ways of tackling them. This is going to be critical in the twenty-first-century work force. Is the appraisal system designed for say-so and input? If it is not, then any system you do have in place will not give you the desired result. You could potentially evaluate your company right out of business.

Abolishing performance appraisals is not an overnight process—it can easily take a few years, say Coens and Jenkins. What they say has merit. It is more a form of coaching than evaluation. I am pleased that Performance Coaching is now being accepted as a method of the future. Viktor Frankl continually addresses the issue of each of us taking responsibility for our actions and says it is up to us to discover our individual paths. What makes this approach new is that Coens and Jenkins' approach supports Viktor Frankl's research and applications. Employees need to know how they are doing and where can they improve. This is not something that is done once or twice a year but on a regular basis. Why shouldn't management see the need for, and benefit to the organization of, the well-being of the employee? This is the exercise of free will and stresses the importance of individual responsibility.

So who are the voices of communication in your organization? Are the communications processes just lip service or are they truly a communication gateway? Is your organization structured so employees have say-so and input on a regular basis? How does your company listen to the employees? Are those who are doing the listening able to understand what is being said? How is the information used?

Questions

- Do you have say-so and input in your current career?
- Do you work for a listening organization?
- If you are a leader, do you dedicate time to speak to employees on a regular basis?
- When was the last time you had one-on-one conversations with your supervisor?
- What is the greatest communication void you currently have in your life?
- If it is a person, who is it?
- Would you rather be evaluated or coached?

- Do you have clear and defined expectations of all responsibilities?
- Do you feel empowered?
- Are you able to review your progress periodically?
- Do you take the time to listen to others?

What does true-life compensation mean to you? It isn't always money. In the next chapter, we will look at what we call a fair wage.

If you work for someone, act like a leader. If you are in college and write a paper or are working on a project, act like a leader. If you give a public presentation and share your passion, act like a leader. Leaders must accept responsibility and listen to new ideas and at times tell people "no." Only as a leader will you share with the world what you believe, those you will protect, and why you are meant to be a leader.

Chapter Six

Is My Career Providing a Fair Wage?

The human spirit needs to work and to discover.
Compensation is more than just money.
It is growing and discovering the investment
of who you are as a person
and your investment in the world.

If you want to hit a sensitive spot with a working person, talk money. I don't know who said that money is the root of all evil, but it does tend to complicate things. I do not know if that is true, but it sure does add much to the conversation. We all want to get paid a fair wage.

You noticed I said *want.* What we want and what we need are two entirely different things. We are told that money is what will make us happy. We also say that we need a certain amount of money. Marshall McLuhan, renowned Canadian professor and writer whose theories on mass communication have caused widespread debate,[1] said we have become "slaves to the message."[2] That message is coming from positions of authority.

The twenty-first-century workplace will evolve and be different. One area in particular that has preached a continuing message is collective bargaining agreements. I will never make a dent in that line of thinking but I must agree that the mind and body needs compensation—that can be salary and benefit—but I challenge collective bargaining units to think about heart-and-soul issues.

As Plato reflects, that opinion is not knowledge and yet, contract after contract comes down to whose opinion is more powerful than the others. That is the irony. Opinion does not foster clear thought nor does it support knowledge, let alone wise decisions. Collective bargaining is like watching television. We again find ourselves in a situation that, when we walk away from a bargaining position, all we have left is the person in charge of the remote control. What we now must face is that the remote control may be in the hands of someone halfway around the world making the same product you are with 30 percent of the labor cost.

We have long overlooked the issue of wages. Not only will foreign markets require us to look at the designs of our organization, they will definitely require us to look at what it costs to deliver a competitive product. Those issues relate to the very design of the organization. We are in a global systems economy. That means not only will we be changing what we do but how we do it. Wages will be on the table and fair wage will be open to many an interpretation. Because of the global marketplace more jobs will also be on the table—or already gone. This is a fact of life. The twenty-first-century workforce is in a constant state of design and redesign. The twenty-first-century workers must now look at two types of investment portfolios, a portfolio of their assets and a portfolio for their possibilities.

This will be a sensitive issue that will not be going away anytime soon. My personal belief is that wages consist of more than money, which means we have a responsibility to earn what we are being paid and an obligation to bring an attitude to the workplace that merits the compensation.

Wages Consist of More Than Money

Again, wages are more than dollars. They, like the other five Needs, are directly related to Meaning. It would be more accurate to say that compensation is *linked* to Meaning. That is why I prefer to use the term *compensation*.

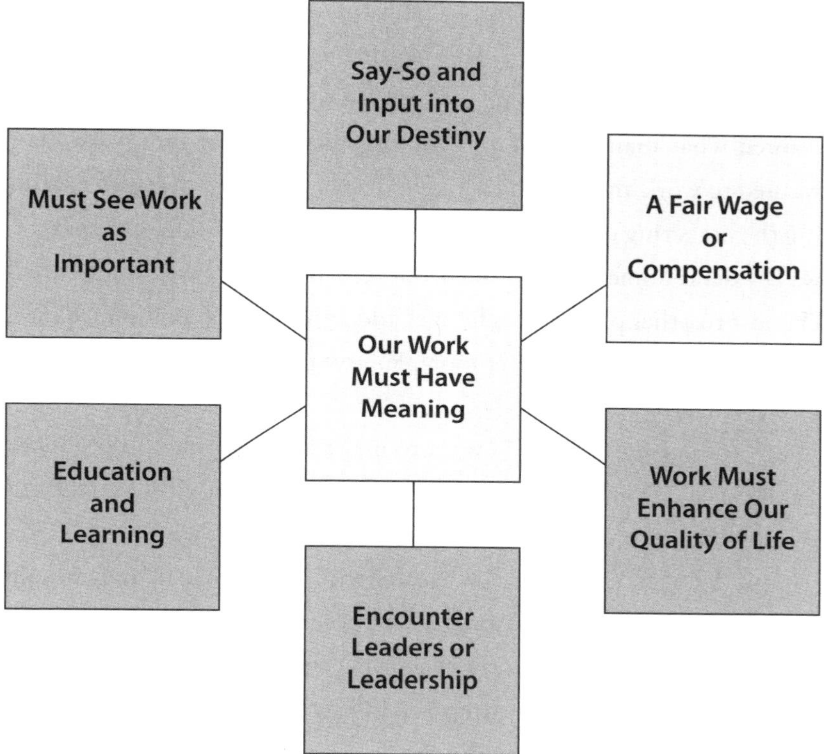

Figure 4. The Seven Needs for Personal Productivity—A Fair Wage

One does not need to have a vast number of conversations before encountering discussions about compensation or money. While the needs and approach of people vary quite a bit, there is one area where a pattern emerges—people want their bills paid, their mortgages up to date, and money in the bank. In other words, they wanted their immediate universe designed with a sense of balance and harmony with a direct road to a terrestrial ATM. In the twenty-first century, how this is done will also be on the table. If you are only investing in your financial portfolio, then you are not making yourself a marketable commodity. A commitment to lifelong learning will definitely enhance your portfolio of possibilities.

While I've had discussions with many entrepreneurs who love risk and see financial issues as a key motivator, the majority of people that I've spoken to were in their work for many and diverse reasons. They were realistic individuals who understood the need for wages, and they wanted what management and the organization had promised. They wanted to work and get paid for it, and I sensed little interest in capturing the brass ring of the CEO or any other senior position. One process was evident. Someone who starts out on a money-focused career often changes to other priorities as he ages and as his goals and vision change. Other things begin to matter more. Fair wage is a broad term and must be treated as such.

One person told me, "I want to make the most amount of money in the least amount of time in the most efficient way." I applaud his tenacity. Again, that was not what many people told me.

If I could capture a few words that were spoken, they would include words such as consistent, fair, communication, good leaders, and pride. It was abundantly clear that employees expected managers to keep their word. Nothing would get a rise out of the employees faster than management reevaluating wages when the employee was not involved in the process.

What Do Organizations Offer to Employees?

One of the major options that organizations offer is promotion. There is nothing wrong with promotion as long as you understand that getting a promotion does not mean that you are getting better. We have created this horrible cultural illusion that we measure our self-worth by a vertical ascent in the organization. It becomes almost a fetish to rise through corporate cubicles and call it good. In Newtonian principles when your process is ascending, you have to exert more energy to overcome the force of gravity. The higher you go the more energy you expend. I don't care if you are climbing flights of stairs or the corporate ladder. Apples don't lie. The higher you ascend the more energy it takes to stay there. No results can ever be guaranteed.

The sinister part of this process is that managers design the organization so if a management position is available, it becomes an unspoken law that those who have worth will go for the promotion and, once there, resistance will stop on the assumption that the right person is in the position. Again, keep this in mind: a manager who exerts energy or force from a position will receive an equal and opposite force from the other end. Don't try and solve that with your people from HR. Newton wrote the policy. This again becomes the great illusion because only one person can get it but you are judged on the number of times you try.

It also becomes a dysfunctional process because the culture of the organization is one where only those inside the company are qualified to do the job. In some cases this is true, but many management positions would be better off if outside applicants had the opportunity to apply for the job. Again W. Edwards Deming relates that a system cannot understand itself.[3]

Again, we have myth supported by company culture. It is almost impossible for an organization to declare itself impartial. Change to any system is an external process. What Deming called profound knowledge comes from the outside and by invitation. (Deming also relates that a system cannot manage itself.[4]) How many companies do you know that invite change from the outside?

The idea of the message/messenger becomes totally lost in the system and traditional thinking. This is not an environment where leaders can promote the balance of the leader, scientific management tools, and an environment where employees can develop the human spirit and see their efforts as a means of compensation. Plants can't grow and forests can't survive unless they are influenced by external sources. Why would a business be any different? Where did we develop this illusion that what might be perceived as a successful business means it must be self-contained? This is an excellent example of confusing organizational behavior with some basic rule of science.

What else does your company offer? We first must define the

term *wage*. This word means many different things but, in general, it is defined as receiving compensation for what we do. A fair wage, however, is more than money—it is opportunity. It is the opportunity for the employee to not only work for but experience other forms of compensation.

What else does the workplace provide? I am referring to things other than the standard benefits package. Maybe what work provides is not in the workplace. Your work can give you access to community organizations that offer a plethora of community opportunities.

Many jobs have benefit packages that can consist of health insurance benefits, good location, good leadership, a learning environment, vacation, retirement, and a variety of options. That too, may be changing. Some people choose a job that may not have the monthly take-home pay they want but offer great benefits. Again, most people's idea of wage relates to a package of benefits. I would like to suggest some other forms of wage.

How about the job itself? Other ideas are having time each month to commit to community service or the opportunity to have time each month with a mentor or other learning environment. No economy is consistent. Productivity, like the faucet in a sink, has two handles, hot and cold. Economies are the same. The key is to find that specific setting, where the right amount of each temperature comes out of the faucet. If an economy is good, then many people will work. In those instances, many skills are needed.

Skill Is Not Enough

As we know from past experience, as an economy cools, certain skills take an immediate hit and others cool off later. The key with any career is to have a portfolio of skills. I believe employees of the future should have skills that many relate to an old saying in the entertainment industry. In that field, you had to sing, dance, and act. It was said you had to be excellent at three and outstanding at two. In other words, you had to have a portfolio of skills.

I do not believe that, in the twenty-first century, one skill will be enough. That does not mean three separate skills have to be learned. You could have a variation of specific interests but multiple talents will win the race. One thing is for sure: multiple skills will be a requirement and being adaptive will be crucial. Add in the realization that a successful career will also mean lifelong learning. This may be the key to the receipt of a fair wage.

I was reading a business publication and found an article where the writer was addressing career change. I associated this with my own experience because the author addressed the need to add skills to his portfolio. This struck a personal note. I changed careers in 1998 and left a structured organization with definitive guidelines and a set methodology for completing assigned tasks. I believed I could take those skills and turn them into a new career. I felt it was time to make a change.

I started Compass Rose Consulting Inc. and became mesmerized by what was happening in other areas of the workplace. I knew I wanted to work with organizations and their employees. One of the catchwords of the day was "reinventing" something. It was used with wanton abandon in the HR field where everyone was to reinvent him or herself every few years.

I was never comfortable and still am not comfortable with the term. So, with stars in my eyes and ego between my ears, I left the security of twenty-three-plus years for a new adventure. What I discovered was quite profound. First of all, life is different when you have to make all the decisions. As I soon found out, I needed to make some changes and the term *reinvent* did not have a solid ring. I had to make changes but radical change was not the answer.

What I needed was a different perspective, so what I did was one of the greatest compensatory moves I have ever made. I had been reading for relaxation when I came across a quote from Peter Drucker, "The most common source of mistakes in management decisions is the emphasis on finding the right answer rather than asking the right question."[5] I didn't need radical change. What I did need to do, however, was to not be afraid to ask radical questions.

I knew that asking questions did not necessarily mean I was challenging everything. What I had to do was look at what I was doing and what others were doing from a different point of view. The best way to describe it would be like looking at something outside through the window of a particular room in a house. Instead of having the same view, I decided to look at the same object but from a different room. In other words, I would look at it from a different and often challenging perspective. I had to ask life what it was asking of me. Life now became the messenger. My influence was external but I had to change my attitudes and perceptions.

So what did I look at? I was fifty-two years old and profoundly aware that life is not infinite and I was not indestructible. I became acutely aware of my mortality and had this inner sense that certain things in life no longer had meaning. What I did realize was relationships, for one, became incredibly important. With that I began to find different issues rising to the surface.

One was a need to start documenting what I believed. I had no plans for publishing a book on the American workplace but *Each Human Spirit* couldn't wait. It was the result of a completely unrelated project. What I did notice was my work with other organizations. I couldn't forget Peter Drucker's quote. I kept thinking about how many times we are trained to immediately head for the conclusion when we do not know if we have asked the right questions. I knew that I had to make sure I asked the right questions for my clients, and they, in turn, had to ask questions of themselves.

What realized leads us back to compensation. My approach was not going to bring me significant riches. It would, however, give me a new type of wealth. I was sensing a deep satisfaction in knowing that the honesty of asking the right questions builds better companies for the people who work there. If smiles and hard work are what I get from my clients, then I am the richest man in the world. I am also realistic and feel part of that is fair compensation to pay my bills.

I find I have a deeper spiritual satisfaction from my life changes. I have a greater sense in appreciating what is happening around me. My wife also sees the difference. She shakes her head when I get up at four in the morning and write. I know it means something because I will be sound asleep and in a moment my eyes open like saucers and the words are in my head. I consider that compensation. It is as if I can't wait to put the ideas in the computer and see what happens.

I look at things in a different light. For example, one day I was mowing the lawn and I became aware of the pattern the mower was making in the grass. I saw the similarity between the grass being cut and a new idea in an organization. The grass is mowed, the yard looks nice, and the family is pleased, but change starts immediately. The wonderful moment is short-lived, the grass starts to grow back, flowers need trimming, flower beds need to be edged, and weeds need to be pulled. So it is with a company. New ideas and products enter, everybody is excited, patterns repeat themselves and you wish the moment would stay. It, too, starts to change. Both scenarios mean constant work and challenges. One deals with people and the other relates to my lawn. Both examples are organizations and both are in a constant state of renewal.

I am sensing an awareness of the message and messenger. I believe I am coming to the fusion of both ideas. I have days when I am asked to be the message to an organization. In other words, I sit and listen to what they have to say. On other days I must be the messenger. I must deliver a presentation and listen for feedback. I believe this duality of purpose relates directly to the principles of quantum theory and the particle/wave relationship. We must be adaptable in our expectations because our compensation may not necessarily be in the form of money. It is knowing what we need to live on, yet understanding that compensation can also be in the form of a recommendation, good word, a satisfied customer, a happy family, or positive attitude on your part or someone else's part.

We Have a Responsibility to Earn What We Are Being Paid

I must again return to the principles of wave/particle duality and message/messenger. This duality of purpose is a new twist to the traditional Newtonian laws, which are predictable. In subatomic particles this duality becomes adaptive. It is as if they create their own sense of purpose. This, to me, is the true workplace. Newtonian physics has the mind and body as part of the equation. It is where many HR managers have centered their thinking and remain mired today. But in the twenty-first-century definition of the adaptive nature of the employee, we have a different set of laws. Here we have the ability of both particles and people to optimize their purpose and become the message and the messenger. This means being able to demonstrate and deliver the message. I think one of the most underrated principles is the power of attitude that I address throughout this book. This leads to money in our spiritual, professional, and emotional bank. How would you measure that on a performance appraisal?

Remember what Thomas Aquinas related when he said free will does not know either right or wrong. We have the power to decide how we are going to feel. If we take that power and focus it on attitude, our compensation can be significant. The employee can become the message and the messenger. That is the good stuff. What Aquinas was describing was a theological remote control.

The challenge comes when we realize that we will default to habit and a conditioned environment, such as company culture. This environment can be created through habit, complacency, or regulation. Companies today have a plethora of manuals that spell out exactly what is expected. An example would be the current plight of the union movement. Collective bargaining, which can illustrate both the best and the worst of intentions, can be the other double-edged sword of the workplace. In either scenario, we are entering a period in our history where we will be redefining the meaning of wage and its implications. We will be able to be financially successful and have more options. How we do it may not have as many guarantees.

We have come to believe that we must earn our wage and nothing else. And the term *earned* now takes on a new meaning. We are becoming conditioned to believe that wages are a pecuniary result of our efforts. Yes, we are paid a wage in the form of a piece of paper, a deposit slip, or direct cash payment. It doesn't matter whether or not you belong to a collective bargaining unit, if you agree to work for a company then you have an *ethical* contract—it may not be a written one or even one with a bargaining unit.

By working for a company, you have told your employer that, for a salary and applicable benefit package, you will perform a designated set of tasks. For doing that, you will be paid. And this is where conventional thinking may be reaching a fork in the road. We have an obligation to bring an attitude to the workplace that merits the compensation. I really take heat for this one and I stand by my statement.

We have entered the era of attitude of change and not business as usual. Just look at the economy. It would be wise to start thinking about what would be fair wage, and I truly mean issues in addition to dollars. The twenty-first-century workplace will be chaotic, creative, surprising, multidirectional, rewarding, adaptive, and elegant. Fair wage will be what you make of it.

Questions

- Based on the work you do, are you being paid a fair wage?
- Is work the only source of your wage?

- What other compensation package might life be offering you?
- Might you be getting compensated in other ways and neither realize nor appreciate it?
- Is compensation linked to your attitude?
- Would your compensation change if you had a different attitude?
- Is money the only type of income you receive?
- Are you happy with your total income package?
- What positive change are you willing to bring into your life to make a difference?

So far, we have had Meaning, Say-So and Input, and Fair Wage. So, does what we do for a living enhance our life experiences and quality of life?

In the next chapter, we will take another step on our journey of Needs.

Chapter Seven

Does My Career Add To My Quality of Life?

Organizational behavior is probabilistic in nature. We do not know the paths the human dynamic can travel or what the human spirit can endure. We must accept it as an infinite range of possibilities. The path we observe with our five senses may not be a choice; it may simply be an observation based upon existing conditions.

Our career choices are an integral part of the equation of total potential. This equation adds to our quality of life. Productivity is not an external manifestation of order and accomplishment, but of knowing the *importance* of opportunity. In my book, *Each Human Spirit*, I refer to productivity as the internal commitment to see life as an opportunity and spiritual expression of free will. When we look at each day as a magnificent gift, we then take the next step and do something with that day. I make this statement knowing that the word *gift* can have different interpretations.

Gift and Quality of Life

I am going to associate the word *gift* with the words *endowment* and *offering*. When we think of a gift, our culture tends to focus on the receiver. After all, receiving something we did not expect does have a tendency to brighten our day. It is when we switch our focus and look at the giver of the gift that I believe a more focused picture develops.

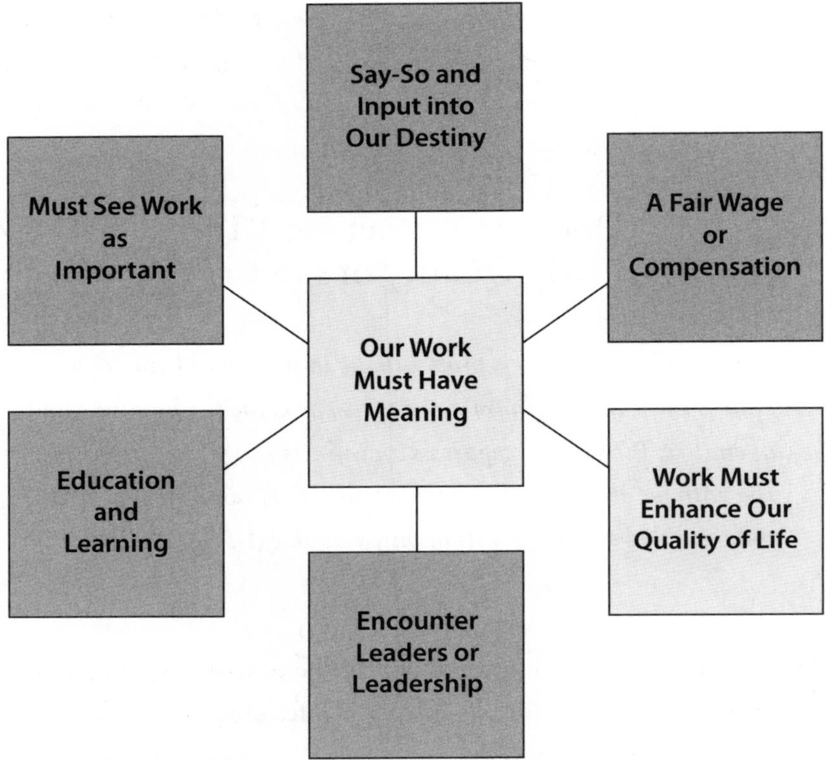

Figure 5. Seven Needs For Personal Productivity—Quality of Life

A true gift is given to us unconditionally. In that context it is what makes each day so important. We are given that incredible commodity called a day. This offering now turns the gift into something we can turn into an asset or a liability.

We have the free will to make the difference. As Thomas Aquinas relates, free will is a power and a gift to us that can be used for good or evil. It is ours to choose. It is an endowment that is ours because we are human; we embrace the reality that adversity can be part of the gift of today or any day. In his writings, Thomas Merton said, "Every moment and every event of every man's life on earth plants something in his soul."[1] I believe that both Aquinas and Merton saw these processes as a journey and not specific events. Life does not stand still.

Merton says we must focus on how the gift of life nurtures and imprints our soul. He never mentions only the good will imprint, or those certain events make the difference. He tells us that all the events we experience in each of our lives will imprint.[2] This takes us to the next step: knowing that life gives us events that may not be fair. They happen anyway.

Life Is Not Fair

These are the shepherds who know no discretion; each of them goes his own way, every one of them to his own gain.
—Isaiah 56:11[3]

The more precisely the POSITION is determined, the less precisely the MOMENTUM is known.

The Heisenberg Uncertainty Principle and the Workplace

I believe that what we are discovering in the behavior of subatomic particles is part of the voice of the human spirit and enhancing the quality of our lives. Wouldn't it be exciting if leaders and managers may have been looking and studying the wrong principles with the best of intentions with marginal results? I believe productivity, like Newtonian physics, may have reached its level of application and it is time to look in other applications. Traditional laws of physics are not holding up to quantum theory, as leadership models struggle to deliver the needed levels of effectiveness in today's workplace. Letting the employee enhance productivity with heart-and-soul commitment makes the possibilities endless.

We are a goal-oriented society. Everything must have a goal otherwise nothing will be accomplished. Goals are set for profit and not-for-profit organizations. We rely on goals to tell us whether or not we have made it. It may be a balance we want in our IRA or sales quota at the end of the month or year or the touchdown at the college football game. We have been taught that goals are success. Yet, we find that when it comes to quality of life, goals are part of a larger process and it is the process, the movement, the momentum that seems to hold the most meaning.

At work, evaluations measure our goals. Sometimes we get a bonus when we reach a goal. We measure a team's success based on when it reaches the goal line. Even when we die, our obituaries tell the world what goals and milestones we accomplished. We feel so comfortable with goals that we even measure our children with them. Where would our kids be without goals? We entrust our children to the local learning institutions and view their success by their ability to reach goals. We call those grades.

We love our goals. Goals are like caffeine. We have to have our fix or we don't feel rejuvenated. What we must remember is this: *a goal is a point in a process.* Once we reach a goal we are confronted with Maslow's Hierarchy of Needs. Once a goal or level is reached it is no longer a motivator. In other words, we must have a new goal. So this begs the next question, how many goals are enough? And do goals measure success? I believe we have become too dependent on goals as a measurement of success. Picture it like milepost markers on the highway of life. The highway is the process and the marker is the goal. It tells us where we are. What goals do not tell us is how fast we are going or what our potential is at that moment. Driving on a highway is momentum. Again, the marker is the goal. It may be in our best interest to look at goals as part of a process.

Hypothetically, we can measure both at the same time. Businesses try to do that every day and they do so with a potential for accuracy. Newtonian physics says we can with limits. This works as long as you don't get too precise. What we cannot do is measure both with a *great degree* of accuracy. We didn't have to in the past. Life, however, is changing and so is our need for accuracy in our nano world. Vast journals and documents tell us how to reward our stockholders based on the momentum and movement of the company, while we measure the success of employees based on their specific goals, or points in the process.

In reality, this may be causing more damage than thought possible. What we have difficulty doing is measuring both with a great degree of accuracy. We do, however, run into a problem that is probably the greatest insight into human behavior. We cannot measure both at the same time—accurately. In other words, the word EXACTLY becomes a nemesis. It is here that we again enter the quantum world where strange things start to happen.

Ladies and Gentlemen, Meet Werner Heisenberg

One of the issues of quantum mechanics is that it cannot give exact results. It does, however, give us the probabilities for a variety of possible results—it gives us options. Quantum theory deals with particles that are so small that their very existence is a probability. We have not even seen some of them. *We have only seen the results of their efforts.*

Why is this even an issue? Because I believe that behavior has direct application to the workplace. It is also relative to our quality of life. How many leaders have actually seen all their employees work? What they see are the results of their work. In other words, we measure employees on a point in a process. We measure outcomes. We reward results. This does produce an end result. However, the traditional laws of human behavior, when applied to subatomic particles, may cause your people in HR to take some very long coffee breaks. Strange things start to happen.

Werner Heisenberg, one of the founding fathers of quantum theory, challenged the notion that every cause in nature is followed by the resulting effect. That statement alone would send plant managers in corporate America into extended closed-door meetings with senior management or their therapists. Outcome-based managers would be filling out job applications by the dozens.

Here is a twentieth-century scientist who unknowingly fired a shot right across the bow of one of the basic thought processes and assumptions in the traditional workplace and he wasn't even aiming! Heisenberg aimed his quantum theory at the scientific community. What he didn't realize was, he hit another target called organizational behavior that was firmly cemented in the principles of Frederick Taylor. He fired the shot and the workplace still hasn't heard the bang but they are seeing the results. They just haven't realized they have been shot at!

OK, let's get into Heisenberg's Uncertainty Principle and its application to the workplace. If we know a set of facts, then we not only know what the result is going to be, but probably where it will be. Isn't that the principle behind the assembly line and the Industrial Revolution? If we look at this from the view of Newtonian physics, what he was saying was that motion of an object could be exactly predicted or determined from knowledge of its present position and momentum and all of the forces acting upon it.

We have file cabinets full of charts and graphs that tell us so. Heisenberg's Uncertainty Principle says not so fast. Heisenberg said we cannot know the precise position and momentum of a particle at a given instant, so its future cannot necessarily be determined. In other words, we cannot measure location and movement at the same time. One cannot calculate the precise future motion of a particle, but only a range of possibilities for the future motion of the particle. Everything varies.

One should note that Heisenberg's Uncertainty Principle does not say everything is uncertain. Rather, it tells us where the limits of uncertainty lie when we make measurements of subatomic events. Take heart: the parallels between some of the behaviors of subatomic particles and our human behaviors can be eerily similar.

So as a leader, worker, or the HR manager in an organization, why in the world should I even begin to try and understand how my job relates to a subatomic particle and a guy named Werner Heisenberg?

The laws of classical physics are based on providing a determined result. The time, conditions, and location may change but the laws are the same. The human spirit, however, has a range of possibilities and it is NOT completely predictable, as in quantum mechanics. A human being may see a given situation and respond differently, based on his principles, values, and ethics and his response over time may not be the same. Humans, like subatomic particles, behave differently under the same situation as classical physics, and the results can differ.

Much of our traditional business thinking is grounded in determined results. Traditionally, performance can even be dots on a line graph. You are evaluated, marked, graded, scored, merit paid, and tenured on determined results. That is not the real issue. How we measure for those issues is!

Measurement in the workplace IS a big thing so why shouldn't it be accurate? Traditional managers are under the illusion that you can take quantum employees and put them in a Newtonian workplace, and get the same result time after time. Heisenberg says you can't. Taylor tried, and when the process or assembly line didn't get the desired result they changed the worker. Why? Because the behavior of the worker varies!

If it truly works, you wouldn't need all those manuals filled with rules. It doesn't work and it won't work. If it did, we would be able to take outcome-based education and predict with certainty what each child will accomplish and have a determined result. Traditional management principles teach and rely more on evaluating cause and effect and less on the notion of a range of possibilities. We have endless focus groups trying to look at these problems and they are all trying to make the numbers work. They can't. As long as the human spirit is involved you will have variation and that variation is in every man, woman, and child. It is built in; it is not added on.

Employees are expected to produce predetermined numbers or points in a process. Subatomic particles, like employees, do not respond to these laws, but to a range of possibilities. I believe employee behavior is more like subatomic particles and should be seen as a range of potentially endless possibilities; it can be predictable to a certain degree.

The human spirit adapts to conditions—that enhances quality of life. Try to show that on a flow chart. Leadership must be open to this notion and to utter surprise when the human spirit delivers or their creativity takes the company in a direction it has never been before. That adds to the quality of life.

Subatomic particles, like many employees' behavior, often are seldom seen in an organization. They are, for the most part, taken for granted. So is the human spirit. And yet, here is where we are discovering our biggest surprise—that people, like particles, can become, deliver, and show up in areas never thought possible.[4]

In order to help us get a better understanding of my point, let's look at a couple of terms: momentum and position. These help us tie in Heisenberg with leadership and decision making, the measurement of human behavior, and quality of life.

Let's say you hit a golf ball (particle) and it is moving through space down a fairway. Look at the golf ball as your company moving down the fairway of productivity toward a goal. Newton says we can define its position and motion by telling you where it is (position) and how fast it is moving. We will call that momentum.

What happens next is far too similar, I believe, to what happens every day in our businesses and organizations. Twenty-first-century businesses want and need EXACT location and MOMENTUM for each employee, product, process, and account balance. Even our stock quotes for day traders need real-time data and information. Newton can't deliver that. His laws produce a close number but it isn't what you would call super accurate. It is close. In the past we needed *close* and we accepted it. Nano businesses cannot accept that notion. The playing field is changing and *close* might not be an option in the highly competitive twenty-first-century workplace.

In the strange world of quantum mechanics, the idea that we can measure things exactly breaks down. People who study quantum theory are dedicated souls with strong stomachs for the unpredictable.

Let's go back and state this Heisenberg idea more precisely. Let's say a particle has momentum and a position. In the quantum world, I would not be able to make this precise measurement. This is because, whenever I make either measurement, I must disturb the system. If I measure momentum I disturb position. If I want to measure position then I disturb momentum. (In order for me to know something is there, I must *bump* into it to make it STOP so I can measure it *accurately*. Picture it as bumper cars with subatomic particles.)

If I want to measure exact position I must stop the motion. If I want to measure the rate of motion I cannot know where the ball is exactly because it is moving. Got it? What this means is the size of the uncertainties in our organizations and businesses are not independent, they are related! Traditionally, we measure the company performance *as movement* and the employee performance separately *as position* and often with different expectations. Heisenberg's Uncertainty Principle says that won't work. Let's apply this to employees.

We cannot predict where an employee will be with 100 percent certainty; we have to look at probabilities. Yet, one manager expects an employee to be at one level and another manager sees the employee as not productive and this employee should be elsewhere. In other words, in the workplace, the word *momentum* can be replaced with the word *opinion*.

Employees can only be measured by the opinion of the manager in control of the system. I can say this today. (Werner Heisenberg said it decades ago.) For example, I can say that an atom or golf ball will be at some location with a high degree of probability, but there will be a small probability it will be somewhere else. (In fact, there is a small but finite probability that it will be found across the universe or, in this case, across the golf course or, in the example of an employee, not up to expectations because of a fluke in the organizational system.) This is strange.

A consequence of these principles is that particles can appear in places where they have no right to be from an ordinary, common sense point of view. Some may call that thought. Some would call it thinking. In the workplace I would call it creativity. It is what the human spirit does best.

Some managers and HR people would say you are not following your job description. This is brought up every day in many businesses when something out of the ordinary and totally unexpected happens. Have you ever heard in one of your meetings, "Where in the world did that idea come from? That wasn't supposed to happen." Sure it was! (Have another doughnut.) Heisenberg said it would![5]

Here is another example. Let's say a car is your business. We are driving down the highway at seventy miles an hour. We know this by the data and information from the speedometer. In other words, we are measuring rate (i.e., movement). If I say I want to measure specifically a point on the road where employees will be so I can accurately measure their goals, I could do that if I set up a designated position. If I want to be truly accurate I must stop the car in order to measure *precisely* where I am with any degree of accuracy. When I reach that point, I have accomplished my goal. The problem is I had to stop the car (business) in order to do it accurately. If this is the case then I wouldn't give your cell phone number to your stockholders.

So what we have done is set up two scenarios. We can measure the rate something is moving, or we can measure the position. To us that is a no-brainer and we do it all the time. If accuracy and real precision are necessary, like in an industrial process, the playing field changes. What Heisenberg says is, we cannot measure both at the same time. You can measure precise location or momentum, but not both. If you do, the system is changed and NEITHER number is accurate!

Traditional management is under the notion that employee productivity and production in a company are parallel processes. This means that if a company sets goals, then everyone should focus on the goal and work in the same direction and with the same purpose. They expect the process for reaching that goal to be the same. Quantum theory tells us that productivity has a range of possibilities. In other words, it can bump into other forms of productivity and become random, and spin off in another direction and change in the process. Trying to measure both at the same time is physically jarring process. *Remember the Einstein-Brownian Principle?*

Heisenberg said, if you measure a product then you cannot measure the momentum or process that made it. You can measure both but you cannot measure them at the SAME TIME because one or the other would have to stop in order to be measured!

Let's apply this to the workplace:

- The more you put your efforts in trying to figure out where your customers are, the less you will know about how fast they are learning, changing, or going somewhere else.
- If you try to define how fast your customers are learning, adapting, or changing, you may miss where they really are and miss a potential market.
- The more you focus your resources on achieving a particular benchmark or a performance measure based on a given percentile, the less you will know about how the relative issue is changing, adapting, or no longer significant.
- If your resources address a given condition or set of circumstances, you will not know how that condition is adapting, changing, or implementing other conditions based on the identified conclusion.
- If one part of your organization is focused on process improvement and another is specifically focused on results, your

> production costs may actually increase because these two nonparallel processes may actually be causing your system to operate inefficiently.

Managers try to get a handle on where employees are and they measure their productivity at the same time. Newton called that science. Heisenberg probably would call that a shudder or collision in a system. It is not accurate nor does it tell you what you need to know. Traditional thinking in organizational behavior has roots in deterministic principles, meaning the theory that a given set of calculations and plans will produce a specific, accurate, and measurable result. If this is true, does that mean the universe has free will? If the universe is probabilistic then we could assume that, with quantum theory, the universe has choices or a range of possibilities. Might that also apply to your business?

Let's say that your boss tells you to get a project done by a certain time. You work on the process and focus on the rate you are working and want to make sure you will finish on time. You will get results. The measurement of either, however, may not be accurate.

Causality in nature is not a given. This would mean that a set of circumstances, like marginal leadership or a butthead for a manager, won't necessarily produce the same results over time. The DNA of organizational behavior and the human spirit can develop a defense mechanism to reject the outside intruders.

If you direct your managers to measure results, ALL had better be measuring for the same thing and the same way! If some are measuring, based on their individual management styles, for momentum, and others for position or location, then the quality and quantity delivered may not represent the design of the process. If some are measuring for a specific point, then they will cause the system to shudder because another measurement bumped into it to get their result.

Others, however, may want to measure how smoothly the system is working. They have the best of intentions but could actually cause the organizational resources to collide, resulting in very unhappy employees. In other words, you could be causing your company to wind up in some other part of the business universe and wonder how it got there!

Accounting personnel may see the first indicator in the numbers but might not know what they are looking at. Remember signal to noise? They may or may not be telling you something, and you may be listening to the process in a completely different way. Your front-line employees could be working as hard as the system lets them but their energy is not working in one direction. What they are really doing is working in a company where energy and productivity are colliding, and they are not channeled in a specific direction.

Understanding what Werner Heisenberg said may hold a significant clue. Remember, measuring a point or goal while, at the same time, trying to accurately determine the rate, causes a system to shudder. Goals may be much more expensive and harder on a system than measuring the process the goal is associated with. Picture this as a freeway with all traffic moving in the same direction, but periodically they all have to stop to measure position and then resume speed to measure momentum. Think of how much gas it takes to speed a car up and slow it down and the chaos it would cause on the freeway! In your organization, substitute money for gas.

Are the charts, programs, and processes in your company designed to shadow just predictability? Is predictability the only indicator of profit in your organization? How do you measure surprise? Is your company or organization comfortable when the unpredictable happens? Don't get caught up in the moment. Remember: when you stop to relish a point of success, your company is still moving. In fact, it may be moving to the next level of unpredictability. Are you ready for that? Just because you stop and admire the work of the organization does not mean the company should too!

The human spirit has choices and is obligated to make them. It is critical to quality of life.

Organizational behavior is fusion. It is the demonstration of the spiritual and physical energy, mass, and reaction. Picture a freight train standing still on a railroad track. We can accurately measure its position. All the cars are standing still. This is traditional physics. Now, have you ever been near a freight train when it starts to move? What happens? The train has slack. The engine starts to move, and then the first car takes up the slack and starts to move, and then the second car and so on, until the entire train moves. It sounds like a long series of controlled crashes. It is!

If we had an employee riding in each of the train cars how would you measure each one's productivity? Employees in the front of the train would be moving while employees at the rear of the train might be standing still. Who is correct? Who is productive? Which is more accurate? We can measure one or the other. We cannot measure both because neither is truly accurate in relation to the entire system. Another example: is any division, section or unit in your organization standing still waiting for data and information from another section that is moving? Which one is successful? How would you measure it? Neither measurement will give you an accurate picture of the process.

Can you measure position accurately? Not anymore. Can you measure momentum? Same thing happens—the momentum of the train starting to move is slamming into the train standing still. Both are in a state of transition and neither can be accurately measured. From the traditional law of physics, we can say we are at a certain milepost. That is OK for trains. If you are in a situation where you must be VERY specific in a manufacturing process, such as the exciting world of nano technology, all bets are off. Neither is accurate. The processes have collided. That's Heisenberg!

We have created the illusion that what appears to be a smooth-running company means everyone and everything is working in the same direction at the same speed. I believe traditional management does not realize it is causing controlled crashes every day. We try to identify any system or person who has pulled over to the side of the corporate highway and find out what the trouble is. We see a slowing of the system or a person as some sort of defect.

In reality, it may be the system telling us that a successful organization doesn't necessarily work that way. Maybe some processes progress at a different rate? That instability may be part of the creative process.

Much of what happens in organizational behavior is like patterns of behavior in our universe. We seek balance and harmony in our lives by understanding that life always has stress, and balance and harmony are what we make of it. We seek balance and harmony as individuals and can have that in our workplace to a point.

Objects in the universe are like people in an organization—at times we run into each other. This may not be bad. We have been taught, however, that conflict is bad and we must all get together in our hallowed hallways and seek karma through a group hug. Our lives are stressful and so is the universe. Even our spiritual commitments and their impact on our workplace productivity can cause us stress. Again, I believe we run into Heisenberg.

We focus on workplace collisions or points in a process, and measure productivity by reducing accidents. In reality, we may have a system that is designed to produce a certain number of accidents, no matter what we do. What we should focus on is the process and improvements. To measure with accuracy and come to a conclusion again causes the organization to shudder at every measurement. The sad part is that, while all this is happening, nothing is able to measure the heart-and-soul work habits of the employee's efforts.

The Heisenberg Uncertainty Principle, Leadership, and the Titanic

I believe today's scientific thought has relative principles that were taught by the early prophets and in the Old and New Testaments. My point is, I do believe that Scripture and science are separate entities. I do not believe that all of science is new frontier. We need to start making the connections. I believe not only are they connected, they are interdependent. Scripture has supported certain scientific principles for thousands of years. Both Scripture and science are giving us fresh views of ourselves, the universe, and a deeper spiritual connectedness. It is our responsibility to make the connections even if some of their leaders choose not to take us there to enhance our quality of life.

A Lesson from the Titanic

I have used the terms *message* and *messenger* from Moses in the Old Testament, and what I believe is its relevance to wave/particle duality, modern-day quantum theory, and theory of leadership. I have talked about how one of the ways we find meaning in our lives is our attitude toward unavoidable suffering. I have talked about the decision-making model that uses data, information, knowledge, understanding, and wisdom as its roots. I discussed how the majority of our decisions are made with just data, information, and knowledge.

I discussed how it is important to reflect and consider the ethics of understanding our principles and values, and to wait and make decisions that enhance our quality of life. That is our goal.

I have also talked about the importance of attitude in our work ethic. I would like to give you an example of this strange but interesting relationship that ends in tragedy. This tragedy occurred because a society refused to take responsibility for its attitude. What it created was an era that proclaimed a superior quality of life. That everything was predictable. It was intellectual arrogance at its best. They didn't understand the message and the messenger. And they made history in doing so.

At the turn of the century we were in the throes of the Industrial Revolution. It was the Edwardian era, an era of decadence, invincibility, and ego. I believe that some of the changes made became a metamorphosis of the human spirit. We systematically compartmentalized each worker (particles) and determined what that worker should produce (waves). If employees wanted to get paid, let alone keep their jobs, they had better be predictable, even if they may be producing a flawed product. We did not look at workers as a range of possibilities or potential for duality; we only saw outcomes. Some managers still hold that notion today.

We had little focus on the rate of change or the speed at which it could change. Output was everything. Damn the process! Outcome was everything! Workers were a constant (Newtonian principles). We thought we could measure both outcome and rate and be accurate (Heisenberg Uncertainty Principle). We were wrong, dead wrong, and that is the basis for my story.

One accomplishment alone exemplifies the height of the industrial arrogance of the driven Edwardian era. This single product took history and froze it in time. Even today, we are still mesmerized just by its name: Titanic. Back then, we didn't have to discover scientific principles—we could make them. It was the era of invincibility and we exploited it.

If our industrial will was strong enough, we could defy spirituality, nature, and all that the past or future did and could produce. This arrogant attitude christened the Titanic with the curse of the current thinking. We even went so far as to call her unsinkable.

The Titanic was the ultimate liner of the seas (message, particle). Yet, she carried with her that which society refused to acknowledge. She was also the industrial statement and voice (messenger, wave) of that same era. She carried the socially chosen. Her lower decks carried the common citizens who paid the real price. The Titanic was nothing more than a cultural coffin.

The Titanic's role was to lead the transportation era into the Promised Land. It was as if we smashed the tablets of common sense (message) in order to make her a reality. She embodied all that science and technology had to offer. All the data, information, and knowledge of the day were encased in her riveted hull. She was the biggest, fastest, and most opulent form of transportation. Even the many immigrants seeking a better life could afford to occupy her space below decks. The Titanic could do it all. It was as if she could create and write her own science. Who would want to spiritually challenge her purpose? She was the ultimate statement of her time. It was as if she could do almost anything.

Let us lay some more groundwork before we leave on our journey. When we talked about our five-step decision-making model, I related how data only tells you where you are—single data sources do not tell you where you came from or where you are going. Data does not always tell the truth and it has no conscience. With information being multiple sources of data, you could say that information could be a harbinger of bad data. The Titanic went one step farther. She represented the current state of knowledge.

Remember from our model that knowledge is information with theory. The Titanic was eight hundred eighty-five feet of floating theory and unbridled Edwardian arrogance.

Records Are Meant to Be Broken

On the 11th of April, 1912, at about 1:30 in the afternoon, the *Titanic* finally set sail for New York with just over two thousand two hundred passengers and crew. She departed Queenstown Harbor headed for her day of infamy. She represented the thinking and populace of her time. It was inevitable that something so new had to set the standard. It was expected!

It was the practice that each new ocean liner set a new record for a Trans-Atlantic crossing on her maiden voyage. The Titanic was no different. Her captain and crew had one goal: to cross the Atlantic in record time. After all, she was the flagship of the White Star Line. All that mattered was getting to New York fast.

On that fateful day, the Old Testament, message and messenger, quantum theory with wave/particle duality, the Heisenberg Uncertainty Principle, and five-step decision making and numerous other teachings and natural laws all sailed into history. They were all on board but none of them were on the passenger manifest. The reason you could not see them or meet them is because they were built into the system.

No ocean liner had ever traveled as fast. Titanic was doing so well that even her crew was amazed at her progress. In fact, her speed already was beyond expectation. I would imagine the attitude of the crew was almost euphoric. The goal was everything! And everything was a city called New York.

Enter now the Heisenberg Uncertainty Principle. Remember what that said? In layman terms, this means that it is physically impossible to measure both the exact position and the exact momentum of a particle at the same time. The more precisely one of the quantities is measured, the less precisely the other is known. So you can calculate how fast something is going or you can calculate the exact location but you cannot do both at the same time.

So what was the priority for the Titanic? It was to cross the Atlantic in the shortest length of time. All focus was on speed and momentum. The goal was the record and the record was a number. Numbers are data. Data has no meaning unless the cumulative information and resulting body of knowledge lets you improve. This meant the priority, New York, was more important than where they were at any given time. Its speed became a given. It was a matter of routine, an expectation of an unsinkable ship, and unsinkable thinking. *You cannot jump from data to understanding and wisdom.*

The Titanic's location was taken for granted. You had tens of thousands of square miles of ocean. Surely nothing would dare interrupt or interfere with this ship. By the time the crew realized its mistake, it was too late. You see, when the Titanic struck the iceberg, the data, information, and knowledge were all focused on momentum. What it did was run into a specific position, literally. Remember, the goal was New York (particle). Captain Smith, not understanding his role (messenger or message), had simply done the proper thing. He had a choice when he left port. He could have sailed with the focus on momentum or he could have sailed with his focus on strategic points for accuracy, safety, and specific locations. He could not do both. He took his ship and flew off into the universe of unpredictability. What are the statistical odds of one ship running into that one iceberg in the Atlantic Ocean at that given moment? When he went to full power to accomplish his goal, it was as if he broke the stone tablets of understanding and wisdom. He was in uncharted territory. He should have studied Moses.

Moses and the Titanic

Spiritually, the Titanic suffered the same fate as Moses. Captain Smith and the crew did not understand their roles as messenger and message. The Titanic was the message of the age and the messenger of the evolution of travel. What it did not understand is that you cannot change Scripture while traveling over twenty-four knots in an ice field.

The rules, Scripture, and science were in place before they left port. The natural laws of science took effect on the fateful evening in the North Atlantic. But Scripture laid the foundation thousands of year before. Captain Smith smashed the stone tablets of wisdom. Scripture would have taught him more about navigation than the stars on that eventful evening.

The Titanic disaster was a series of interdependent events built into a dysfunctional system. Each system had a language and that language spoke to anyone who listened and understood and knew what it was listening for. The Titanic event spoke in many tongues. The sound of the data, information, and knowledge was screaming at anyone who would listen. It spoke the language of spirituality, quantum theory, and psychology. The culture of the day turned a deaf ear. More than that no one was listening, I believe that no one knew what they were listening for, let alone looking at. The system was shouting at them in its own respective language and the powers that be did not listen. This was a classic example of signal to noise.

We say in the Heisenberg Uncertainty principle that the measurement only applies to subatomic particles and that the difference is not noticeable in everyday occurrences. Yes, you can measure location and velocity at the same time with some degree of accuracy. You have to admit, that iceberg was pretty small compared to the size of the entire ocean. After all, why would you need that measurement in the first place? Heisenberg's theory would be relevant if, instead of subatomic particles, we substituted the subatomic particles for the human spirit. In other words, man would be the particle and human behavior the wave.

The Titanic set sail and all they had in mind was the goal: to set the record and reach the destination. All the systems of the Titanic were directed toward that purpose. What they did not pay attention to was *where* they were. The speed of the ship nullified their ability to measure position accurately. They were not in harmony. Probability became an issue.

The crew was so focused on the destination, a point in time, that they paid little attention to their position. All they cared about was the record. Their scenario has an eerie similarity to what Werner Heisenberg relates. The crew and owners of the Titanic focused on the destination. It was their rate and unknown velocity that killed them. The system truly shuddered. Quality of life was truly an issue.

Quantum theory struggles to measure wave function and its predictability. Managers suffer the same scenario trying to measure the position of an employee in the system, much like a letter grade for a child. Each is identifying a moment for inspection. What they may really be doing is failing to get the most accurate reading of either.

What some managers are trying to achieve was proven a failure in the North Atlantic over one hundred years ago. I believe both systems are saying the same thing. We have not identified the indicators nor do we recognize the language they are speaking. The behaviors of employees and productivity in corporate America had kindred spirits in the North Atlantic in the early part of the twentieth century.

The Iceberg Called Results

We were so focused on the results of the Edwardian era that we failed to listen to the true voice of the system and what our arrogance was telling us. And that was the behavior of the people who designed, built, managed, and sailed the Titanic into history. They were doers. They were the message of the times and not listeners. They were under the illusion that quality of life was an absolute.

More importantly, when they did listen, it was to data, information, and knowledge from the past. They did not listen for themselves to what the system of the time was telling them. They did not listen to the floating system of arrogance they were creating. They did not listen to the noise created by a system under extreme pressure. All these issues were individual points screaming to be heard. They did not have to—after all, they were the leaders. They only wanted the final result.

The anguished cry of the human experience is always heard near the end of a dysfunctional process. It is then we find that we have collided with something along the way. The system tried to tell us and we failed to listen. By then it was too late.

Committing to Free Will

The just man perishes, but no one takes it to heart; devout men are swept away, with no one giving it a thought.

—Isaiah 57:1[6]

I gave up long ago thinking life was fair. What is fair is that we have the power through free will to look at that adversity and decide how we choose to see it and let it impact our lives. That, I believe, is part of our misunderstanding of the term *free will* and its application to quality of life. That message was quite clear with the Titanic.

I believe we must commit to free will. It does not commit to us. If we decide to understand free will, then we must also commit to accountability, ability, and attitude. What is our calling? Talent is the external manifestation of a set of behaviors or processes. I believe our calling has less to do with talent and more to do with ability. I do not believe they are the same.

I know many talented musicians, artists, and authors who have given their lives to the pursuit of their craft and have spent many hours pursuing their goals. Ability is different. Ability, to me, is taking something we have a love for but are not necessarily good at; it may even cause anxiety. And yet, we rise to the occasion to transform ourselves to a higher level. What the world asks of us is most likely something we are not good at!

I believe everyone has talent but not everyone has the ability to pull it off. One only has to look at emerging and developing nations. They have very talented and resourceful people who bypass the system to make a meager living for their families. They, too, want something better for their families and a better quality of life. It is an international tragedy when third-world people are exploited when they reach for a better quality of life. They do have a very dysfunctional system that keeps their ability to succeed at a minimum.

Hidden Capital

We have something else going for us in this country that other parts of the world do not have. We have a form of hidden capital—let's call it equity—that strikes at the core of why our success is what it is. It is directly related to our quality of life and greater opportunity for the human spirit.

In *The Mystery of Capital: Why Capitalism Triumphs in the West and Fails Everywhere Else*, Hernando De Soto says, "The major stumbling block that keeps the rest of the world from benefiting from capitalism is its inability to produce capital. Capital is the force that raises the productivity of labor and creates the wealth of nations. It is the lifeblood of the capitalist system, the foundation of progress, and the one thing that the poor countries of the world cannot seem to produce for themselves, no matter how eagerly their people engage in all the other activities that characterize a capitalist economy."[7] Again, these people are only as good as the system they live in lets them be.

In Western culture, we have learned that all levels of society have potential. And that is the key. We understand that all parts of our culture have potential and, in a true capitalist society, that potential is used to reflect free enterprise. In third-world countries, many citizens have dived into the entrepreneurial spirit. One only has to look at many developing countries to see the vast array of home-based and store-front businesses. But capitalism does not seem to work. In fact, it has produced a system that is in chaos.

What they haven't learned, according to De Soto, is they believed money can exceed the human potential and lead to success. Many of these former socialist and third-world countries did not grasp the concept that capitalism is the human spirit and is a significant force. Look at capitalism as a type of intellectual ecosystem where the key is potential and not money. Potential is a self-renewing resource. I believe that potential is the human spirit. The system and the people are interdependent with quantum results.

Again, the secret of capital is not money. Money is the by-product of the system's potential. It is the ability to think we can! We tend to think that money is the driving issue behind capitalism. This is a debate in itself. Much has been written about capitalist countries being selfish and materialistic. To some it is. It is also a very efficient system of renewal.

Western culture has realized that, in capitalism, the money is not the deciding factor, it is the potential of what that money and entrepreneurial spirit can do. Potential is a spiritual and personal form of internal capitalism. Capitalism is our ability to leverage the human spirit. The real fruit of the venture is the potential that made it. The philosophy that capitalism is process oriented has deep roots in eastern thinking.[8]

A Quality Watch Does Not Make Us Productive

In our culture we have chosen to mark each day with a reference to time. And time has been tagged as the nemesis for quality of life. I was recently watching a program on television about a watch repair business that has been in the same location for five generations.

One of the salespeople was commenting on how many of their customers have been having their watches repaired for generations. He also related how some people come to them saying, "My watch needs repair, and it is running six seconds slow." And that was over the course of a year! I wonder how six seconds has an impact on this person's life over the course of that year. I wonder if more quality of life is lost worrying about the six seconds than doing something else.

The interesting twist to the dilemma of the six lost seconds is that they never existed in the first place. Time is something we have invented in our universe. It does not exist anywhere but right here. Einstein understood the perspective of time and I think that is why he was not in the watch business. Time has absolutely no independent existence other than the events by which we measure it.

What that means is, the more we focus on time, the more we lose our quality of life. That brings to mind the wonderful story of the passenger riding the train in Ireland. As the train entered a small Irish village, a passenger felt the quaint and idyllic atmosphere of an authentic Ireland. As he was getting off the train he noticed that the train station had two large clocks on the outside of the building. One clock said one o'clock and the other had twenty minutes past one. His curiosity got the best of him and he asked the conductor why they had two clocks with different times.

The conductor looked at the passenger in mild reproach and said, "Well now, if they both said the same time, then we would only need one of them!" Our life is relative. And neither clock could change that!

The watch customer could have been doing something else instead of spending so much time worrying about the six lost seconds. (How many other potentially important events did he miss by worrying about six seconds?)

What one realizes, of course, is that in our culture, our day has significant restrictions but it does not have to limit our quality of life. In a twenty-four hour time period, we must sleep, work, and have time for family, friends, and fun. It may not happen every day nor may it happen in that order. And even though we try to save time, time cannot be saved. Time is something we have thought of to put some sort of perspective on who and why we are. I want to address some of what we do and why we do it.

Productivity Is Not an External Measurement

We base our lives on the measurement of twenty-four hours, when the sun rises, sets, and then rises again. The measurement of the earth's movement is relative to the universe and not to us. We are bystanders in a scientific and spiritually infinite cosmic stadium. The twenty-four hours is something we have done.

We create a problem when we measure our productivity based on an external measurement. If I build a portion of a house, and I measure my progress in a twenty-four hour period, I can call that success. If I do it out of frustration and use poor quality materials, but no one is the wiser, then what have I accomplished? If I wanted to work on the house, but have the opportunity to spend time with a friend in need or spend quality time with a family member, my external accomplishment may appear less but other things have happened. Remember the message and the messenger?

A wonderful example of the anxiety and the unbalanced equation is Mother Teresa. Letters are now being read where her accomplishments are being measured by the incredible difficulty she encountered. What has caught the attention of people reading the letters is how much she accomplished despite her feelings at times of almost being abandoned and forgotten.

Mother Teresa wrote many letters and made references to her interior darkness. The true mark of her greatness was how she accomplished all she did while facing an almost overwhelming environment of adversity.

In a 1961 letter to the Missionaries of Charity, Mother Teresa wrote, "Without suffering our work would be just social work.... All the desolation of the poor people must be redeemed and we must share it."[9] Here was a woman who was the twentieth-century example of quality of life. She experienced words we do not want to hear: doubt, abandonment, and a humble faith. And yet she prevailed. Try to find those words in any book or manual on customer satisfaction.

She never listened to the twenty-four-hour clock. The only clock she listened to was her spiritual calling. This was her gift to the world because she was listening to what the world was asking of her. I believe Mother Teresa did not like the trappings of Western culture. I also believe she lived a concept of capitalism in knowing that the secret lies in the potential of others. And that made her timeless. Her compassionate wealth as a human being was infinite.

With Age Comes New Meaning

In our quest for quality of life, I am increasingly aware of the need I hear our aging work force describe for increased meaning and for clarifying their definition for quality of life. They are very aware of their continued momentum. They want to live life to the fullest. They do not want to stop. I believe some of those questions will be answered through the "unavoidable suffering" expressed by Victor Frankl and Mother Teresa's "suffering in our work...and interior darkness." What I also hear from the aging work force is their sense of perspective of their youth and their ideas about life.

With the infancy of the techno age, I believe we will see new definitions of life's meaning and skills. The aging work force is now showing signs of not quitting at a predetermined retirement age. Many are looking into secondary and some even third-phase careers into their sixties and seventies. We have an aging generation that will want to accomplish tasks and confront issues their predecessors would not have dreamed of. They will be a testimonial to Heisenberg's principles.

Baby boomers will have their share of darkness and so will the following generations. I believe they, too, will have a sense that the illusion of time that society has created will be held against them. I can't wait to see the baby boomers in their eighties and nineties! It will be interesting to see the quality of life choices that will be made. I don't see the boomers as passengers on the Titanic of old age.

Aging, of course, always does bring us closer to the truth. And many are choosing to live that journey and apply their talents right where they are. One of the most profound experiences of importance one can have is the opportunity to give back your talents to a cause or community. It is a delight to see the increasing numbers of people who are getting involved with community projects and local government issues.

What Are the Questions Life Asks Us?

Productivity and quality of life are not measured entities. They involve seeking one's role as a constant state of adaptive situations where we live our principles, values, and ethics through listening to what is being asked of us. I believe that the more we understand who we are, the greater steps we take in understanding why we are. Our inner self is not a given. This is a system in search of harmony. Einstein would have liked that.

I believe we must identify, develop, and nurture those skills. It cannot be legislated into productivity and get switched on by telling ourselves we want it to be so. Inner productivity was never meant to be a level playing field. Rather, we find our inner purpose through the turmoil, unfairness, and ambiguity of life's actions.

If this is true, then people like Mother Teresa wrote the operator's manual. Our heart and soul become the better. It is as if life becomes an unbalanced equation and lets us jump back and forth over the equal sign. We then realize that there can be just as much peace and harmony in experiencing the process. But that is not what we are taught. We are led to believe that we have guaranteed expectations and success is measured by a set goal. And if the guaranteed expectations do not occur, then we have been wronged.

What we have really done is a terrible injustice to ourselves. We have been taught that success and life are linear. They are not. Life is adaptive, constantly evolving, and fraught with huge risk and constant self-organization. Life is not a logical sequence of events. It is more like a cloud on a sunny day. It is constantly self-organizing, and changing shapes, and it can move in different directions. These random patterns and chaotic state can still hold hundreds of tons of water. It is also capitalistic in its design. Its organization and beauty lies in its potential. It reminds us with the ability to become who we are and realize our true potential. It never stands still. It wasn't designed to.

Again, our Declaration of Independence gave us the basics. We have the right to life, liberty, and the pursuit of happiness. Even these are not balanced equations. All these rights give us is the right to try. The rest is our ability to become adaptive to life and its calling. It is as if each of us were a cloud, individualistic, random in nature, adaptive, and always moving toward a meaningful quality of life.

That quality of life experience is even more meaningful when we encounter good leaders. And that is in the next chapter.

Questions

- Does my work add balance and harmony to my life?
- Does my work charge my life's battery?
- Do I bring work problems home each day and discuss them with my family?
- How do I measure my successes?
- Do I measure them by the goals I have reached or the obstacles I have overcome?
- Am I too focused on the destination and facility to enjoy the process?
- Is my work affecting my health?
- What positive change would I bring into my life to make a difference?

Chapter Eight

Does My Work Provide Leadership and Professional Relationships?

Interaction of thoughts, emotions, and ideals is a fundamental of life. Our need for professional relationships is critical for the development of the human spirit.

If we look back at all the great writings of man, we become acutely aware of the power of the interpersonal relationship and its application to leadership. The great spiritual writings reflect the ongoing process of the human spirit's being nurtured, challenged, and led by interaction with others. I often read scientific articles and am struck by one person of science being influenced by someone or something someone else did. Both disciplines are grounded in the need for leadership.

Life presents many different challenges for human beings unless they have the opportunity to interact with others. What is interesting is, this influence may occur generations apart. We receive insight or a message from someone else and then we become the messenger for the new thought. We personalize the message and can become the leader for a new thought, idea, or way. It is an example of the duality of the human spirit.

I am struck by the number of great scientific breakthroughs where one scientist or inventor looked at someone's work and saw its use or potential in a completely different way. Here again we have idea/wave turn into message/particle or new concept. The wonderful part of the scientific/spirituality equation is that it can occur at an early age. It is called being a kid. Life was simpler for kids but the reverse is true. Can adults learn from kids they never knew? Sometimes leadership can come in different sizes.

Being the Message and the Messenger at a Very Early Age

This is a true story. I know it is true because I was there when it happened. It is the story of a truck accident, and a lifelong lesson in never underestimating the obvious, and the power an adult can have on younger people. It is also a story of being the message and the messenger. This story takes place in the 1950s. I think that is about right because I was about ten years old. I was at that age when everything was neat and life was one new adventure after another.

The incident happened in my hometown of Brookfield, Wisconsin. At that time, it was still quite rural. I was having a typical adolescent life and attending St. Mary's Catholic Grade School. I liked school because the nuns who taught me said I would. After all, the nuns knew everything. And if they didn't, I was not about to ask. At that age, I believed they were hired by God.

Our house was situated about a block off the main road, North Avenue. About two blocks east of our house was a railroad track. The track was on top of a wood and metal-beamed railroad bridge that crossed North Avenue.

Our neighborhood gang used to watch the freight trains pass over the bridge on a regular schedule. We used to get up close and wave to the people who hopped the trains in search of a better life. I always thought that was cool idea. I just couldn't figure out how I was going to do that and make it home each night so I could sleep in my own bed and not miss supper. That was the limit of my creative thinking when it came to travel. Life was a daily adventure.

The Laws of Physics Can Be Loud

Let's go back to the bridge and my lesson in life, Newtonian science with its specific laws, and a jolt into quantum theory and its range of possibilities. The bridge was an imposing structure that passed over a two-lane suburban road. It was a favorite target for local youth who liked to hang over the side and paint the high school logo on the wide support beam. That was the cool part.

The bridge was built in the early part of the 1930s when trucks were shorter and ten feet six inches was high enough. As the height of the trucks increased to eleven and twelve feet, they got a lesson in math and physics. They were the problem. And once every four months or so, some truck would try to rewrite the science of physics and mathematics and run into the bridge.

What was even more interesting was what would happen to furniture trucks. As they drove west for deliveries, the load was heavy enough to compress the springs and the truck would pass under the bridge. But on the way back, the truck would be taller, and one can imagine the surprise of the truck driver as he tried to pass unsuccessfully under the bridge.

Now here is what happened on one warm and humid summer afternoon. For someone who is not used to it, the humidity of a Midwest summer afternoon can be devastating. Sweat runs into parts of your body you didn't even know existed.

When we heard the crash, we instinctively jumped on our bikes and headed for North Avenue and the bridge. When we got there, we knew immediately what had happened. We saw a delivery-type cargo van with about a twelve-foot box that was missing about half of its roof. Debris was all over the road and the truck was wedged under the bridge. It could not move forward or back.

Sir Isaac Newton would have shaken his head. The driver, who was shook up from the accident, was trying unsuccessfully to get the truck unstuck. As an adult I later learned to call that denial. Our excitement grew when we heard the sirens. There were police cars, fire trucks, and debris everywhere. The road was completely blocked, and no one knew if the bridge was damaged.

This was great stuff for us—no one was hurt and all we had to do was sit in the neighbor's front yard and watch the unfolding series of events. When traffic was finally rerouted, we saw the largest tow truck in the world back up to the rear of the truck that was stuck.

We saw some of the police and fire people all in a huddle and pointing to the tow truck. It was hard to tell who the leader was, but it was pretty clear that the heat of the Wisconsin afternoon was taking its toll. We watched with interest as a long, thick cable from the tow truck was attached to the back of the stuck truck. I believe Sir Isaac Newton would have had his fingers in his ears about this time. Every action does have an equal and opposite reaction. How many times has an idea, project, or information gotten wedged or stuck in some section or department in your organization? How many times did groups of decision makers get together and try to get it "unstuck"? If you think the workplace is special, kids can face the same problem too.

Everybody was told to stand back and it was either a police officer or a fireman who said, "You kids stand back in case this cable breaks." Well, that sounded pretty impressive to us. We all backed up. The tow truck pulled until its tires started to spin on the pavement. The stuck truck stayed stuck. This was getting real exciting and rated high on our list of neat things. Our usual level of excitement consisted of getting our pants cuff caught in the bicycle chain and getting unloaded into loose gravel, or seeing one of our dogs give the neighbor's cat some exercise.

It was obvious that nothing was happening. The tow truck was now letting the cable go slack between attempts to take a running start. The cable tightened but nothing happened.

The emergency crews were now gathered in a huddle on our side of the road. We heard swear words that even made us look at each other. This was no place for a field trip for my St. Mary's religion class. We sort of eased our way to the edge of the lawn and close to the huddle and watched the very important uniformed people with sweaty brows making all kinds of facial expressions. They were obviously concerned.

It was then that it happened. I don't know who said it, but when I heard the statement I just froze. I know it wasn't me. All I remember is hearing someone say, "Why don't you let the air out of the tires of the stuck truck and then back it out?"

It is these moments when one contemplates if a bird flaps its wings in a park, can it affect the behavior of person a mile away? In the same vein, can someone's comment at an accident scene affect the behavior of a group of adult supervisors and Newtonian physics a block away?

The world seemed to just stand still and be silent. All those men sort of looked at each other. And then all we did was get the hell out of there!

I cannot help but look back on that hot afternoon and see how the message was also the messenger on how to solve the problem. Sometimes we get so caught up in our businesses or a team problem that all our training and education becomes a barrier to being a leader.

It was the same with Werner Heisenberg, Niels Bohr, and Max Planck. They looked at traditional Newtonian physics, which was "stuck" in traditional thinking, and saw something different, and saw that something in a different way. Much as with their view of physics, they saw that traditional thinking was stuck. It was their leadership that set the example. I have become aware of the many times in my life when I was the messenger for an issue and yet, I also remember the times when being the message was also significant. It always seemed to relate to an experience where I learned something from someone else.

When I started to collect my notes and examples, I remembered this story about the bridge. Again, I am struck by remembering a story that I had not given a single thought to for over forty years and then it comes back as if it were yesterday.

The bridge is still there. The house and front lawn where I sat and watched one of life's lessons also is there. I have grown older and the road has been lowered to accommodate larger trucks. I imagine, even today, that it is possible for a truck with a very high load to hit the bridge and scatter its contents all over the road. That sound probably would sound as sickening today as it did back in the 1950s.

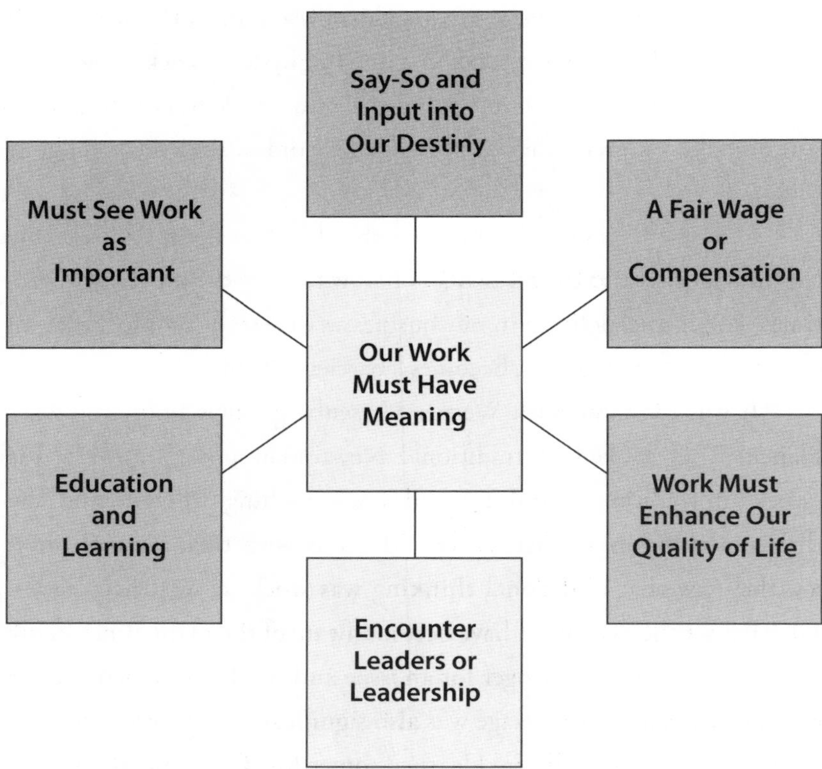

Figure 6. Seven Needs for Personal Productivity—Leaders

Positive Relationships Are an Asset

In my consulting business, I now look at myself as the message/messenger role. Some of my clients want me to listen to their ideas and offer some feedback. I see this as being the message to my clients. They want me to be there for them. They see me as an environmental asset to their organization. To me, this is a foundation for building professional relationships. I do know that our workplace is in desperate need of more leaders.

In this case, being the message means I am in an active mode. I am present as a listener and doer. I am expected to offer significant observations and, if the trust level is established, wonderful things can happen. My clients feel comfortable with my attitude and know that I will offer direction if needed. Some call on me to be a messenger. The challenge becomes knowing the difference between the two and knowing that each may generate different results.

These calls are often a signal for help. I see the messenger as a presenter of information and knowledge. With established relationships, knowing when to be the message/messenger can be critical to a lasting and dynamic association. I am drawn to words like *harmony*, *angst*, and *surprise*. All of these words can describe such a relationship. They can also be used to describe a spiritual and scientific journey.

One of the strongest memories from my professional career is from talking with leaders about career and life issues. I think the vast majority of those instances were just over a cup of coffee, but that brief contact formed the basis of lasting relationships and professional contacts.

When I look back, I think about validation, which gave me the opportunity to get positive feedback and relate to others with similar or even different experiences. Whatever the case, just being around others seemed to create a positive environment. What was most important was the opportunity to learn. It is as if we are hardwired for the influence of leadership and relationships. The challenge is whether or not we choose to use that ability.

I will talk about learning and education in another of the needs. What I wish to relate now is the importance of positive people as a support in the foundation for personal productivity and professional workplace relationships. This sounds like a no-brainer. I am amazed, often daily, how many people continue to associate with or refuse to recognize the toxic people in their lives.

It's Nice When a Leader Sticks Up for You

I want to share another story about leadership, one which I will never forget. Like other stories, it happened in Alaska while I was in the United States Air Force.

I spent two cold, impressive, unforgiving but exciting winters in Alaska. You did not screw around during the winter. Everyone knew what was needed to survive and work was taken seriously. While I was on the flight line, we serviced aircraft day and night. Some flew in and stayed, and others landed just for fuel, maybe maintenance, and a rest.

What made their stops interesting is that many of the aircraft flew nonstop from their home base. Some came from as far away as Louisiana, Texas, and North Carolina. Now you have to remember, if you leave North Carolina in March and fly to Alaska, the temperature at your home base is fifty or sixty degrees. Fast forward eight to ten hours and you get off the plane in temperatures that might be twenty-five or thirty below zero. Those flight crews really got a shock.

One very cold winter evening I was working swing shift. It was about 11:30 p.m. and we received word that a KC-135 aircraft was about thirty minutes out and was going to stay the night. The KC-135 is a four-engine jet aircraft that is used as an in-flight refueler—an airborne gas station. The civilian model of the KC-135 is the Boeing 707.

Well, this evening the unexpected four-engine guest was going to need service, meaning that it would need about an hour and a half to two hours of service in order for it to be ready for departure in the morning. The nicest part of this type of work was helping a flight crew get accustomed to a strange location.

After the aircraft landed, and as the flight crew was finishing getting their gear off the aircraft, I asked the crew if they were hungry. The crew chief related that they had experienced a long flight and were starving. I told him that I could get them a ride to where they would spend the night and I could also arrange to take them to the flight crew dining hall. He thanked me and said that some crew members would stay with the aircraft.

Being about twenty below zero and close to midnight, the crew was very anxious to get to their quarters. After about an hour, I took the two remaining crew members, including the copilot, to the flight dining hall. They asked if I would like to join them for dinner. I told them I would check with my supervisor. This would work out great because we did get a meal break and a chance to eat in the flight crew dining area was a real treat.

It is important to digress for a moment and share a few facts. Officers and enlisted personnel eat in different parts of the dining room. Flight crews ate together in a different location in the dining hall because many of the flight crews had both enlisted and commissioned officers. Their dining hall was open twenty-four hours a day.

All dining halls were cafeteria-style. In the case of flight crews, specialty items like omelets, sandwiches, and other foods were prepared by the staff as you went through the line. One thing that I found out is the United States Air Force and, in particular, the Strategic Air Command, ate very well. I was an enlisted noncommissioned officer (NCO), a sergeant, and could not eat in the flight crew's dining facility unless I was invited. On this evening, I was invited and would have been nuts to pass up an opportunity like that.

It was not uncommon for a member of the flight crew to ask for something that was not on the servicing line. If the cook could get it then, "Yes sir," was all he heard and the specialty item was prepared. This was truly a treat because I, too, was hungry and this type of opportunity did not happen that often. It was great opportunity to get omelets made to order.

So here I was, an NCO in the flight crew dining facility. I showed them where the line was and what was available. The copilot told me to go ahead of them in the line. There was a cook standing by the grill.

As I approached, I said, "Hello." What happened next is the reason I am telling this story.

The cook's first response was to not acknowledge my greeting. By that time, the copilot, an officer, was standing next to me. I again offered a greeting to the cook and asked if we could have breakfast. The cook looked at me and said, "What do you want?"

The tone of his voice was one of bother. He was not impressed that an NCO was in this line and he probably thought I belonged on the other end of the dining hall where the enlisted men eat.

I asked if he could make me a ham-and-cheese omelet. Without saying a word, he made the omelet, put it on a plate, and gave it to me. I thanked him and moved along the line. I felt sort of bad because I had been telling the crew how great a place we had. I hoped the copilot hadn't seen what had happened. I was wrong. He had, and what he did next reinforced my belief in the human spirit and stayed with me all these years. Good leaders are a real asset—treasure them!

Now, the copilot didn't have to say anything, he could have just gotten his meal, moved on, and not said a word. One gets used to people saying things and one does understand that some people have a hard time in the military. I didn't see it that way—I wanted all the people I met on the flight line to get great service and know that we had a great base.

As the copilot stepped up to the cook, the cook's body language and disposition changed. He said, "Yes, sir, what would you like?"

The copilot looked him in the eye and said, "I want the same thing that sergeant ordered and I am wondering if you are going to give me the same look you gave him?"

I had never had anyone stand up for me like that before. This was one of those little moments that no one ever sees or, for that matter, ever remembers. But I did. I never forgot that. I told myself that day that, as long as I was responsible, I would treat people with respect and let them know they mattered and that the work they did was important to the organization.

This copilot gave me the opportunity to show them that I respected what they did, and what he said to that cook told me he respected what I did. That was one of the greatest compliments I have ever had in my life. I knew from that moment on the importance of relationships.

We got our breakfast, sat together at a table, and never said a word about what had happened. Nothing had to be said. It was done. I do not recall the copilot's name, but he taught me a great lesson about respect—that it meant standing up for others. It is one of the greatest lessons I have ever learned. He was not only an officer and a pilot; he was a leader who believed honesty holds the hand of angst and creative thinking.

Attitude and Professional Relationships Are Critical

I think a tremendous analogy relating to the workplace is a sports team. And I am not just saying any sports team; I am talking about successful ones. I want to make clear that I believe there is a difference between winning teams and successful teams. I have seen winning teams where the players and some coaches left much to be desired. And then you have the teams who may not have the best equipment, facilities, or schedules but have a sense of purpose and drive. They play with all the intensity of teams in larger categories, but they see their purpose as more than winning. Theirs is one where it is not winning at all costs. And to the players, it is that great opportunity to play and be around people who make it different. I think those opportunities occur every day. It is called the American workplace.

I had such an opportunity in the 1990s when I was the manager of a training team. Our responsibility was extensive and the pace became intensive. I had the most diverse group of associates one could ask for. All were good at what they did, though some were definitely grounded in a stronger opinion of things. But when it came to their work and the way they treated each other, something special happened. Was I the reason? No.

I believe I created and ferociously protected their environment so they could be the best they could be. I believe I was being an *organizational environmentalist* before I even coined the term and that I had the ability to know a good thing when I saw it. I studied each person individually and paid particular attention as to how they communicated with me and how they interacted with others.

I routinely asked their customers how they did. I gave the employees feedback and told them what I knew. I believed then and now that they had the knowledge, skills, and abilities to make a difference in someone's life. If training was available and they wanted to attend, it was up to them. They were in charge of their own destinies.

They also knew that destiny carries a tremendous level of responsibility, and they rose to the occasion. One area was of particular importance: I encouraged them to seek out their peers and become involved with other professionals and let them know that they represented me and our training team when they did it.

Looking back on this one area, I believe it was instrumental in their attitude and productivity. It was during this time that I was formulating my final theory for the Seven Needs. It became apparent to me that when the employees interacted with other professionals and had an increased level of responsibility, those relationships became key to their productivity.

Two of my employees in particular were responsible for a program that was both critical and had the potential for high liability. Over time, they gained a great deal of respect from other employees and, eventually, other organizations. I encouraged them to share their information and expertise. In fact, when I had the chance I flaunted the abilities of all my employees.

What happened next is a manager's dream. I say dream because it was and still is a dream of mine. I believe a true test of a manager and leader is to create an environment where employees gain both internal and external recognition for their skills. It is not only important to have an environment where the employees become a source for other employees in the organization, but to me, the ultimate compliment to them and the manager is when they become resources to other organizations and experts in their fields. Both employees did just that. Now, to some managers that is a daring statement to make and it leads me into another story. This, to me, was a dream come true.

What Is Wrong with Teams?

The message/messenger scenario requires me to share its relativity to what we have done with organizational groups and teams. I must admit that I feel like I am beating a dead horse. I give many public talks and love to follow up with questions and answers. I frequently ask groups, "How many of you work in a team concept?" Many raise their hands. I then ask them to describe it. When the conversation is finished, I can see by the facial expressions that they have some questions that need to be answered.

I believe what we have done to teams and their purpose has been destructive. W. Edwards Deming would be chastising the American workplace if he were to see some of today's teams.

Companies adopted teams with the best of intentions during the 70s, 80s, and 90s. They were, and still are, critical tools to continuous improvement of processes and systems. Many companies avoided teams like the plague. Those, however, that did use them in a constructive fashion reaped the results. What others did is a horror story.

They saw the team concept as an easy way to keep employees busy. This is truly sad. Some companies have teams so they don't have to hire more managers; teams were used to default from the principles of leadership. A team in the hands of the wrong people limits control.

The team thinks they are doing profound work. The boss, who makes the final decision, often is not supported by the team. The message is sent. The team becomes the substitute for a person needing to make the decision. The result is self-evident. Either decisions are not made or the decisions that are adopted become a special interest or the political average of the group. This is not a team; this is a committee.

A team should never be used as a substitute for leadership. Let me share an example.

I did some work for an organization with an executive director and an advisory board. The director's role was to conduct daily activities and to update the board as to its overall operations. The director, in turn, would ask the board for opinions and input.

What happened was both subtle and disheartening. The director left the organization for a different position and a search was conducted for a new director. What happened next became their challenge. Instead of stepping up the search for a director, the advisory board became the governing body. The board actually added members to show a balanced and fair representation.

What they had great difficulty with was finding solid direction. Much of the board became factional and multi-centered so what materialized was an organization plagued with leadership by consensus. They governed and tried to do it without offending any member's point of view. In the end, they lent new meaning to the word *average*. I left.

Here is another example. Communities pride themselves on the involvement of citizens and listening to the public for a better vision of what to do. The result usually is the development of boards and commissions. This approach lets members of the communities become involved in issues they see as both civic and social concerns. That is good.

Communities, however, must make sure these boards and commissions stay focused on their purpose. These groups must remain advisory. They need to bring both the good and bad to their respective council and members. If they really have purpose and direction, this becomes their driving force. They must also have strong leadership. That is the purpose of teams.

What happens, however, is the team becomes so involved in its purpose that it subtly becomes a special interest group that loses its focus and direction. The team can easily assume the identity of ultimate survival. In other words, its survival becomes paramount to the concern and needs of others and no longer serves its issue—it becomes an issue.

A team must remain objective. When it begins to see its purpose as "us versus them," then its purpose is purely an outcome-based process. The team has abdicated any sense of message/messenger and no real knowledge can emanate from this situation. The team has created its own world and reality, and its purpose changes. It begins doing what it was not meant to do.

My advice to companies thinking about teams: if you do not understand the principle of teams and do not have a strong leadership training program, then don't go there. You will do irreparable damage to your company and the employees who work for you. Teams are designed to assist strong leaders in finding out what is wrong in the organization, and to improve the system. This includes the employees.

Let me give you another example, and I will refer to flying an airplane. When I was getting my pilot's license, my instructor always told me to fly the airplane. No matter what happens I was responsible for all souls on board. *I had to fly the airplane.*

I use that analogy in some of my seminars. I tell the participants that companies, teams, and organizations need leaders. They are not productive if they are run by a committee. And this is the example I use. I tell participants that the next time they fly on a commercial carrier and they are getting on the airplane, I want them to look to the right where the passengers are and then look to the left. If the cockpit door is open then glance in the cockpit. If you see a conference table in the cockpit, then get off the airplane!

Here are some questions for you to consider regarding teams:

- Are the teams in my company working? If not, why not?
- How do you collect and analyze your data, information, and knowledge?
- Do your teams have strong leaders?
- How active are the leaders?
- Do they know when to talk (message) and when to listen (messenger)?
- Are processes and systems improving?
- Have the teams had training on how to find root issues?
- Do a few members on the teams do all the work?
- Does the team process involve opportunities for education in order to proceed?
- Are the teams inundated with eleventh-hour bright ideas?
- Are the teams' directions clear and understandable?

Conversations Are Never Out of Style

When we establish relationships, I would like to believe that the norm of the day is face to face. That is changing daily and we are replacing one-on-one relationships with the digital divide. One issue I wish to make clear: I don't believe communication by cell phone, texting, pager, e-mail, and conference call is true communication. The medium used is designed as a conduit. We must use all types of information assistance. It does not mean, however, that we should use it as a preference over one-on-one communication.

The manuals for my laptop and cell phone are great tools for using the medium but they do not tell us anything about communication. We gain that experience by presenting ourselves to other people and taking the time to check the electronic guns at the door.

I believe that managers should constantly talk with all their employees. Where they stand is critical to what they will do next. If you want them to do honest, positive, and ethical things, then why would you not want to frequently have honest, positive, and ethical conversations with them?

On one occasion, I was having an informal and periodic conversation with one of my employees. He was bright, dedicated, and loaded with ability. He and I had frequently talked about certain areas in his portfolio of skills that needed attention. He knew it, I knew it, and we talked honestly about it. During our conversation, I asked him where he saw himself with the company and asked if there was any job that he saw as attractive.

He looked at me for a moment, looked away, then looked straight at me and replied, "I would like to have your job."

I looked him right in the eye and said, "Well, I am in it right now and I won't be in it forever. Let's see what we can do to create that opportunity."

I was honored and also challenged. I was risking a lot. Here was an employee who had great potential, heart and soul. If I chose to be a butthead and close my mind, I would have felt threatened and thought his comment arrogant and not appropriate.

If I chose to be one of the Eighteen Management Behaviors mentioned in my book *Each Human Spirit,* and was truly insecure, I could easily have been reaching for the policy manual as I thought of different ways to stunt this person's career.

What we did was develop a plan for this employee to get the skills he needed. This employee made frequent visits to my office and our conversations were quite candid. Over time, this employee transferred to another area for the career training he needed. Eventually he returned and found that his experience gave him the opportunity to apply and get a different position and promotion. I believe I had something to do with it. Being candid can work the other way.

My openness with my employees was a wonderful experience. To this day I miss them deeply; I miss their energy, dedication, and just plain guts. I did everything I could to protect their ability to do their jobs as best they could. That philosophy comes with a price.

If you are in such a situation, others may not look at it the same way you do. For instance, in order to get the job done, I sometimes cut a few administrative corners to make it happen. This was not well received by those higher up in the food chain. In fact, some tried to make my life as miserable as they could. I did pay a price but it was worth it and I would do it all again for my employees. Employees like that are worth the wait and the effort of any manager.

Some Bosses Are Jerks

I had a student tell me a story where being candid had the opposite effect. This person addressed his job with vitality and a sense of purpose. He always wanted to know more. Realizing that his present position was not offering the training opportunities needed, he approached his supervisor with an idea.

During the course of the conversation, the employee looked for common ground in the conversation. Realizing that many training opportunities meant being away from the workplace, the employee suggested a popular program called mentoring.

This employee had heard that his parent organization offered career mentors for those employees who wanted to explore other areas and apply them to their present positions. An informal request was made to the supervisor and the employee left the room.

Several days later, the employee was asked to come to the supervisor's office. What happened next stunned the employee. The supervisor said he had considered the request and would process it further, however (and here is where the hammer dropped), the supervisor then stated that he felt that if the employee still wanted to pursue the mentor option, then he should also consider looking for a transfer to another area of the organization.

The supervisor felt that the employee could no longer be loyal to the company because he was looking for outside assistance and that, as a supervisor, he felt the transfer would be best. The employee was shaken. The boss should have been shaken, and then fired.

Knowledge and the process for acquiring it has become an organizational two-edged sword. *Attitude comes from inside the organization, but change comes from outside.* Learning and having the employee informed of expectations are part of the process. However, any supervisor, employee, or person in a position of authority, who sets an expectation and uses that expectation as a way of measuring loyalty to the company, is doing a horrific disservice to the employee and organization itself.

This idea, that only certain people have the necessary knowledge, can actually be detrimental to a positive working relationship. Employees want to learn. Why would any manager or leader (there is a difference), ever want to stifle the learning process? The human spirit has free will and, as Thomas Aquinas relates, is obligated to do something with it.

I have never understood how a company could build a health and fitness center or membership opportunities, and then forbid or limit an employee to attend a training seminar for her mind. Management must shed the yoke of fear and give employees a range of learning experiences and learning relationships related to their jobs. Each experience should be reinforced by having the employee explain how her experience connects to the company as a whole.

Interact with Other Professionals

Interaction is a learning process. It is also part of the *Seven Needs for Personal Productivity.* If you have to interact with someone who is a jerk, the process is fundamentally one way. If, however, you have opportunities to interact with other professionals and learn from them, and they from you, a more vast range of possibilities begins to happen.

My Alaskan experience speaks for itself. I am not advocating peer communication as signing up for every training program that may present itself. Getting on the seminar circuit should be used with moderation, unless it is the only training available. Seminars will give you skills. Your goal is knowledge, understanding, and wisdom. You are also obligated to use that knowledge wisely.

Education is a life experience, but if work pays for your education, they have the right to get the results. Find someone who can teach you something. Those leaders are worth their weight in gold. Too many people in leadership positions choose not to teach you anything. Avoid them. I have deep convictions regarding relationships and leadership and knowledge. To put it bluntly, we easily become whom we hang around with.

Stay Away from Negative Influences

One evening, I was watching my local public broadcasting station and my attention became focused on a motivational speaker. I do not recall his name, but he was talking about relationships. He then said something that really caught my attention. He said that, if we are to succeed, we must get the toxic people out of our lives.

I cannot count the number of times I have had a supervisor or manager saying how they spend the majority of their time with a small group of employees who cause the majority of problems. I make the next statement out of personal experience and take responsibility for my own opinion. I believe we will associate with people who think in direct proportion to how we think about ourselves. I use the word *think* instead of *feel*. If we have negative attitudes and thinking, then we will seek out others with like processes.

In the 1970s, my parents extended their home to help a family member who was having a difficult time in his teenage years. Life was a challenge as he struggled with learning issues and a background of emotional and physical abuse. My parents gave him a new start. He was in his early teens. They enrolled him in the local high school, bought him clothes, and gave him a stable environment so he would have a chance.

After I left the Air Force, I returned to my home town. My parents were very optimistic and had put their heart and soul into making it work for this young man. He was not aggressive and was very respectful of my parents. It was sad to see that hard work and the best efforts do not guarantee success.

After a few months I went back to my local high school to see the principal. He invited me into his office and, after catching up on old times, I asked him how my young cousin was doing. He told me, "Art, I have twelve hundred students in this school. Of those twelve hundred I have about fifty that cause the teachers and staff the most problems. Of those fifty I have about ten to twelve who are constantly over the line. That dozen are a daily problem from the time they enter the building. After your cousin arrived, within two weeks, that dozen were his friends."

I got the message. It was the same on the home front. No matter what my parents did, this young man fought them at every step. He was not a mean kid. He just looked at the world with a very misdirected set of values. He measured his success by whom he associated with. And poor choice followed poor choice. No matter what was said or done, it didn't matter.

He left my parents' house and moved into an apartment. He wanted to be on his own. He died tragically of a medical condition at eighteen. They found him several days after his death.

I learned several lessons from his death. I had seen similar situations in the service and it held true through my working career. One must remember that the power problem employees exert on other employees is just as dynamic and forceful as any positive and directed efforts. In some cases, their negative influence can be even more powerful and destructive.

The sad part of the situation is that problem employees become a magnet for employees who are searching for leadership and meaning in their own lives. The problem develops when those people in search of acceptance and direction find it in a group of negative people. Knowledge of decision-making skills and core values are fundamentals to any sense of true identity.

I know that, to this day, my parents wonder if they did all they could. They and many others tried desperately to teach this young man some of life's basic tools. The hard part is when we realize we still do not want to give up trying, even after a person's death has occurred.

What I say next is not a new idea: no one is ever too young to have positive role models. Growing out of it is not something to take for granted. Today's workplace is in desperate need of mentors, role models, and grass-roots leadership.

You will hear how an employee admires, respects, or has positive words for certain leaders. I think that says something. I believe this requires that we again address the area of leadership. I believe leadership should be taught and mentored at all levels of the company. I hope no one believes that leadership should only be taught to those people who manage the organization.

Patience With Leaders

I did consulting work for a professional organization with a government contract. A large public sector organization facilitates the contract. The work requires regional travel, which means the standard measure of records and vouchers for reimbursement. I began to notice a change in the level of service from this organization. Their checks were taking longer and longer to process, vouchers were now taking over forty days for processing, and, in one instance, the paperwork was lost.

Being an avid student of Dr. Deming, I knew that something was not right with the system. Forty-plus days had passed and I had not received my funds. I had a staff member make a request for someone in the finance department to give me a call.

The person who returned my call made a number of references to his system being broken with several employees on vacation. I knew prior to my conversation that the person I was talking with had been on vacation. I was informed in a previous phone inquiry that the voucher was in his in-box but had not been processed.

During the current conversation, he informed me that my funds were sitting on his desk and he asked me what I wanted him to do about it. For a nanosecond, I wanted to take off my hat as a business consultant and take thirty seconds to be the nightclub entertainer that lurked within. Ethics took hold and became the guiding force.

I told him to mail it to me and expressed my concern with future transactions. I asked how we could keep this from happening again. What he stated next was quite interesting and would have made Dr. W. Edwards Deming launch into one of his famous dissertations.

The supervisor said, "I am not going to take responsibility for this."

Well, then who is? And here is where leadership comes in. I have no doubt that this supervisor knew his job. I again believe he did not understand his job. By that, I mean having a grasp of how his position was interdependent to others, especially the customer. If I had mentioned the term *interdependent components*, I probably wouldn't have gotten a response.

I also believe that this person did not have the slightest grasp of the concept of customer service. What is for certain is, I will remember him long after he remembers me.

Leadership needs to be taught and encouraged at all levels of the organization. Even employees who process checks should be taught to give outrageous customer service. Why wouldn't they? Leadership is more than interpersonal relationships. It is the physical movement of an object from point A to point B. It is Newton and Heisenberg at their best. It is also the deep understanding of when to be the message or the messenger. Wave/particle duality is the foundation of leading with action.

Leadership is critical; it is not enough. Great organizations are learning organizations. It is now time to explore our need to learn.

Questions

- Do I have a clear and defined leadership program in my organization?
- If I am a leader, am I providing an environment where employees have the opportunity to network with other professionals in their field of work?
- Do I have the ability to interact with other working professionals in my career field?
- Does my organization encourage interaction or do I have to do it on my own?
- Does my organization have a mentor program?
- Does management walk the talk?
- Am I taking positive steps in my life to address my personal issue?
- What positive change would I bring into my life through professional relationships?

Chapter Nine

Is My Career Providing an Educational Experience?

If you have to ask someone's permission to be creative, you are in the wrong job.

Life, of course, is a continuous educational process. Some of our educational experiences give us true enlightenment, while other events may cause nothing more than intellectual injury.

I am remaining cautiously optimistic about educational opportunities. I have been seeing some companies looking into the crystal ball of the bottom line, and willing to make the investment. One company offers its employees an undergraduate degree and master's program that is company paid. They will pay for the entire program if the participant's grades meet their criteria. If not, depending on the circumstances, they will pay partial tuition.

This is heading in the right direction. Can every company do this? No. Should something be offered? If you want to be competitive, yes. You have to keep in mind that being a learning organization means a broad commitment to the human spirit. Education should be viewed as an investment. The expectation of twenty-first-century employees is way different from twenty years ago. Employees want to do a good job but their motivators are different.

If you want to have a successful twenty-first-century business then you had better listen up. I believe employees are asking one of the most fundamental and much-needed questions: do people learn in this company and how is it done? What is the attitude of your company toward educated employees? Does the company foster employee education? Does the company mission include the education of all employees?

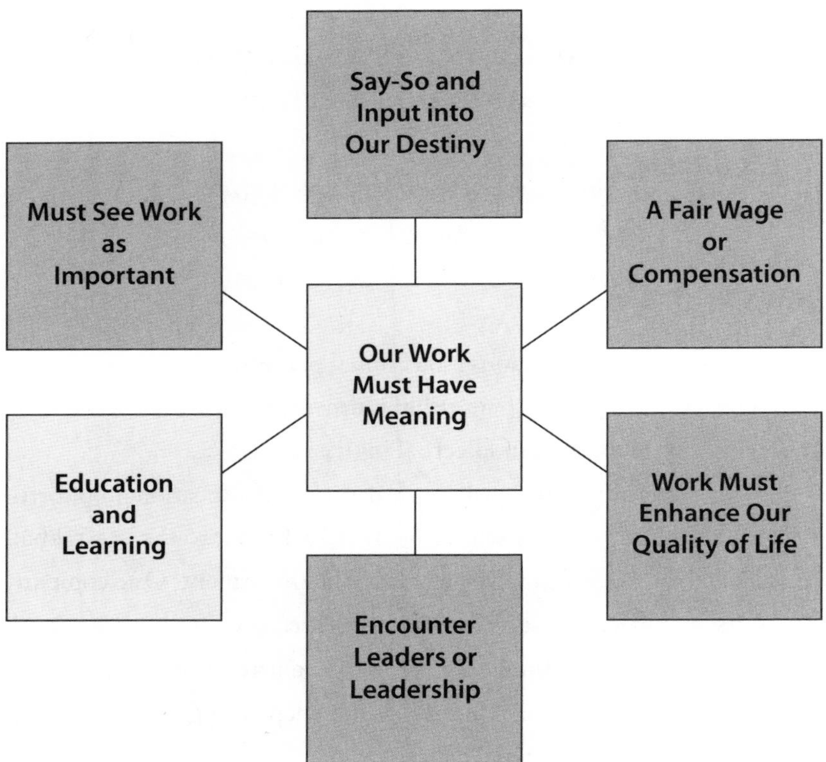

Figure 7. Seven Needs for Personal Productivity—Education and Learning

Learning Processes Are Built into a Company

A company's learning environment is much like ordering an accessory for a car. Is it going to be added on or is it built in? What about your company? Is education part of the natural order of things, or is employee education and training something that is squeezed in where it can and will be implemented? Is the learning environment the responsibility of a certain few, or is it a company-wide policy that is a core value?

I have a rule of thumb. If a company's strategic plan does not include a committed and built-in learning experience for all employees, then approach with caution. Your career will be short-lived in that operation. That may be what you are looking for, but I would have a personal plan for your educational experience. Remember, this is also a two-way street. We want to work in a learning environment, but you must also ask yourself a fundamental question: do I want to learn?

We are becoming a more informed society. That also means we are becoming a more demanding society—that has a higher price tag and is less forgiving. The rewards are there. When I use the term *informed* I have grave misgivings when that issue spreads to our culture. I refer to the vast amount of overwhelming information that bombards us. Information is like food—not all of it is good for you.

I believe information is not knowledge. With knowledge comes the responsibility of an associated theory. Knowledge changes as a theory is disproved. As I describe in another chapter, this is learning. My concerns grow by the day as I see society moving in the direction where we base our decisions on too much data and information. An informed society is not necessarily an educated society. Are we a society that understands the difference between signal and noise?

I believe a future case will be made where we find little educational value in this information. And when I say educational value, I apply that to the expansion and solidification of life skills. Nowhere is this more important than in the workplace.

Our work is part of our lifestyle, culture, habits, and people that involve our association. In *Each Human Spirit* I related that the human spirit must be exercised as much as the body. Our minds must have the opportunity to develop, exercise, stumble, question, discover, and we must have the opportunity to love what we do.

I also apply my point to one's own career. How many people are actually doing something they love to do? Haven't we all heard someone say, "Someday, when I have the time I am going to . . . "?

And they don't. That tells me they have been informed about some issues they may feel strongly about but they never implement a plan to do it. That tells me they are informed but are not educated. If they would take their information to the next stage, they would apply it and find out if their initial belief was correct and a new theory developed. That is why the evening news informs and does not educate.

The Human Spirit Has Scientific Applications

As I stated, I believe the relationship between some quantum principles and human behavior and learning is seamless. For example, in quantum mechanics we say that a particle may not have a particular position or velocity. This, of course, defies traditional science where everything must be measured and it is only understood when we can put it in some type of intellectual compartment, law, policy, procedure, or past experience. Here, too, the workplace guides itself on the principles that not only everything, but everyone, must be measured. This also means that some executives will lose sleep knowing job descriptions might not only be counterproductive but potentially impossible to measure. Employee potential does not have position or velocity. Is your organization hiring and educating for potential or for a position? In the twenty-first century, status quo means you enjoy tread marks through your workspace.

Job descriptions are designed to measure results. An educated workforce gives leaders a better picture of a range of possibilities. In my entire professional career, I have never seen a job description or training program mention the words *human spirit*. We will be traditionalists to the end. I believe some organizations will always defend the idea that some compartment, any compartment is necessary to rank, define, measure, or merit increase every employee. If you have to measure it, then it may already be too late.

Remember Heisenberg? If you measure everything EXACTLY, then each employee, project, assembly line, and project must come to complete standstill in order to be measured. Do you bring your organization to a standstill to measure what you have learned?

How many people did it take to measure? How was it measured? And if you are seriously into continuous quality, you have to ask, "Did it need measuring in the first place?" Are your employees being measured on data, information, and knowledge, or understanding and wisdom? How would you want to be measured for what you know?

HR has a tough job to do. I do believe they make it way too tough, but it is the way they've always done it. How do you measure the human spirit? Then again, how do you educate it? It is brought to the workplace every day, and yet it is stifled, ignored, demeaned, and denied by the very lack of education. That is like looking at the human spirit with a rear view mirror. We assume that satisfaction comes from building a product or an idea, but a far greater satisfaction can come from working and learning together, and improving the process and work environment. Tell me about a product or project you designed, built, or manufactured twenty years ago. What gave you the most satisfaction, the end result or the learning process that developed it?

Knowledge of the job to be performed is taken for granted, or it is a data entry on a spreadsheet or personnel file. Productivity and the human spirit are nurtured by learning. Education is the DNA of productivity.

The Work We Do Has Many Interpretations

If I choose to look at position descriptions, outcome-based processes, and then quantify my view of a company, I must ask, "What is the position in the organization, and velocity or potential of the employee?" Drop those questions at the next staff or HR meeting and see what happens. Pay particular attention to body language. I am talking about the ability of the employee to do the job and live up to his potential with surprising expectations.

An employee and customer will learn something faster than the company can adapt. What intrigues me is, in the quantum field, particles (like people) respond differently. Instead of the traditional concepts of predictable behavior, the potential of particles have a range of possibilities—they are adaptive.

I believe that true productivity and employee educational opportunities can only realize their potential when they are given the opportunity and a range of possibilities. This means the organizational chart must be less of a form and function operation; it must almost seem fuzzy to the outside observer. The employee's goal would be a realm of possibilities.

If the employee's goal is a realm of possibilities, she then has the opportunity to develop her mind, body, and spirit. In order to maximize employee and organizational potential, true leaders must educate their employees beyond their position descriptions. If you only educate for the position description then you have proven Heisenberg correct.

You decide to educate and test for a volume of knowledge at a certain position or level. Don't forget that, all the while you are testing the employee, the organization is growing, moving, learning, and adapting. In other words, a static assessment of the employee cannot measure the distance between where the employee is educationally and where the organization has gone.

I find it interesting that, in a true learning environment, the job description becomes almost secondary to the discovery of potential. Does your organization's performance appraisal have a section that measures "surprise, creativity and momentum?" The current measurement system looks good on paper. It is predictable, gives a bottom line everyone understands.

If an organization considers itself a true learning environment and offers training, different opportunities, and cutting-edge products, but it measures the employee in the traditional performance evaluation, we open ourselves to another paradox. We try to measure, through traditional evaluation tools, a quantity that is adaptive with a portfolio of possibilities. What we need for employees is to seek a truly productive system where an employee experiences a learning environment. Then his potential is not a single series of criteria, but a range of potential and the relative probability of productivity under a series of situations.

Too many organizations measure employee potential for a given position but that potential is validated only under the current structure. What is the potential of the organization itself? *Are we truly an adaptive and learning organization?*

Learning Is Food for the Soul

In late 2001, I had the opportunity to talk to an attendee at one of my seminars. After the introduction and pleasantries, we started to talk about work and careers. This person related to me all the aspects of her job, responsibilities, and potential.

After I inquired whether or not she liked the work she did, I began to see a slight change in her demeanor. I then asked, "Are you learning anything in your work?

This question obviously caught her off-guard. She then lowered her voice and said, "It doesn't thrill me. I enjoy my work but I am not thrilled."

In the course of our conversation, we were able to identify that she was working for an organization that was informational but it really wasn't what you would call an educational experience. She had a specific job and had to learn about that job. That was her focus. She was not given the opportunity to be adaptive.

I believe she would have thrived had she been given the opportunity to explore a range of possibilities in her company.

We must learn to learn in our organizations and seek those areas that provide the knowledge, skills, and abilities to better others and ourselves in our lives. Absence of a learning environment will produce not only a predictable behavior, but also an unstable one. I believe this is one of the most misunderstood principles: predictability does not guarantee stability.

One only has to look at the feeling of being bored. Attitudes change and, carried with our attitudes, is our productivity, thinking, relationships inside and outside of work, and our direction. We lose sight of the future. We live in the present but we dwell on the past. After all, past behavior now begins to drive our future results. Some companies actually hire people based on that principle.

Learning Is Not Just for Managers

Once again I am going to climb on the soapbox of personal experience. I want to relate one of the most counterproductive, costly, and totally preventable behaviors in the corporate world. I refer to the education of management and its impact—or lack of impact—on the organizational process.

For over twenty-three years I worked for a great organization. I am not singling out the company I worked for because I have heard employees from other companies relate similar stories. Here is my issue: many managers have educational opportunities that are not available to front-line employees. This includes completing bachelor's and master's degrees, and other types of professional leadership programs. I am not talking about one-day seminars.

I relate in *Each Human Spirit* a destructive and costly management behavior, MBFOM, Management by Flavor of the Month. This is the significant investment in education over an extended period of time. What concerns me is, when these people return or complete their experience, they submit a memo to their boss, thanking him for the opportunity and they probably talk about it to other managers at the next staff meeting. And the rub is: not one single professional paper, presentation, seminar, or workplace-related project is presented to the front-line employees. This also applies to the latest trends, knowledge, or new ideas. Also suffering is the training department, HR, and other areas that may benefit from the material as future references and resources.

In far too many instances, this educational expense does not benefit anyone except the person who attends it; he simply adds it to his resume or portfolio. What I find more disturbing is that many of these same people do not have the ability to relate it in the first place. If this is the case, who won or who lost?

One might hear the statement, "My education helped me do my job better." How do you measure *better*? The issue is, you can't measure it. And because it is difficult to measure, it also means that many of the systems designed by HR people also are not productive. They will produce numbers—data and information. This is measuring success by measuring the manager's position at that moment. That, again, is Heisenberg.

Education is a behavior change. If a person has been attending school and gets a degree, what has improved if his behavior is the same after he gets the degree? If you own a business and you let employees obtain a degree and you pay for it, then you have a right of expectation for their performance. Will their getting a degree really improve your system?

Managers Must Do More Than Manage

Some important thoughts about managers or leaders and learning environments:

- All managers who attend career development courses or complete a degree program should be required to deliver a professional paper or training program to the organization and employees. Bottom line: if you are going to be in a responsible leadership position then you must publish and teach your craft. Publishing can be limited to a trade or professional paper. I believe you have an ethical obligation to pass it on.
- All leaders should learn the Seven Needs for Personal

Productivity and how they relate to their organization, employees, and the customers they serve. This includes using the Seven Needs as a communication tool each day and, specifically, for performance appraisals.
- Be assigned to the training and development section for a working sabbatical in HR development and employee education. This would include loaning a manager to another section, organization, or community project.
- Mentor company employees for six months to two years after the completion of training. This would include mentoring outside students from college-level business and graduate schools.
- Complete an in-house project approved by senior management as part of the education curriculum. This would be in addition to the professional paper and teaching requirement.
- Complete a designated number of classroom hours as an instructor in a related topic acquired in the education program.

What Does a Manager Really Need to Do?

I think it is time to thoroughly examine the role of managers and what they are supposed to do. It is becoming quite clear that organizational behavior and a manager's role are facing new challenges. More companies are becoming adaptive and flexible in their operations. The term *global connection* is more than reality—it is going to be our way of life.

What does a manager really need to do? I believe, first and foremost, that a manager should be creating and sustaining a continuous learning environment. I believe many companies hesitate at the idea of changing their management philosophy because of the impact on job descriptions. This narrow focus has kept many managers and employees myopic in their careers and obligations. Twenty-first-century organizations may need to hire more educators as managers.

I believe managers should be disciples—teachers—for the organization. That means they must be open to new ideas, they must be lifelong learners and, most importantly, they must be teachable. If managers are not teachers, then they should not be exposed to the company work force.

The American workplace is not a college classroom—it is a classroom with consequences and higher stakes. It should be a seamless continuation of formal education. Employees should be challenged to understand the language spoken by each system and the company.

Education Never Ends

I attended a business luncheon and one of the topics was the recovering economy and jobs. One person sitting at my table worked in the high tech sector and was talking about job applicants and their qualifications. He related that he had lots of applicants with good credentials.

He then said something I found interesting. He said that a person with a college degree looking for high tech work needs to stay on top of his education. He stated that the average four-year degree was good for about a year in the private sector after employment. I asked him if he wanted to go on record, and he said he did not. He did say that a four-year degree in certain areas of high tech might not be enough because the industry is changing so fast that continuing education is a must. I believed he helped build my case for my next topic—fluid organizations. This is chaos at its best.

Fluid Organizations Can Work Well

I believe the term *fluid organizations* works well with an educated work force. Fluid organizations relate to any group of people who join forces to start a company, project, or segment of a project. The people meet, identify, learn, develop, produce, and market a product. This could include operating within the context of a larger parent company.

After the product or project is complete, they disband and assume other roles. This type of behavior crosses the line of traditional job descriptions. It is skill-based and also requires a high learning curve as well as a high level of risk.

But then, when do we learn the best? Is it not when we reach and have the opportunity for significant growth? Education by doing raises the level for all employees. It forces one to shed the bonds of traditional job descriptions. I do believe that true learning organizations are not for everyone, such as someone who chooses to be sedentary in his or her career.

I currently belong to a professional business group where many of the members work out of their homes, have national and international markets, and have participated in a fluid organization in the past year. They are redefining meetings and procedures, and seriously question the need for brick-and-mortar buildings in their operations. This concept is not for everyone and has special applications.

What message it does send is profound. New ways of doing business provide a concept of real-time education. The curve is steep and the amount of information may be overwhelming, but the rewards are huge. Job descriptions may only be as relevant as a specific role or task which may last as long as seventy-two hours.

Never Assume Employees Know What They Are Doing

We assume our employees know their jobs and understand their purpose in the organization. We are challenged when we must also be able to relate our purpose, tasks, and mission to others. This fundamental skill in communication is critical. If a leader, manager, or employee does not have the acquired knowledge, skills, and ability to relate and inform other employees in a professional environment, then why was he selected for his position in the first place?

It also begs the question, "What process got him there?" If he does not have that ability, then work needs to be done in the selection and hiring process.

I make my living as a consultant, and my suggestions and ideas take away from my career field and may cost me business! I prefer to see an organization use internal talents coupled with external resources for a balanced education program. Managers are a natural vehicle for the delivery and improvement of workplace education. Taken together, leadership, supervision, and management are more than a title or function. Leaders must be able to educate and create an environment to motivate employees for a greater understanding of their work and true organizational development. To me, this relationship is the cosmic "goo" of the workplace. A twenty-first-century work environment should lead to teach and teach to lead.

Questions

- Do I work for a teaching and learning organization?
- Am I using my professional education to "give back" to the company?
- Am I given the opportunity to continue my education?
- Is the same opportunity open to everyone?
- What significant addition have I added to my educational portfolio?
- Am I satisfied with my current career track?
- What positive change could I bring into my life to make a difference?

We need to know that what we contribute to the workplace
has merit and is important; that what we do
has value and that we are valued!
This is part of the DNA of the human spirit.

Chapter Ten

Do I See My Career and Work as Important?

What we say is our language.
What we believe in is our voice. How we live is the essence of both.

We all want to fit in. In our youth we wanted to be one of the kids in the group. It was important to know where we stood. Sometimes it was called the pecking order. Whatever the term, knowing where you belonged was important to any relationship. As we grew older, high school became the scenario for the term *in-group*. Little did we know that would evolve even more when we entered the workplace. This is part of the larger scenario called *organization*.

Life, like the universe, is encountering and surviving organizations. It can be a simple alliance of like ideas or a complex structure of cultures that applies to an international corporation with thousands of employees. It can also be that strange and fuzzy relationship between science and the human spirit. Either way, where we fit and belong in that organization is important to the individual. One element, however, is essential. What we do, contribute, or manifest within the organization must carry with it a sense of merit.

We need to know that our contributions are important to a particular project and the organization. We also need to know how they fit into the grander scheme of things. The little important sums are essential to the success of the cosmic whole. We need to apply these principles to a working career.

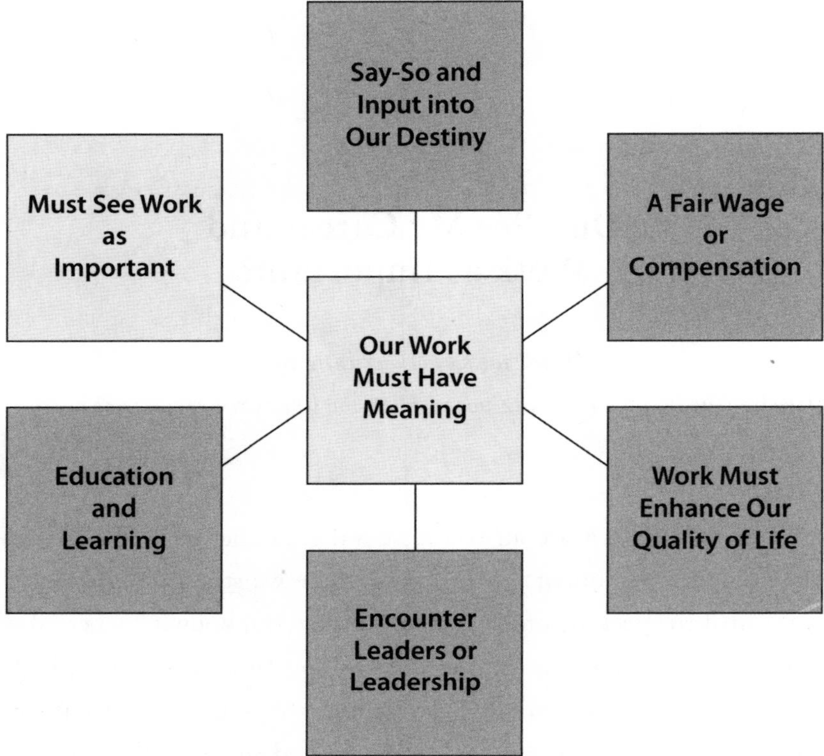

Figure 8. Seven Needs for Personal Productivity—Work Must Be Important

Being Valued Is Part of the Human Spirit

I would like to share an important story that relates to this issue. I believe it is not only a profound example of the need to feel important, but it shows how the organization and management behavior can derail the process.

This is about a group of community volunteers who were asked to look at a particular problem. They were given direction with their project and their process was checked along the way. What resulted was an entity that changed not only the rules at the eleventh hour, but the scope of the project as well.

This group took pride in their commitment to citizen input. They expressed their delight by forming many groups to help officials deal with public issues. This one group had a very responsible role—to advise a public body on policy issues that related to a large public facility.

The volunteer advisory group was told to come up with a new policy for the lease. The group asked three knowledgeable citizen volunteers who were familiar with this facility to explore designs and formulate a lease procedure. What happened over the next year is the result of the best of intentions, dedication, volunteer spirit, and sense of purpose all being exposed to a nightmare of bureaucracy and shifting priorities.

As the final draft was presented, the managers questioned the purpose of their findings and then added further criteria that rendered the document meaningless. It was a classic example of eleventh-hour "bright ideas." The process basically started over again. The conclusion of the process showed that the administrators used inaccurate assumptions and had based their decision on flawed data. In the end, a product was delivered. Do these people trust the system? Probably not. Will they respond if asked to volunteer again? I doubt it. Did they feel they and their work was important? It probably was not.

I find this interesting and of concern. We may find we truly do love our jobs. If it is a positive experience then it will have a benefit. If, however, you are emotionally attached to a job out of fear or intimidation, one enters a whole new school of thought. I would have loved to ask Werner Heisenberg how he would have measured that one. No performance evaluation system I am aware of could capture the essence of that situation. This would be a situation where an employee is in total chaos and assumes message/messenger for survival, not creativity, in the work.

Employees Need to Know They Are Important

If you are in management, how many times a week do you talk with your employees and tell them you value their work? If I came into your company today and asked your managers, "On a blank piece of paper, please write for me your company's Attitude Statement and core values," how many could do it? Another example might be, "Please write on a piece of paper the purpose of the project you are on and its relationship to the goals of the organization."

What if I also asked, "When was the last time you talked to your employees about what the Attitude Statement is and the importance of those core values? Did you do it in an environment where the signal was clear or did you do it when the 'noise' of the company—like voice mail or cell phones—interrupted?"

If these two questions are important to your company, are you teaching them? Employees see their work as important because they filter what they do through their value systems. They are looking for the company or project to connect through their validation process. If they are Generation X, then they will see a greater connection with projects and specific areas of their interest. In either example, are you letting them know they are critical to the success of their project and the organization?

Do you, as a leader/manager, make it a point to talk to employees before they go on vacation? Do you value that time and encourage them to disconnect? When was the last time you told an employee, "You are doing great work; enjoy your vacation." Again, we are looking at particle duality. Are you as a leader saying one thing and then doing something else? Is being the message of a leader in harmony with being the messenger of supporting behavior?

It is easy to put out a company E-mail, letter, or annual report touting how the company is people-oriented and the importance of the employees. You must remember, there is nothing more powerful in organizational behavior than the power of the spoken word between a manager and an employee. Are your employees making the connection?

Yes, you tell employees that they are key to company success, but how do you tell them? How do you inform employees that their individual work is critical to company success? That their work is relative to all the other company jobs? Do you use the word *value*? Do you verbally make the connection with them that their work must be put into perspective, and that family and other life issues also are important? Do you leave them in doubt? If you do, why are you doing that? You, the leader, are now the message and the messenger. You are not accomplishing a leadership role if you do not understand the duality of the position.

Are your company's leaders given training on employee communication, or is that something you assumed was included in their personal portfolios? This sense of importance crosses the bridge into our personal lives. These are not mind, body, or just HR issues. These are front-line employees giving their hearts and souls to their work. As a manager, it is critical to understand this dynamic. The power here is immense and many employees are participating in a costly game.

The Puzzle Lady

When I was a child, my mother would set up a card table in corner of the living room and do jigsaw puzzles. If I looked around the house and didn't find her, I knew the card table was a sure bet.

I was always amazed at the size of the puzzles. One thousand pieces was the norm. She would sit with the utmost patience and hold one piece in her hand and just look. Eventually she found the match. This was one way she would relax.

As I look back on her strategy, I wonder if she was practicing lessons for teaching her children. Pick up each one, and search the world for where he will fit. Where will he connect with other people to fit into the grander scheme of things?

I think mothers are like that. I remember a comment she made one day. She had been looking at one piece for the longest time and her eyes just moved over the puzzle. Sometimes I thought her eyes weren't even moving. But I learned later in life that moms saw everything. I asked her why she didn't just put the piece down and work on another one. She said in that quiet and caring voice only a mother can have, "Each piece is important."

My mom could have been a CEO or a criminal investigator. The title of Mom made her both. She has the heart and soul of one who has the patience to look at all the pieces and will not rest until they all fit together. I sometimes wonder how she would have done as a scientist in a laboratory. She loves to explore and look at pieces of a puzzle from different points of view.

She knew that the picture could only be appreciated when each piece was connected. It took patience, time, and the discipline to know when to get up from the table, leave the problem alone, and work on it later. She did that with her children. She never gave up. My mom is now in her nineties and still works crossword puzzles. She says, "Those help me practice my spelling."

Maybe we should learn to get up from the table and let a fresh perspective develop. I found that what I needed to do in my life often seemed like a puzzle or it was like gazing into the night sky. Where do I fit in? What should I really be doing? My mom held the piece of the puzzle—me—in her hands for many years. My parents then handed that responsibility over to me. I was given both control and the responsibility to figure out where I fit in the puzzle.

What started to change my thinking was looking at the puzzle of life in a different way. I used to look at myself as one of the pieces in a large box with a description similar to the other nine hundred and ninety-nine pieces. One star in the universe may be minute but it does fit into the system and the grander scheme of things.

What I have learned over time is what I saw my mom do when I was a child. Be patient with each piece and look at the universal puzzle of life as a whole. To her, each piece was unique and special and contributed to a much larger system. And when she found the home for each piece, it made the connection with the others around it. Each piece was held gently with lots of patience. With time the answer came. It usually fit in an area she had not considered.

I am often amazed at the sense of accomplishment one can feel just by getting one of life's pieces to fit. And, with one small success, a little more color is added to the world. Galileo would have liked my mom.

Moms Are Great Teachers

I now see my mother's actions in a completely different light. Her puzzles helped her organize and focus. Again we have the paradox. Random, scattered processes and systems gave her great joy, though they were not random and scattered for long. She rearranged them one piece at a time and saw how they fit. Chaos gave her skills in adaptive behavior and looked at her project as a range of possibilities.

To this day, I can safely say that my mother has never heard of quantum mechanics, Albert Einstein, Werner Heisenberg, Max Planck, wave/particle duality, or chaos theory. But her actions gave meaning and, most of all, importance to her life and to mine. Her knowing when to retreat to her puzzle project was part of her calling. Whether she realized it or not, she was going to school. And the universe was her classroom.

I don't know if she realized that she displayed one of the most fundamental principles of true leadership and management. It is our goal to show how each piece is unique but fits into the organizational whole in a significant way, lending its design to the total picture.

Why does someone find solace and relaxation in total chaos and random concepts? Again, the paradox: the challenge is in what appears almost insurmountable to some. It is safe to say that looking at one thousand fragmented pieces would cause one's heartbeat and blood pressure to rise. I believe my mom's actually slowed down. It is as Viktor Frankl relates—how we understand what life is asking us by looking through the window of adversity. She needed to know how each piece fit. And she wouldn't give up until she gave each one a home. She needed to know that it was important.

I think management-training seminars should put away their laptop computers, iPads, and cell phones, and work more jigsaw puzzles. It is unfortunate that today we mostly find jigsaw puzzles in group homes, hospital waiting rooms, and garage sales. I think they should be part of every boardroom in the working community. More businesses should have them in the lobby for people waiting for appointments.

Frankly, I believe any person who sits at the conference table in any corporation and doesn't understand the true dynamics of a picture puzzle shouldn't be sitting there. To me, jigsaw puzzles are the ultimate organizational chart. Each piece is a part of an employee, random in design, and clearly defined but not productive unless it is shown how it is interactively connected to the pieces around it. Everything is relative.

Dr. W. Edwards Deming stressed the importance of understanding that organizational systems are interdependent components. Each piece is an individual employee and, therefore, important. Employees' talents cross the boundary lines of the piece. In other words, an employee's name can be linked to several pieces—adaptive—and each piece has a range of possibilities and potentials. Then the employee begins to know he is important.

Each area develops its unique image and perspective. Several areas do not make a picture—areas linked together begin to make the whole. Each piece is different, important, random, and significant. I would like to see the participants along the way observe how putting that puzzle together relates to the human spirit in the workplace. Why is each piece important? How do they let employees know why they are there? How do they fit into this random concept called the workplace? Our goal now becomes one of connectedness to all that is around us.

Recognize Employee Potential

Leaders and managers must understand that, to design the successful organization, they must have a passion for employee potential before they figure out what the organization will look like. This may be a complete reversal of current thinking. How can the organization understand how it is going to do something before it understands why? This is letting the people shape the ideas first and then letting the ideas shape the people.

Many companies start out this way but, as they evolve, the opposite takes place. It becomes more important to preserve the structure than the idea it was meant to serve. That is like saying you understand the universe before you look through the telescope.

Cutting costs becomes letting people go. While this may be part of a redesign, it should be the last resort. Individual people make the organization. The organization does not make the individual. The organization can influence individuals. Trees, plants, animals, and clouds contribute to the whole. The whole then becomes the design necessary. The design must also adapt.

Let's use the example of a garden space. We plant and visualize what it will look like. The problem is that we tend to choose the plants with the space already selected. We limit the plant size and eventual growth to a predetermined design. We stifle our sense of surprise.

What would happen if we chose the flowers first, then looked where we could use them? We would then let them become a part of the yard and environment, and would not stifle their potential by what we had already done. They would no longer be destined for a predetermined area, but would have the opportunity to adapt. Why can't corporate training include designing and planting gardens, and landscape design?

The possibilities of new and even stranger partnerships become possible. I am becoming more intrigued and comfortable with the term *strange partnerships*. It says "yes" to the world of new possibilities and their potentials. Life then ceases to be chosen by what we see in the rear view mirror.

What I am asking you to do is to know the people before you know the design. Traditionally we design and then fit in the "right" people. That is like hiring a group of carpenters to work on a finished house.

What we now have is great potential (people) in a design that may not work. I may be asking the ridiculous. What I am saying is, have an idea in mind and a goal to accomplish. Now hire the people but let the design of the organization take care of itself.

Before you screw someone into a tightly skewed job description or cubicle, the employee may show other potentials previously not known to you or others. Talent ALWAYS crosses the lines of job descriptions, just as the picture on a piece of a puzzle cannot become whole unless connected to another design. That is why one of my personal virtues in life is that I never ask anyone's permission to be creative.

By the way, my mom had a working career outside the home. As a cook-supervisor for a larger high school, she directed the cooking for hundreds of students each day. She did that for twenty years. Each morning she would get up and be at work before six o'clock. She opened the giant refrigerator/walk-in freezer at the high school and began the tedious process of fitting all the products and recipes together to create the daily menu. She never stopped putting together puzzles.

Questions

- How does my organization let employees know they are important? Is it in the form of a statement or policy, or is management verbally communicating it?
- Is my work so important that I must take a cell phone and pager with me to stay in touch?
- Do I know how my work relates to the big picture of the company?
- What other ways do I stay in touch with work when I am not there?
- What price might I be paying?

- When was the last time someone in the organization told me that my work was important and they valued my services?
- Is this job my life commitment or would I like to do something else?
- What positive change could I bring into my life to make a difference?

Review Of The Seven Needs For Personal Productivity

1. Does my work and career provide a sense of meaning in my life?
2. Do I have say-so and input into my destiny?
3. Am I adequately compensated for my work? What is it costing me?
4. Does my work enhance my quality of life?
5. Do I work for and does our company have true leaders?
6. Do I work for a learning organization?
7. Does what I do relate to the organization and is important? Am I told how it relates?

If five of the Seven Needs have not been present in your career for at least the last year, then you may wish to dust off your resume!

Our attitude is driven by our governing values.
Attitude is a choice.
Choosing each day to be a benefactor
or a butthead is up to us.

Chapter Eleven

Attitude, Leadership, and Listening

Attitude without ethics is arrogance.

Attitude is a way of thinking and behaving. Leadership, whether it is personal or professional, is the result of taking appropriate risks in order to overcome obstacles and to have faith in the abilities of your people. Having faith is another way of saying one has a conviction that some of what one sees as instrumental may not yet be known—it is a future outcome.

Leadership also is the result of *attitude*—the first step in critical communications. I teach people how to inventory their attitude. To do this, you must assess who you are, what real issue is coming to bear, and why you are taking a certain position. I have come to believe that the single most important quality we can have is our attitude. Viktor Frankl said it was critical to finding meaning in our lives.

I could write a book about hostile work environments and what they do to our attitudes and related issues. We get into trouble when we let others impact and control our attitude. In doing so, we default our behavior to others. Our external situation may be one of despair and hopelessness, and shifting blame and behavior will likely send us into a downward spiral. We cannot control others—we can only impact their behavior, just as they can impact our behavior. It is only internally where we have control.

I often hear people say, "My organization has a morale problem."

Another way of saying it is, "Our attitude stinks." As an attempt to change this, many organizations hang up snappy slogans and increase employee incentives. These are short-term attempts at a fix. What they must realize is that employee morale is a symptom of a much larger problem.

I am dismayed when I see youth of today who seem to have given up hope as to not only who they are, but why they are. They appear to be in a struggle for some sense of identity. It is as if they are not being taught the skills to overcome obstacles.

I have always liked this quote from George Bernard Shaw. "People are always blaming their circumstances on what they are. I don't believe in circumstances, and the people who get on in this world are the people who get up and look for the circumstances they want. And if they can't find them, they make them."[1]

A word of caution: if you bring who you are to the table, you have an ethical responsibility to conduct yourself accordingly. If you do not want to bring who you are to the table, then I do not believe you want to communicate, and other issues may be at play that could cover a chapter in itself. You may also find yourself in a conflict with the purpose of the group. This too, requires action. If this is true in either case, then you have an ethical responsibility to give up your seat.

Organizational Structure—The Mandelbrot Set

I am inspired by the work of Polish-born French mathematician, Benoit Mandelbrot. I believe it is the foundation for one's attitude, leadership skills, and the ability to listen.

Mandelbrot coined the term *fractal* to describe complex geometric shapes that, when magnified, continue to resemble the shape's large structure. Stay with me, this has *everything* to do with attitude, leadership, and listening. The exciting thing about this is that, when you look at these smaller patterns you find that the larger structure has the same pattern as the smallest scale of the same formula. This behavior of repeating the larger shape down to the smallest scale is called *self-similarity.*

The marvelous, mystical aspect of this discovery is in the field of nature and, more importantly, the workplace and the human spirit. We are literally surrounded by the principles of fractals! We can find them in leaves, computer screen savers, clouds, and seashells. We find them in ferns and even the geometry of the seashore. Anywhere the same pattern is found—both in the large and small structures of an object—a fractal has occurred. In some respects, it is simply a new perspective on realities we have viewed previously, but to me, it adds a sense of imperative. Once the pattern was established at the smallest level, the larger structure was predetermined, even if it didn't yet exist. And the same is true of investigations going from large to small.

How does this relate to attitude and leadership? Traditionally, we view formal organizations as hierarchies where leadership and power emanate from the top down. If we apply the fractal phenomenon to our Judeo-Christian value system, then we should see the patterns repeated as we go into the smaller structures. After all, Genesis teaches us that God made us "in His own image," and yet, there is the concept of the omnipresent God and "God in us." Newtonian physics looks at the larger part of our scientific laws and quantum theory looks at subatomic particles. Again, we have the top-down process.

I see evidence of fractals in the business world every day in attitude, leadership, and listening, which are replicated in organizations large and small. Is the attitude that is replicated in your business or organization positive or negative? Employees mirror both behavior and the relative attitude that drives it. Mandelbrot would be thrilled. Do your good leaders teach others their craft? Is it part of your company policy that leaders MUST teach others?

We must keep one thing in mind. Fractals are replication, not ethical replications. Fractals, like, mathematical formulas have no conscience; they do not know right from wrong. Therefore, a bad idea at the top of the organizational food chain will be replicated perpetually until someone—or the system itself—changes the equation or formula. If you feed bad data and information into a formula, the formula will replicate a flawed process.

A strong leader replicates positive abilities by allowing and encouraging those qualities in the employees who are below them in the organization. Likewise, when I see negativity and poor service at the front line, I can draw a lot of conclusions about the quality of the person at the top.

Self-Similarity in Organizations

I experienced self-similarity firsthand a number of years ago when I taught Franklin Covey TimeQuest for more than nine years for the State of Oregon. During that time, I had the opportunity to attend a conference in Salt Lake City. It was not so much the conference that was memorable, but the company employee I met who drove me to the conference.

In my usual fashion, I engaged the young man in conversation. "Do you like your job?" I asked him.

"Yes, I do. We help people gain control of their lives."

I was immediately taken by the sincerity in his voice. He worked in shipping and receiving in the stockroom, and yet he clearly understood the mission of the organization and how he fit into the process. To me, this meant that the organization was run in such a way that not only ensured that this young man's manager understood the corporate mission, but that the front-line employee who moved boxes around all day had integrated it into his heart and soul. This is an excellent example of the fractal principle at work from the top down. To me, this mirrored the attitude of the company.

Due to the nature of fractals though, we can also expect to learn something from looking for self-similarity from the bottom up. I believe that the building blocks for the success of an organization are in the integrity and commitment of the people who perform the most elemental functions. Here again is the quantized application of attitude.

The productivity and pride evidenced at the most basic levels of an organization can be replicated from the bottom up to the highest level, building success, unless some destructive force (e.g., misguided middle or upper management) gets in the way.

You must understand that part of the formula is the system within which the employees work. Employee improvement alone is not enough to change the system. Management has control of the final equation and sets all the parameters. Individual employee productivity can stand alone as an elegant design. If the management systems do not provide or accept the opportunity for a change in the formula, then no amount of employee effort will work. The formula or equation will not balance.

The attitude and actions of dedicated, loyal people are like a wave. That is why I believe the Seven Needs for Personal Productivity give that energy equation a "conscience." The Seven Needs are grounded in value-based decision making. They can make a huge difference to those around them and, therefore, they create a surprisingly widespread ripple effect of positive results. If you have negative energies or attitudes emanating from the top, however, there are going to be some powerful cross currents, and waves will be rolled under and swept out to sea. Either way it is a process of replication.

People won't always respond in the same way to a rule or regulation, quota, or incentive, no matter how consistently it is applied. That is why attitude is so important. When attitude partners with leadership and listening, we have a garden for Mandelbrot to grow.

If we haven't figured out a way to deal with this quantum reality in the workplace, we do what humans tend to do in confusing situations—we apply the old solutions more vigorously.

I like the idea of looking at the unexpected aspects of our work environment. We must personally look at the smallest of the parts in the workplace, i.e., each individual employee taking responsibility to assess what he does. Again, we are asked to be stewards of our natural resources.

I would like you to consider a new leadership term, an *organizational environmentalist,* which complements a quantum career. To me, this is twenty-first-century attitude, leadership, and listening. Employees have to determine and look at what they can control and choose to influence and adapt. This is looking at the wave/particle duality of their work and asking these questions. It is also a fundamental goal to encourage and be stewards of the renewable resources of the human spirit.

A Leader with Attitude

Positive leadership is like a string of DNA in the workplace. Many of the individual components—the people—have specific duties that relate to the entire string. Like DNA, no two workplaces are the same. Each workplace has its own scientific and spiritual fingerprint. It is these markers that give each workplace its respective design and outcome. We have the potential to see the day when the workplace can share with science and spirituality the term *elegant design*.

I had the opportunity to talk with Mike DeRoshier, a senior executive with a large Oregon title company. I was referred to Mike because I was told he had a great attitude about his work and his people. Mention the word *attitude* to me and I become intrigued. I was looking for an example of Mandelbrot and replication and I found it.

We played telephone tag for a few weeks but finally had mutual time. Mike is a very busy man. I like interviews because I get to see people in their roles and assess how comfortable they are. Talking with a manager on his home court can be quite revealing. As our interview progressed, I began to see a deep commitment. He was good at what he did and he had his opinions.

My first question to Mike was, "What are the greatest problems you believe leaders need to understand?"

His reply was immediate. "First, it is critical that all staff understand that, number one, delivering products and services is not so much about policy or papers, but it is about the people behind the transaction—the buyers, sellers, realtors, and lenders. Second, the manager's role is to create an environment where staff can thrive."

I started to like this. Everyone says that people are the connection, which is true. What I was hearing was the connection, both internal and external—meaning that anyone who put his hands on the work or was involved—is part of the success. Mike was saying what I advocate: that it is important to have the policies in place, but they should not hinder or limit the creativity of the people, and that the organization and managers must create the environment for creativity and change. That means management responsibility.

I asked Mike what advice he gives to managers.

His reply was, "You can do it (regardless of what it is). I have confidence that you will make the right choices at the right times for the right reasons. You need to have confidence in yourself and act." What I was hearing was a leader with attitude who verbally communicates with managers on his belief in their ability. This was Mandelbrot's process.

Our conversation continued and I was curious as to what he thought was the greatest lesson that was taught to his company.

He grew pensive for a moment, and then replied, "At the end of the day, one's reputation is all you really have. Therefore, don't compromise, don't cut corners, and don't cave in to demands that will diminish or tarnish that reputation."

This was an interesting message. I believe if we were to apply the concept of the message/messenger, he was stating that when you walk in the room, all you have is your reputation. That is being the messenger.

What was interesting was the order of his strategy. We must be the message to our customers and employees. That is the actual delivery of our attitude and product, the doing part of our work. When we evaluate at the end of the day, we traditionally look at our product and what we have done. Mike said something different. Product/message was important but our reputation/messenger was critical. Our actions are the particles and our reputation is the wave.

My next question was one I ask all the organizations I work with, "What are three gifts your organization possesses?"

Mike did not hesitate to answer. "We have a commitment to excel and be successful and not be willing to settle for anything else. We have a commitment to provide a superior environment for our employees so this is the best place to work. Commitment to our communities—involvement, generosity, and support."

I then asked one of my all-time favorite questions, "What has been your greatest mistake?"

Mike gave simple but informative advice. "Go after the market. Companies deal so much with what is coming in that they do not position themselves for what is to come."

I liked his answer. It is so easy to get caught up in what is here and now and to not pay attention to trends and future possibilities. The true leader will see the necessity to educate and inform the work force of where they are going and how they are going to get there. The Great One, Wayne Gretzky, on advice from his father said, "I skate to where I think the puck is going to be and not where the puck has been."[2]

I attended a seminar where the facilitator remarked that we change our lives when we change our attitudes and our perceptions. I, too, believe the two most important assets we have, that get us in trouble the most, are our attitudes and perception of the world. When things really get tough, those two qualities can make or break us. The Book of Wisdom 6:12 says, "Or as when an arrow has been shot at a mark, the parted air straightway flows together again so that none discerns the way it went through."[3]

An important example of attitude is seeing loved ones deal with terminal illness. We see the external loss of form, function, and quality of life. They no longer are able to care for themselves and will soon be gone. But they still live each day with attitude. They have accepted their lives and issues but refuse to let the illness and external issues control the way they look at life. That is attitude.

We again see the paradox where some people handle their own terminal illnesses better than some people handle their jobs and the workplace. This shift in situational identity is both complex and fascinating. It will remain a challenging and interesting area. I remain fascinated by people who want to have a positive attitude and look at life with a sense of purpose.

When the topic turns to the workplace, it is as if you just moved a switch from on to off. Sometimes the change in attitude is profound. We try adjusting our attitude to compensate for someone else's behavior, whether it is good or bad. An attitude of denial is part of the dying process. We may be mourning the loss of a work environment we may have had or wanted to have.

Again, the adaptive nature of a particle and wave come to pass. The actions and our attitude are like the arrow and the parted air. When they are gone, we do not know they were there. How sad to have positive attitudes, good leaders, and missed opportunities.

I believe this also references our lives on earth and our actions. What did we do with our lives? Were they well spent? Did we live in a way that showed and helped others, or did our pride enable us to default to some other motive or action?

The Elements of Leadership

My conversation with Mike progressed to the topic of leadership. Mike wasted no time in saying, "Elements of leadership should be taught. We must help others to grasp the principles and give them the experience of leading. I'm willing to try things. Why one person is, and not another, is an interesting dynamic.

"Traditional models are gone. We have generational change with new models and new competition. Older people are good at what they do. The generations coming up do not have skills, but possible talent."

I was having a lot of fun with this so I asked him, "What do you see in the corporate crystal ball?"

Mike replied, "Different technology will bring trading partners. Employees must have confidence in their abilities. Do not fear what is coming. This is the time to become excited about the future."

I had to explore the area of our existing and future work force. "What void do you see in the work force?"

His answer, which was direct and to the point, did not surprise me. "I see a lack of commitment by employees to sacrifice a bit. They are not willing to give something up now versus the future."

New employees do not see the organization as the role model and a sense of commitment. They see themselves identifying with projects and ideas and focusing their loyalty in a closer perspective. This attitude may cause them some anxiety.

We were basically finished with our interview but I asked if he would like to add anything else. I noticed he had a pensive look. He was focused at the top of his desk for a moment, then looked up at me and said, "I love to garden. We have to create the greenhouse for people to thrive in." This was such an insightful statement. Are we as leaders creating a greenhouse where our employees can grow and prosper?

Remember that leadership is the result of attitude. Good leadership in the hands of a person with a positive attitude replicates. Bad leadership in the hands of a person with a negative attitude also replicates.

I like to describe attitude and leadership as the way a leader's mind works with the world. The first step, however, requires attitude to make the next significant step. I believe it is a physical condition, and doing something with that condition. It is more than the way someone thinks. It is the condition of a series of beliefs, behaviors, actions, attitudes, and processes. It is also accepting the outcome—whatever it is—and making any needed changes.

Leadership is not just the will, it is the dynamic response to a set of conditions that asks questions of us and then implements a process. And we are obligated to respond. How we respond, our beliefs, values, and thinking create the action. That is why leadership is a calling to a certain set of conditions. I believe those conditions are both spiritual and scientific. It is a response and responsibility to a way of life.

If you have a bad attitude then leadership is not for you. History has taken care of bad leaders in the past and the future will hold the same. The workplace already has enough buttheads in leadership positions. Attitude is an internal condition and we have control of it. Our attitude is ours alone. We wear it like a garment and it drives who we are. If we are to lead people and take risks that will have an impact on them, then a positive attitude is mandatory. If it is not, then look for another career.

Implementing the Seven Needs

I want to share what I believe are the relationships between more unlikely partners. My goal is to give a deeper understanding of those partners and their relationship with the Seven Needs for Personal Productivity. I believe every journey requires certain conditions or tools to experience the event to its fullest. The Seven Needs are key to the journey. Remember, the Seven Needs are: meaning in our lives, say-so and input into our destiny, being paid a fair wage quality of life, leadership, education, and importance of work.

To implement the Seven Needs in one's life or business takes attitude, leadership, and responsibility. Responsibility means taking risks. Taking risks means listening. What greater risk can you take than to sit in the presence of another human being and just *listen* to him? We must be leaders if we choose to take responsibility and control of our lives. That does not mean you have to be a CEO of a corporation or in a management position.

This direction is as much an internal journey as the external manifestation. I believe that any sense of leadership or personal development does not come by accident. Granted, we may find ourselves in what one may call a chaotic life, but internal and personal leadership will understand the harmony of events that make us who we are. And the goal is the understanding and application of the Seven Needs for significant personal and career leadership and development.

Too many people believe that if they are not a leader or in management, then it will not do them any good to study leadership. Lesson one: leadership is not what someone else says you are. The opposite is true. I cannot count the number of people who are in leadership positions and should not be there, and the many who should be and are not.

First of all, four statements need to be made.

1. Leadership is the result of attitude. You must be open to unlikely partnerships, chaos, and suffering. Your attitude toward those situations is important.
2. Sources and books on leadership are numerous and are not always found in the business and management section of your favorite bookstore. Look around you. Some of life's best examples are meant for experience and never make it to the bookshelf. Also, look for books on science, nature, and spirituality. Understand their role in leadership—how they complement each other and are not adversaries.
3. Be prepared to be surprised from unlikely sources.
4. Leadership is not a job description and doesn't have a budget.

I look with definitive caution when I hear of a morale problem. You do not have a morale problem; you have a management problem that is showing itself as low morale. Morale problems are symptoms of larger issues in your organization. Employee behavior is data and information on the Decision-Making Model. It is external.

Let's take it to the next step: what knowledge does that data and information support? Remember, data, information, and knowledge are an external manifestation, or behaviors.

Leadership must intervene during the next two steps, understanding and wisdom. What are you doing so that your leaders can further understand the issue? Are you then encouraging them to make wise decisions and to stand by those decisions? Remember, management controls the system. They are responsible for the environment for employee productivity.

If we ever look at ourselves in any type of leadership role, then we must address pride. I say this because, under a time of stress, we confuse pride with attitude. I have yet to find anyone who has not, at one time or another, let pride get the best of them.

In writing this book I, again, found many similarities among our actions, scriptural teaching, and scientific information. Pride is a good example. Pride can be good. I am proud of my relationship with my wife. That is very good. If I refuse to communicate with her and let my pride get in the way, that is bad. The Book of Wisdom 6:8–10 has much to say in reference to pride:

> *What did our pride avail us? What have wealth and its boastfulness afforded us? All of them passed like a shadow and like a fleeting rumor; like a ship traversing the heaving water, of which, when it has passed, no trace can be found, no path of its keel in the waves.*[4]

I believe this is an excellent example where the use of a ship (particle/message) glides through the water and the water is the carrier of the ship (wave/messenger.) Again, both the ship and the water can be adaptive. They can be a message by their presence or a messenger with their ability to carry and transport relative cargo. This principle fell on deaf ears on the bridge of the Titanic.

The Book of Wisdom 6:11 continues, *"Or like a bird flying through the air; no evidence of its course is to be found—But the fluid air(wave), lashed by the beat of the pinions, and cleft by the rushing force of speeding wings, is traversed; And afterward no mark of passage can be found of it."*[5]

The passage of the bird leaves us with the memory of the moment. Here we have the bird, (particle/message) leaving us and now it has turned into the memory (wave/messenger) of that beautiful moment. A particle now acts like a wave and the wave of flight acts like a particle with the memory of the bird. The duality of their meaning is the goal.

What Listening Can Accomplish

When was the last time you listened to another human being with no cell phones, computers, blackberries, iPods or MP3s? Is it part of your daily routine?

Here is a true story that shows in a timeless way how ordinary people can say and do extraordinary things. In this case it started with an attitude that shows how faith in beliefs and ideas can truly change the world. The critical element, however, was how they listened to what the data, information, and knowledge of the time told them, and how they used it in a different and creative way.

Wilbur and Orville Wright were not aeronautical engineers. The words *aeronautical engineers* had not even been created when they built their first airplane. No one had told them about the Bernoulli Effect or the vertical and horizontal component of lift. The last thing on their minds was *vx* or *vy*, which represent best angle or rate of climb for an airplane.

While the Wright Brothers built bicycles, airplanes were their passion. The only thing they understood was their love of flight. They had attitude. They also took responsibility for their talents and did something with them. They didn't have a corporate headquarters and an HR department. They listened to what the world was asking of them.

I can say with a degree of certainty that an employee-of-the-month parking place did not exist in the sand dunes of Kitty Hawk, North Carolina. The Wright Brothers' belief window dealt with bicycles. Their dreams were somewhere else. It was their dreams that made them leaders.

When the Wrights were as young as eight years old, the passion for flight was taking hold. It was strongly mentored by their mother. They designed crude helicopters and other things. Their dream did not exist at any airport. They had no aviation museums or college courses in aeronautical engineering or, for that matter, other airplanes. If they wanted to fly, then years of waiting and other sources of income had to be obtained.

When their bicycle business was established and they knew they wanted to build an airplane in earnest, they encountered many technical problems. They were, however, quick to discover one mechanical problem in particular that had to be overcome. It had to do with one of the most fundamental principles of lighter-than-air travel. This was beyond passion. This had to do with staying alive.

How do you turn an airplane? This was something that was basic to their success. They wanted their machine to have the ability to change directions. Versatility was the answer in creating a flying machine. Again, something so basic did not have an answer. And that answer would come from the unconventional.

The Wright Brothers did not consult the great twentieth-century industrialists for the answer. They simply kept looking up, and listened with their hearts and souls. They went to the most logical source for this type of knowledge—they studied birds. They sat by a local river and quickly observed that, when a bird wants to turn, it warps its wings. Not only does it warp its wings, it warps them in opposite directions. In other words, if the bird wants to turn left, the leading edge of the left wing is warped down and the leading edge of the right wing warps up. One wing drops, the other rises, and the bird turns.

That was all well and good, but how do you do that with a man-made wing? Remember, Boeing and McDonnell-Douglas and NASA were decades away. I believe what the Wright brothers did next demonstrated sheer ingenuity and created a brilliant solution. I believe it was also one of the founding principles of turn-of-the-century leadership. It is, however, lost to many leaders of today.

They used existing knowledge in a different way and were willing to be surprised. They thought outside the box, literally. In this case, however, they found their answer inside the box. Remember the Wright Brothers made and sold bicycles. (I would love to see this attitude emulated in the workplace.)

One day, Wilbur was with a customer who had just purchased a rubber tube for a bicycle tire. The tube came in an elongated box. Looking from the end, the box was square. When it was held in his hand, it was long and narrow. While handling the box, Wilbur grabbed the box by one end and, in doing so, he happened to pinch the opposite corners of the empty box.

Wilbur Wright then noticed what 99.9 percent of the world would not have given a second thought. He noticed that when he pinched the opposite corners of one end of the box, the other end of the box responded in just the opposite way. In other words, the box distorted in the opposite direction. It warped!

Wright knew that his airplane would have to have two wings in order to be successful. He not only realized that he had to warp the wing, but he had also figured out a way to do it. He knew that he could apply pressure and tension on opposite corners of the wing with a series of cables and they could turn their aircraft. And he did it by looking at an empty box for bicycle tubes.

Wilbur and Orville Wright were dreamers with attitude who took the risks and responsibility for those risks. They *listened* with their attitude and beliefs. They had such a passion for the unknown that they left their minds and organization open to the impossible. There was no institution for higher learning for the problems they faced.

They solved one of the most fundamental principles of twentieth-century innovation, without a hard drive, software program, spreadsheet, or flex-time employee suggestion box. An HR department would have been useless. They had attitude, and were leaders in the truest sense in that they listened!

They threw a huge particle in the existing lake of traditional science, the twentieth century, and created a wave that ripples to this day. That wave has yet to reach a shore. Their innovation in aviation continues. The airplane was the single most innovative principle to date. Their feat has never been surpassed. I would like you to remember the terms *particle* and *wave*. Those two words are critical to the principles of a true leader. Every time the space shuttle returns to Earth, it carries the fundamentals learned in a bicycle shop.

A Butthead with a Bad Attitude

Here's one of my stories about attitude. In the 1980s, I experienced a significant challenge in my career: I worked for a butthead. It got to the point that nothing I could say or do had any impact. This person told me, "I want your undying loyalty." He displayed several of the dysfunctional management behaviors I identified in my first book, *Each Human Spirit: The Transformation of the American Workplace*. He was a butthead, demanded loyalty, and ruled by length of the leash. This was a person who displayed behavior that put him in way over his head.

I knew that it was up to me to survive. I did survive and he became his own worst enemy. He did, however, cause much damage in the organization. This incident was one that I remembered years later as being significant. I survived; he resigned under a cloud of controversy.

When I started Compass Rose Consulting Inc., I used this person's management style as a lesson. I told myself I would use my skills to learn from this experience and teach the opposite. I knew there was a better way. I knew that attitude was critical to my success.

Here is what I did. Each morning as I dressed for work, I made it a point to keep an empty hanger in the closet. As my father told me, "When you wake up each morning, no one can determine how you will feel that day but you."

I think that is sage advice. What I do to this day is look at the empty hanger. Even when I travel for business I always leave one hanger empty. It is critical to each day. On that hanger, I mentally hang the garment called *attitude*.

As I dress, I look at that hanger last. I mentally remove the garment called attitude and put it on. That attitude is what I will wear each day when I walk out the door and face the world. What I want that garment to be is up to me.

My clients deserve a positive attitude. Why would they deserve anything different? If you work for a lousy company, then your attitude may be all you have. You must take positive and ethical steps. What are you going to do about it? Remember, the more advice you offer an insecure manager, person, or organization, the more they will grow to resent you.

Clients Deserve the Best

Attitude, leadership, and listening are something we choose daily and they control our destiny. Life gives us events, some of which we can control, while others are random and can be life-altering. Our attitude toward those unscheduled and controversial events is what makes us who we are. We may not have control of the event, but we do have control over how we will respond.

That hanger has proven to be the most self-motivating tool I have. It took a few years to stick, but the message was clear: we are in charge of our destiny. My father used to say that we are the sum total of our experiences. That was a powerful message from a person who lived through the Great Depression and 1929 crash. We seem to lose that message if we study this time—his generation lived it. Our generation has a hard time understanding, let alone teaching it.

I believe we become educated in school, but we gain wisdom by living. Now we must pass it on to the people we serve daily—our customers. While living, we must adapt to the unexpected. And through experiencing the unexpected, we change.

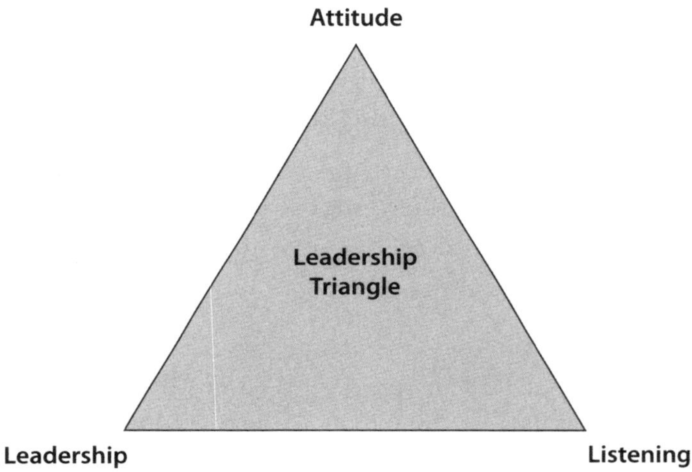

The Leadership Triangle is the vehicle that can make the difference not only for us, but the generations we serve. After all, what is the cost of one coat hanger?

Questions

- How would others describe my attitude?
- Is my attitude replicated in my actions as a leader, and what is the impact on others?
- How often do I spend time listening to others?
- If I listen, is it a habit or is it because I have to?
- What three gifts do I possess?
- What subject could I speak on with endless authority and passion?
- What goal would I like to accomplish as a sense of personal and professional leadership?

- What actions would I use to make it happen?
- What has been my most memorable breakthrough in thinking?
- What person has made the greatest impression on my life? Did I thank him?
- What could I do that would be of service to others?
- If I were able to make changes in my life, what are my fears?
- If I had one hour of prime-time television, what would I say to the world?
- Is the world asking something of me? Am I listening?
- Do I have an empty coat hanger in my closet, and do I put one in my luggage when I travel?

We must now start looking at ourselves and who we really are. We must begin to see that, like the Wright Brothers, we are adaptive beings who become inspired with scientific principles, but relish the human spirit and its ability to go beyond scientific boundaries and replicate our ideas, thoughts, and actions. This does take attitude, leadership, and our ability to listen.

Chapter Twelve

The Twenty-First Century and the Assembly Line of Fear

I have two fundamental rules for leadership
and organizational behavior.
Rule Number One: There is no more valuable entity in any
organization or company than the people who work there. Without
people you do not have a philosophy, purpose, mission, or product.
Rule Number Two: If you want to create havoc
in your organization or business,
start screwing around with rule number one.
—Art Bobrowitz

For in their mouth there is no sincerity;
Their heart teems with treacheries.
Their throat is an open grave.
—Psalms 5:10[1]

Organizations are a series of assembly lines and they will be moving faster with more changes in this century. They are the internal wave within a company that carries the potentially defective parts/particles to the customer. Here is a classic example where a wave (assembly line) can act like a particle and vice versa.

If we say the assembly line is the particle, it then carries the wave of indecision, poor leadership, and fear to the employee and customer.

This is not something that is added onto the product. In many organizations, it is built in and so prevalent that it is accepted as a way of doing business. Everything—and I mean everything—is created and implemented through a process. And the results either come in or leave through the front door or on the loading dock.

Organizational leadership controls all the assembly lines in a company. Leadership alone is responsible for the effects of their products and the process. This process has many influences. I have included other behaviors as part of the process. I want to make it clear that fear is the primary response.

We must also consider supply and demand, raw materials, process time, and labor costs as other influences. I would like to include one of the most critical and expensive commodities that will never show up on a spreadsheet. It is there, but hidden as an unknown. In fact, no spreadsheet has a line item that determines how much this commodity—*fear*—affects production and productivity. Fear has an assembly line all to itself. Like the member of any family, fear also has relatives. It can be a message and a messenger of the way things are and the harbinger of things to come.

Fear, anger, and lack of communication are not only integral parts of the process, but great killers of the human spirit. An organization permeated with fear, anger, and poor communication has little chance of being a host environment for any employee to realize the Seven Needs for Personal Productivity or for the organization to be the platform for any decent decision-making process.

It seems reasonable to assume that an assembly process is required for any product to be manufactured. We must have research, study, planning, cost analyses, manufacturing, marketing, distribution, and the necessary cycle of process improvement. These are some of the external issues. We must also be aware that we have other assembly lines in our companies.

The behavior of each employee, like any process or system, also is an assembly line that manufactures a product. Every day we experience the unseen assembly lines that are driven by employee attitudes. If you have two thousand employees, then you have two thousand products coming down the assembly line each day. This is in addition to the one you manufacture and hope to sell for a profit.

These additional assembly lines and products, which are an integral part of each organization, cost vast sums of money to operate. These are the most devastating costs a company can have. They are hidden, unknown, and possibly unknowable. Many businesses do not want to admit many of these costs, but they are built into the products that are in demand and delivered to customers. Many organizations hope these issues are not part of their product. The original intention was to start the company and deliver a unique product that would capture or impact a market. Wasn't that why the company was started in the first place?

What other assembly line behaviors do you have built into your organization's policies, rules, and procedures? Remember, if they are built into your procedures, then they are also built into the products you sell to your customers. Are your leaders trained to sense that fear, or are they using it as a motivator and calling it productivity? Again, we have the relationship between signal to noise. Your product is the signal. The noise is the fear, intimidation, and anger within the employee.

Here are some ideas you may wish to consider:

- Employee fear is an assembly line.
- Fear in the workplace is one of the most caustic, destructive, and expensive processes. I would have to dedicate a whole chapter just to list the books written on fear and its effect on people in the workplace. One that stands out is Kathleen D. Ryan and Daniel K. Ostereich's *Driving Fear Out of the Workplace, How to Overcome the Invisible Barriers to Quality, Productivity and Innovation.*[2]

In their book, Ryan and Ostereich state: "We cannot quantify the cost of fear to organizations or individuals or the exact impact of the turn-around strategies we suggest."[3] This truly is a profound statement. In order for fear to exist, it must be manufactured. It has the same processes as any industrial commodity, meaning it must follow a process that requires an assembly process.

At the end, the product called fear becomes part of the organizational culture. I believe we again can apply the quantum principles of wave and particle duality. Fear can become adaptive. It can be the attitude (wave) of a manager that creates an environment for generating wrong numbers that has employees cut corners on a product (particle) they know is flawed.

Like the formula of Mandelbrot, fear now replicates. It can spread throughout an organization like weeds in a lawn. Fear, too, has no conscience. It becomes adaptive to its host environment and edges out planned growth. Fear is a cancer in any organization. It also steals needed nutrients. Fear does not have a firewall or virus check because it is built into the system. And here again we have the paradox: fear *becomes* the system. In other words, the farther you get away from the quality principles of your organization, the greater the noise.

The next phase is even more destructive. Fear mutates. It implants itself in its host environment (such as a new employee or manager) and becomes an unhealthy motivator or barrier to personal productivity.

The cycle continues and, all the while, the new company computer system with space-age accounting software never has a clue. Remember: numbers can prove much, but numbers can hide even more. Data has no conscience and in this case, does *not* tell the truth.

In your performance evaluation system, how do you measure fear? When a person is consumed by fear, he has a tendency to freeze or limit his movements. The same is true in an organization. Employees who are in constant fear will limit movement and productivity. The company, however, must continue to move forward or else it goes out of business.

Don't try to measure both movement and those who are standing still. You can go ahead and try, but remember, Heisenberg says you can't.

We may never know these numbers. Dr. W. Edwards Deming relates that the most important numbers we need to know may be unknown and possibly unknowable. We have experts in the field who say that it is next to impossible to determine and quantify the cost in relation to both the organization and the people who work there. I believe this is significant. What would cause that level of fear? Again, there are many books that describe this. I believe it is manifested by the relationship of the people in the organization and their environment. Leadership, however, holds the magnifying glass that must put it in focus. I believe we do it to each other.

Teams Are an Assembly Line and Have Really Suffered

The message/messenger scenario requires me to share its relativity again to the concept of teams. I believe what we have done to teams and their purpose has been destructive. We have run the "bulldozer through the garbage." W. Edwards Deming would again be chastising the American workplace if he were to see today's teams. Companies adopted teams with the best of intentions during the seventies, eighties and nineties. They were, and still are critical to continuous improvement of processes and systems.

As with any tool, like DeSoto's bulldozer, someone always looks for a new way to make life easier with the tool or use it in a way. Teams became that tool. Many companies avoided them like the plague. Those, however, that did use them in a constructive fashion reaped the results. What others did is the horror story.

Some saw the team concept as an easy way to keep employees busy. The team became the substitute for a person needing to make the decision. The result became self-evident. Either decisions were not made or the decisions that were adopted became a special interest or the political average of the group.

I have said this before but it is worth repeating: a team should never be used as a substitute for leadership. Do you remember the story about the organization with the executive director who left and the advisory board that became the governing body? The organization then became plagued by leadership by consensus. The problem was only solved when a new executive director was hired and did away with the advisory board altogether.

Conflicting Values Are an Assembly Line

Ask yourself: are the values of the organization that management is teaching really the "walk" of the organization? Are values displayed in reports, snappy slogans, or regularly framed as wall hangings, but not lived in the company? Does the annual management retreat produce true knowledge that is customer-driven? Or do these retreats only generate symbolic cost cutting and employee shortcuts?

I was conducting a training session for a group of managers. The purpose of the session was to present a training program I was going to give to the front-line employees later. Management heard the program first so they would know what the employees would be talking about.

I did something extra for the managers. When they entered the room and took their seats, I gave each person a piece of paper that was face down. I told them not to turn it over until I gave them the cue to turn it over and answer the questions. I told them this was just a formality and it would not take long at all.

I did my introduction, took care of a few housekeeping issues, then told them to turn over the papers and start. As the participants turned over the papers, I wanted to watch the body language of as many of the managers as possible so I could see their reactions. Their reactions ranged from fear, denial, anger, boredom, and some I am not trained to recognize.

I had written two questions on the papers. The first was, "What is the Attitude Statement of your organization?" The second was, "What are your company values?"

I asked these two questions because, when I was interviewed as a consultant with this company and asked for this information, I was presented with a professional brochure by a very important senior executive. I was told that the brochure outlined the core values and that this organization was very proud of them. In this test, less than 30 percent of the managers could tell me the answer to either question. If they didn't know, how could they teach it to their employees?

These were, for the most part, hard-working and dedicated people who wanted to do a good job and had pride in their organization. They came to work each day and showed effort and commitment. And what was the result? It appears Mandelbrot stopped at senior management. The organization was not designed to replicate. Did they manufacture a good product? Yes. Could it have been better? Improvement is always good.

This process was, of course, to enlighten them in the following areas:

- Your attitude and values are the foundation for all the decisions your organization makes. How do they replicate in your organization?
- Attitude and values are linked to the productivity system and the product they manufacture (wave/particle). All employees should have this knowledge.
- If management does not know the company values, then neither do the front-line employees (key to the system!). How can they know? How can they improve?
- You cannot hold employees accountable for a system over which they have no control. If employees are not improving, then they are not moving. If they are not moving, then neither is your company.
- Management controls the system.

Anger Is an Assembly Line

This topic often comes up in conversations with friends and associates. Think for a minute. How often are you engaged in a conversation regarding workplace issues and somewhere in the conversation the word *anger* is used or maybe displayed?

I am intrigued by the effect anger has on an organizational process. Some managers use it as a tool for manipulation. Employees use it as a threat to the work process. It is used quite effectively by those who chose not to accomplish a task, and those who default their anger and responsibility to someone else. The main point is, anger is not a stand-alone issue; it has an effect on multiple levels. In fact, if we look closely, we will find that many people get angry *because of* the effect their anger will have on someone else. You have just started another assembly line.

Anger is a great tool to avoid confrontation. If someone is angry, do other employees gather round and settle the issue? Chances are, they avoid that person like the plague. Then the angry person doesn't have to confront an issue she most likely is responsible for creating in the first place. This is quite nice for those who do not want to rock the corporate boat. An angry manager is a great way to keep heads lowered in ergonomically-correct work cubicles.

And if you did confront someone who was quite angry, how long did it take to solve the problem—maybe a couple of days, weeks, or maybe never if the manager chose to let it blow over?

Regardless of the circumstances, what has been taught to each employee who is involved is a new assembly line. Anger produces a product that is used by the internal customers of an organization—the employees themselves and the customers they serve. Anger produces a defective product. Quality suffers. They may not like it but, over time, it becomes part of the company culture.

Add to the previous mix the effect anger has when it is taken home with each employee. Remember, the assembly line of the human spirit does not respect the boundaries of the corporate culture. Anger is an organizational odor that does not honor individual environment. The family and personal life of every employee now becomes part of this process. And in the morning, the last details of this dysfunctional trail will return to the workplace to complete or expand the issue.

Poor Management and Employee Training Is an Assembly Line

Several years ago I had a conversation with my brother-in-law, Paul Zollner. He was in the middle of a career change and shared an interesting conversation about one of his interviews. Paul experienced what many others were and are being exposed to in the corporate world. His background was in finance and interaction with large corporations. Not one to rest on his laurels, he made a career change. His assets were many. And with that went the problem many people in the work force face—they are downsized and told they are overqualified for the positions they are applying for.

Paul and I had the opportunity to talk, and one of the areas was the need for the workplace to be an educational experience. We shared many thoughts on working for learning organizations.

He interviewed with one organization and, during the process, he became aware of a rather rigid and formal interview process. At the end of the interview, he was asked if he had any questions.

Paul replied, "Yes, I have several. Does this position have a job description?"

He immediately sensed tenseness in the person doing the interview. He then asked, "To whom do I report?"

The interviewer now was definitely on edge. He was sure it was the line of questions and specific issues that he felt needed to be answered.

The interviewer's reply was, "You will report to me."

The next two questions gave Paul the information he needed. "What is your management style?"

The interviewer tap-danced around the question and never gave a direct answer.

The last question put the period at the end of the interview. Paul asked if this was a learning organization (Seven Needs, meaning, say-so and input, fair wage, leadership, quality of life, *educational opportunities,* and importance of work).

The interviewer's response was, "Yes, you do have opportunities to attend seminars periodically, but you will still have to accomplish the work that is assigned to you."

Paul thanked the interviewer, got up from his chair, and went out the door and on with his life. The interviewer didn't get it. He did not understand what Paul was asking or what the organization was all about.

Paul shared with me that the interviewer did not make the connection between education and a learning environment. He saw that education was part of the process and not a perk. It was more than the opportunity to attend seminars—he was looking for an attitude that said, "We learn here."

Organizations often pride themselves on education. We have a society that touts an educated work force. We also have many groups disguising themselves as organizations that provide no form of training other than an initial orientation. Some of these groups don't want to, and others may feel it isn't necessary. That is their problem. I don't feel sorry for them. This is a sensitive area. Not only is it sensitive, it can be damaging with far-reaching ramifications.

The human spirit needs to be nurtured; it is like planting a tree in the yard. Apply this thought to an organization. An employee is planted in company culture. If a tree is not watered, nurtured, or attended to, it will either die or not develop properly. It is the same for employees. If the organizational culture does not provide the nourishment needed for the employee to survive and thrive, the proportional results will occur. It will also be reflected in the quality of your product. The human mind, like the body, needs to be exercised.

Ask yourself the basic questions of organizational development:

- How do we exercise the human spirit?
- Does your organization offer a course on the human spirit in the workplace?
- Does your organization value employees who stretch their imaginations or their problem-solving and creative skills? This is more than having employees attend designated seminars; this is providing a work environment where the employee grows with the organization. This is Mandelbrot!
- The above also requires us to ask, "Do I want my employees to grow in this way?"
- If I am a leader, do I want to lead an organization that has a learning environment?
- How will I create that environment?
- If this is true, then what am I going to do about it?

Procrastination Is an Assembly Line

You can never say enough about procrastination. Given the opportunity, I also use procrastination as a model for the dysfunctional assembly line. The reason for its importance is that procrastination, for the most part, is driven by two fears—the fear of failure and the fear of success.

When we say *fear of failure* it conjures up a note of caution. It really is quite basic. Our culture does not reward failure. In fact, we have become so fixated with winning that anyone who is not number one is a runner-up, second, or an underachiever.

If we look at fear in the wave/particle relationship we can see fear as a wave. It is pure destructive energy that can bind all our thoughts into not trying to accomplish something in the first place. This can be quite destructive with personal relationships. We may meet someone (particle) and find that, over time, this could lead into a deeper relationship. Fear of past failures can put it on hold or keep us from developing further. This part of it (wave) keeps us from moving forward.

Here is a classic example of attitude (wave, messenger) becoming a product (particle, message). Out of fear of failure, the employee will procrastinate. He will also procrastinate in telling his supervisor what the problem is because he fears he will be blamed or he knows management will not back him up. The cost is huge.

The second fear takes a little further explanation. This is the fear of success. Employees may procrastinate their success. They may become cautious around success because, frankly, it can cause them more work. Now, this requires clarification. In a hostile work environment with vacillating leadership, few employees will respond to any additional type of work. Even the good employees will default to their job descriptions.

In organizations with good leadership and managers, the opposite can be true. Employees want to please a leader who takes care of them and creates a positive environment. (I am not saying that employees are lazy.) That is not true for the vast majority of employees, though sadly, it is true for some.

My point is: good leaders want to reward good work. It is not uncommon for good leaders to give their successful employees more responsibility as a reward. What is interesting is that more responsibility is a long-term motivator. Employees will procrastinate for both negative and positive reasons. An effective leader understands that motivation, sincerity, and consistency play a pivotal role in employee behavior. This is the leader as an organizational environmentalist.

Hiring Practices and Qualifications Are an Assembly Line

The Oregon Employment Department published a document entitled, "Work force 2000: An Oregon Employer Perspective." This survey, a representative sample of Oregon's private sector and many public sector employers, asked a variety of questions relating to recent hires, difficulty in hiring, finding qualified workers, current worker skills, and future needs. It was enlightening, to say the least.

What attracted my attention were the comments by industry respondents who were asked what skills were difficult to recruit. Over half of the respondents related they were challenged with the "Work Ethic" and "Problem-Solving Skills" of the job applicants.

What was even more troubling to me were two other categories that were desired skills but lacking in applicants, "Interpersonal Communications" and "Supervisory/Leadership." These results crossed the boundaries of both small and large businesses. I think we had better pay attention to this message. I still see these categories in today's workplace.

Businesses with a warehouse operation need to have an inventory system or computer database for parts, products, manuals, file systems, etc. Picture, if you will, a warehouse full of parts or computers loaded with information and no system to organize, communicate, or find the right application and potential for all these parts and services.

We know why we have all these parts and services, but how are we going to professionally apply and use them? What are the correct avenues for us to use that will give us the greatest chance of success? In other words, what is our method of measurement and implementation?

"Work force 2000: An Oregon Employer Perspective" tells us that the warehouse is full, but the application and distribution system for employee productivity may not be equipped to handle the task. If applicants do lack work ethic, problem-solving, interpersonal communications, and supervisory/leadership skills as part of their portfolios of skills, then *concern* should be the word of the day. The applicants have the information to do the task, but lack the professional distribution system to make it happen.

The information age and level of current education is supposed to be second to none. Yet, we appear to have a serious void in the ability of employees to apply what they know, even though they are learning in school. Employers may have a hiring system that does not address the issues. In real terms, they may be asking the wrong questions during the hiring process.

The fundamentals of leadership, interpersonal communications, problem solving, and ethics are essential. These are not just job description issues; they are fundamental building blocks for the mission of the company itself—they are the DNA of the human spirit.

Additional Assembly Lines

I have included a variety of additional assembly lines so you can read the questions and add your own answers. You will quickly see the devastation and organizational debris field left by dysfunctional assembly lines. Remember, every assembly line has to be managed. Picture a dysfunctional assembly line as nothing more than a stationary Titanic with job descriptions. Everyone is doing her job with her neck pulled in and not rocking the boat. They are just doing their jobs. What happens when your product leaves their work space is someone else's problem. "It's not part of my job description." That means someone is in control of the process and delivers the result. What other assembly lines can you think of in your organization that I have not mentioned?

Linear thinking and organizational structures are assembly lines.

- Do we look at our problems through the eyes of conformity?
- Are we open to ways of thinking and the opportunities they may present?
- Are we open to using already existing materials and ideas in new and different ways?
- Are existing structures and policies creating barriers to innovative and creative thinking?

The obsessive or compulsive need for managers to control is an assembly line.

- Does management create an environment for change?

- Are we so structured that creative thinking is being stifled?
- De we have to ask permission to be creative?
- What areas in our company are being hampered because of excessive control?

Poor management communications skills are an assembly line.

- What percent of management/employee communications are face-to-face versus machine-to-machine?
- Do managers teach the organizational Attitude Statement, values, and goals?
- How do we check and monitor management communication skills?
- Does our company provide communications training or is it an elective for employees?
- Are managers encouraged to communicate one-on-one and *listen* to employees?
- Do we even have a management training process, or is management training something that the organization expects the applicant or person who is promoted to already possess?

Lack of leadership is an assembly line.

- Does management default decision making to teams?
- Are employees reluctant to find new ways of doing things?
- Do employees have clear expectations and directions in process improvement?
- Is management making decisions that employees should be making?
- Are leadership decisions being made with a level of understanding and wisdom with the assistance of data, information, and knowledge?
- If this is true, and I am your customer, why should I pay for all those other processes?

Every one of these behaviors can be considered a wave in the application of wave/particle duality. Behavior doesn't have mass—it all relates to energy. These behaviors can be both positive and negative. Remember, free will does not know right from wrong. We must decide what we need to do, and make the ethical decisions and accompanying behavior. The decision remains up to us.

Human Resource Management

Henry Neave said he has never liked the term *Human Resource Managers*. He refers to a quote by Del Nelson of McClellen Air Force Base, that what we do with a resource is obtain it, shape it, use it, and throw it away.[4]

The point here is quite clear. Two significant incidents changed the outcome of the last century. The first incident was the births of many post-war baby boomers from 1946 until the early sixties. The second incident will be in the years 2009 through 2015 when those same baby boomers will exit the work force. That means now! Many will leave it for good and others will move on to career changes. And with them will go the single largest volume of discretionary income in the history of civilization.

But something else has gotten in the way. For a while, the downturn in the economy ravaged organizations and pension funds. It also drove a wedge in the middle of the boomers. Many left their organizations due to job loss and early retirements. A significant number stayed on.

Some, however, took another route. They left their jobs with the capital to start their own companies. Some of them are coming back as competition for the organizations they left. These are not brick-and-mortar businesses. These are lean thinkers working out of small offices in homes who are looking at efficiency in a new way.

Some HR people looked the other way and failed to capture the moment. The greatest single lack of communication was the failure of the HR system to interview those who left to gather meaningful data and information to improve their knowledge base. If I have heard it once, I have heard it a dozen times.

When those highly skilled employees left their organizations, they were never asked about their experiences. It is too late to ask now. You do not capture the moment by looking in the rear view mirror. The attitude and behavior of these departed employees may prove to be the greatest missed opportunity in the last fifty years. To the visionary, it may be another inner tube box, like the Wright Brothers', waiting to be altered in such a way to produce a new design and purpose.

All too many organizations, in the name of productivity and efficiency, will develop and implement at-will policies. In the hands of the unskilled, the at-will policy becomes the headless chicken. Loyalty has now gone out the window and fear now collects the paycheck. I am waiting for someone to tell me how at-will is an asset to productivity and the growth of the human spirit. This, too, becomes part of the assembly line.

Not all employees are productive, I agree. Some need to be dismissed because they are a detriment to the system. If an employee is a consistent problem, he should be let go. The at-will issue is much bigger. At-will can have a very dysfunctional effect on the good employees too. Remember any policy, whether good or bad, affects everyone.

Organizations may develop a policy because of the bad employees, but you must remember that it will also have an impression on the good ones too. They are told they can be let go for no reason other than someone says they were no longer productive. In the hands of the poorly trained manager, this is lethal. You have just dug the Grand Canyon of communications barriers in your organization. The best-intentioned policy, when placed in the hands of a poor manager, is a legal landmine waiting to go off. A bad policy in the hands of a good manager isn't much better. At-will policies work well for insecure managers who are committed to corporate fiefdoms and personal agendas.

If you like notoriety, this may get it for you in ways you would never have imagined.

We can see striking similarities between an assembly line process for raw materials and manufacturing, and any employee. It is this blurring of the products that makes one deeply concerned for any company or organization using this approach. This type of thinking reflects directly back to Frederick Taylor and his early-twentieth-century theories on worker productivity.

How can employees improve at-will? Improvement should be based on the employee's contribution to the organization; it should not be a subjective policy with little leadership merit. Why should the human spirit commit to an environment where its efforts will be arbitrary at best? *At-will never promotes good will.*

I find the greatest challenge and dysfunction for at-will policies buried in the development of job descriptions. This is because we have transformed job descriptions into this myopic view of a single person who must perform a specific function. Every person who works for an organization is interrelated to someone else and multiple processes. If you fire someone at will, you are not necessarily solving the problem. The person you fired may only have been doing what she was told and trained to do. How many people today do what they are told, and only what they are told, because they know they can be fired at will for doing something that isn't part of their job description?

W. Edwards Deming has one of the clearest definitions of job descriptions and their purpose. If I could give one lesson to HR managers who choose to understand the purpose of an organization system, it would include this quote from Dr. Deming. "A job description should not only describe what the job is but what it is for. Anybody's job should not merely be to do it right but to do it better. Nobody is doing his job right unless he is continually collecting data to help improve that job."

At the Second Annual Conference of the British Deming Association in Portsmouth, England, in 1989, Nissan stated that they use very little detail in their job descriptions. The example they use relates to the tasks of an engineer. An engineer "should be able to do everything an engineer needs to do."[5]

If you train your employees to find ways of continually improving, managing, listening, and collecting meaningful data and information to improve their jobs, why would you need an at-will policy to get rid of them? At-will wrongly assumes that the problem rests with the employee. While it is true in some cases that the problem does rest with the employee, it is also true that many problems are in the system the employee works for, and over which they have no control.

I would like to know which businesses and institutions of higher learning promote the teaching of such destructive tools. If you do have them in place, then you will get what you deserve. Your work force will produce out of fear; you will end up with office favorites and poorly-trained managers. You will get a product that will be presentable, but it will not be efficient or competitive. It will be delivered over budget and manufactured by various office turfs. I have never been aware of any employee experiencing a firm footing in his career when he has had to dance on office turf.

Let's look at our message/messenger model. The manager (message/particle) sets the tone for the company with an at-will policy. The employee no longer looks at the manager as a resource but as a source of any potential problems and future headaches they may have. Employees learn fast to stay in good grace with that manager!

In reality, the opposite should be the goal. Managers should be the messengers/wave. They should be a resource and magnet for employee communication so employees can improve their work and education. There should be continuous improvement of the organizational system. Managers who adopt the message/particle role create an environment where employees learn to survive where they are.

Managers who see their role as one of mentor and systems-thinking messenger/wave are focused on what employees and their organization can be and methods of improvement to get there. Once the manager has employee involvement in finding new methods, and she has set the tone for leadership, then employees will take responsibility for their work, careers, and collecting new data, and information.

The manager now becomes the messenger/wave. This is taking responsibility for her tasks and obligations. She is now taking risks. *This is leadership.* It is in her best interest for her attitude to recognize the employee's behavior. Attitude is everything when it comes to the leader. Any leader with a myopic or bad attitude has the ethical responsibility to leave her position and assume another role in the organization.

The destruction to an organization caused by a bad manager is no different than building a campfire in a forest and leaving without dousing it. Bad leadership is like a smoldering campfire. Give it time and it will set the forest aflame. In the forest we call it arson. In the American workplace we call it poor judgment.

When an organization moves, it is not a data entry or revised chart—it is a law of physics. And just as Newtonian science predicts, it will continue to move unless someone applies equal or opposite force to make it stop. Here is where leadership gets dicey. Throw the human spirit into the equation—the smallest particle in the organization—and a person may respond as a message/particle or messenger/wave for the new direction.

As a leader, what do you want them to do? You had better know, because the effect of employees not knowing what you want or the direction you want them to take, or who are not listening, can be immediate, costly, and even catastrophic. Just ask Moses.

Questions

- What other assembly lines do you have in your organization besides the product you manufacture?
- If you are a leader, are employees afraid to come into your office? Why?

- Are you a messenger of a better way?
- Do employees come to you for information and answers?
- Why do they come to you?
- If they don't, why don't they?
- As a leader are you teaching a better way?

Scripture tells us to be a servant to others and to lead by example.
Leadership passes through us as light passes through a window.
We need to be a positive example and a light for a better way.

Chapter Thirteen

The Goal: Positive Leadership Behaviors

It is not that someone else is preventing you from living happily; you, yourself do not know what you want. Rather than admit this, you pretend that someone is keeping you from exercising your liberty. Who is this? It is you yourself.
—Thomas Merton[1]

We cannot view the universe with only our physical senses. What else might it be trying to tell us? We must have faith in what we do not yet know. We must look at ourselves and the universe and ask not only who we are but *why* we are. To separate them is the same as saying you will not accept the universe unless it is on your terms.

I want to describe leadership in such a way as to relate it to an object or process. I see leadership as a seamless and evolving process with scientific application of organizational principles and the spiritual belief of the leader of the human spirit. Leadership is a law of the universe. It is a universal process.

The Light of a Prism

How would you describe leadership? In what context do you put the word so you can relate its scope to someone else? As I was pondering this problem while working on this manuscript, I noticed that sunlight hit the beveled edge of the mirror on our living room wall. The light source was divided and a brilliant pattern of colors was created. As I was thinking about leadership, I began to dwell on the idea of a prism and its application.

We know that a prism separates light into a series of colors. To the naked eye, light has no color entering the prism. We could say that it is a single entity. Yet, when it enters and is processed by the prism, the light source is broken down and separated.

Each wavelength is defined by its own frequency, which is displayed as its own unique color. Look at it as a scientific version of stained glass. It is interesting that many great places of worship around the world have stained glass windows. While many of the windows tell a story from the Scriptures, others are simple designs that transform outside light into colors that shine on those inside.

To me, it is no coincidence that light is broken down by a prism or that stained glass windows are in a church, or a leader is someone who understands her employees as lights of many colors and intensities. So, where does this take us with leadership?

Every organization has policies, rules, and procedures. Hopefully, the organization has someone in a position of authority who is also a leader. The leader is responsible for the direction and well-being of the entire operation.

Picture these rules and procedures as sources of raw light made up of different wavelengths and bundled together. Each is designed to have a specific impact on the company. The leader is now in a unique position and critical to the process. Picture the leader as the prism and the spokesperson for the operations manual, like a light source. The policies, rules, and procedures are then broken down or separated and defined based on the principles, values, and ethics of the leader (hopefully).

The level of responsibility that the leader chooses is crucial. The actions now become defined and presented in order, much like a ray of light. If we call that behavior, then the behavior will be in a respective order, just like the colors of reflective light. Remember, different management behaviors have different patterns of policy interpretation of the organizational rules. The results will be a plethora of colors and patterns. Simply stated, productivity will have color.

Let's look at another example using the words of the Scriptures as the light source of a prism. Scripture talks of the oneness of God and His creation of all things. This is hard to understand now; in the early centuries, this idea was even more overwhelming. But it does not stop there. Theologically, we were given a prism which gave us the ability to separate out the different spiritual wavelengths. Sacred Scripture tells us so. These documents give us the opportunity to see the *light* of the Word.

We hear the stories from different points of view because the message is broken into texts, statements of various faiths, denominations, and people, much like the wavelengths of light. The leader now becomes the messenger. The colors, reflected in the many hues, are called free will and responsibility. With the application of our principles, values, and ethics, we now have one light directed through the scriptural prism and the multicolored messages are seen by people of faith. And it is seen from an individual point of view, with each of us having our own view of the brilliant and colorful messages.

If I am looking at the light that has passed through a prism, I may see a different color than the person standing next to me sees. We are looking at the same light from different positions or perspectives. The angle in this case is our individual principles, biases, and points of view. Granted, we are not seeing the whole, only a portion of the light from our points of view.

In order to see all the colors that are displayed, we must change our positions. We may find ourselves resting in a particular color because of its beauty and conviction. It is the same with reading Scripture. We read Scripture from our point of view and see and make interpretations based on the color of our beliefs. In order to get the true spectrum of theological teaching, we are required to look at Scripture from different points of view and gain a deeper understanding of the intensity by our openness to what we are called to do.

We may also rest in our organization because the leadership has set clear direction and purpose. It now provides a sense of harmony for our personal beliefs. True leaders create an environment where employees can find their individual light and still explore other colors of the organizational spectrum.

That thought brings us back to leaders. A leader may see her role as one of rigidity and standing firm. This is true, but the purpose of her obligations and responsibilities is for her to be the vehicle and conduit for direction. Leaders must move their abilities to be able to capture the total light for front-line creativity.

Remember, a leader is the prism. The other light source is the input and communication she receives from her employees. What she is getting is not only words but actions. A multisource display looks different to each employee, depending on where she stands, but it is equal to all. That energy is the true light of leadership. Scripture is also that energy in our words, and our behavior. This is the paradox of the adaptive nature of the human spirit. The light leads us to being the message or messenger. We have the ability to grasp its true meaning or ignore the message.

Stay with Your Path and Vision

The art of leadership is the implementation of scientific principles using the tools wisely, and with a deep understanding of the spiritual assets of each employee. In *Each Human Spirit,* I outlined eighteen management behaviors that stifle, limit and, in some cases, destroy productivity and impact the human spirit.

I want to share with you the other end of the productivity spectrum. It is called making decisions for yourself and seeking out those who display positive and ethical leadership. If we choose to make something of our lives, specifically a career, then we must also carefully choose the leaders we wish to follow. The path we choose is up to us and, along the way, we will encounter obstacles and challenges that may appear insurmountable.

Keeping to your path and vision is critical. That is why I recommend a basic business or life plan to all my clients. What is your attitude statement? What do you value? Where do you want to go? How will you get there? What might you run into along the way? What have you been doing that has proven successful? What do you see as challenges? The point being, make a plan. Once you make a plan, start looking for other people who have made a plan.

Do business with people who have a plan. Look for and work for leaders who have a plan. How will you know? Ask them. You will not stumble into success. Professional speaker Jim Cathcart said it best, "Most people aim at nothing in life and hit it with amazing accuracy."[2]

Those who say they stumbled into success should be congratulated, though it is similar to putting twenty dollars in a slot machine and winning ten thousand dollars. Does it happen? Sure! But does it happen every time you go to Las Vegas? Hardly.

All you have to do to find your answer is look at all the development in Las Vegas. That town was built because they had a plan. Their plan is to defeat yours! That is why your money stays there when you leave. Simply stated, their plan works better than yours does. Do you want to know how good their plan is? They have you convinced when you leave that you had a good time even though their plan defeated yours. You can't fault them. They show you the best time in the world. *Get a plan.* It doesn't have to be complicated or lengthy—only doable—but it must plan for the future. Once you have a plan, find your leaders.

I will describe five leadership behaviors that will help you look for leaders in the twenty-first century. I am sure there are many more. I chose these five. These are positive behaviors—life is too short to look for and hang around the negative ones. These behaviors show direction, purpose, and respect for the human spirit.

We know that taking a scientific approach to leadership can produce significant data and an opportunity for discovery. A person who looks at the same issue from a spiritual perspective may hold a different view. What matters is our behavior in addressing the problem. That is where leadership commitment takes hold.

While some of the following behaviors are quite common, the titles I have chosen to identify the behaviors are not. I did that because I want you to look at these behaviors through the lens of words that one might not think of when dealing with leadership—that is the point of this book. These leadership behaviors are a prism for productivity.

I hope I leave you with unanswered questions. I hope, however, the questions you have are new ones. If they are not, then I have not accomplished what I set out to do: to understand the possibility of creating a work environment that reflects leadership, science, and spirituality.

Again, free will has played its role. Whether we accept it or reject it, the responsibility is ours. It is up to us to see the light and, hopefully, be the light of leadership. With that I wish to give you five leadership behaviors I believe reflect the connectedness of leadership, science, and spirituality.

Five Leadership Behaviors That Connect

Good leaders can be very personal. They understand the weight of responsibility. They are aware of the overwhelming challenges they face, and are serious. The not-so-good leaders are different. Their behavior causes problems and that is why I gave them their own chapter in my last book.

Leadership is like a multicolored window that can be seen from both sides, and the light of data, information, knowledge, understanding, and wisdom is allowed to pass through it. These are qualities we would like to see in ourselves and in others. If you think leadership is something just for other people and not a personal commitment, then skip this chapter.

I believe leadership is both internal and external. When I say that leadership is internal, I refer to those employees who are not in leadership positions or in a defined position description. That is why I believe so strongly in these behaviors. It must be understood that these behaviors do not recognize the defined boundaries of an organizational chart or job description, or are inhibiting behavior of other employees.

I defined these five behaviors because I believe they inspire. They provide two functions—first of all, they attract positive attitudes, and second, they repel those people who choose to work because of an ulterior motive. These behaviors all have a sense of purpose, being, conviction, and fortitude. These behaviors provide an environment for both direction and inspiration, not only for others, but more importantly, for ourselves. The seed must be planted and the fertile soil found within each of us.

I must say something else about leaders. I have found that some leaders I have met were not the best communicators. What was significant was, when they did communicate, they had the ability to say the right thing at that moment, and to listen. It was as if they sensed an evolving situation and knew what to say.

I give you the following leadership behaviors as I have observed them. They are not technical terms. I did not write them to be inserted in a job description, but if an organization chooses to do so, then I commend you for your vision and sense of purpose. Your attitude will be visionary. You will also drive your people in HR over the edge.

I see each of them as fluid design and adaptation. I believe they reflect the connectedness of leadership, science, and spirituality. All require a person to take risks. If you do not take risks in your life or it is not part of your management style, you will not find yourself here. All of these behaviors have one thing in common; their behavior can be put under the umbrella of organizational environmentalist. They are all stewards of the human spirit.

Disciples, Gardeners, Entrepreneurs, Hushers, and Visionaries

The Disciples

A disciple is a teacher. What a noble calling! It is, however, a difficult role to address. I heard a Christian commentator relate a definition of the word *disciple*. He said that disciple is the root word of discipline.

The word *discipline* is now under attack as the nemesis of free expression and educational transformation. It is unfortunate that a word as productive as discipline has fallen into the recycle bin of political correctness. A disciple is one who is open, a lifelong learner, and someone who is teachable. Think for a moment about someone in your life experience who had a thirst for knowledge and applied it with wisdom. That list can be quite short. The issue with disciples is that they are knowledgeable, but what sets them apart is their steadfast commitment to their convictions. These are not people who adhere to the principles of situational ethics.

I think one of the finest qualities any person can have is to be open. It is something we cherish in our friends and relatives. It is something to die for in a leader. To be open means to unlock, release, untie, and unwrap. The antonym of being open, of course, is to close. For those of us who have worked for a closed leader, the answer can be obvious.

One must keep in mind that being open doesn't mean you are not disciplined. One who is open and has strong central beliefs should be admired. One who is open and does not have strong central beliefs is to be avoided. I like the word *open*. In a leader that means looking, thinking, and observing a new way. We live in a world that stresses new ways and ideas. It is then quite another thing to say one is open to new ideas. To me, being open means to see one's calling in a time of adversity.

I think these are the times that build character. It is always nice to learn in a comfortable environment or in other moments of inspiration.

In times of adversity, our willingness to see and possibly act in a way we never dreamt about is challenged.

Openness also means being able to open to someone we may not understand or necessarily like. How open am I, as a leader, to ideas and suggestions from a person I may not like or necessarily agree with? We must be open and listen to someone in those moments when he displays genius, even if he has consistently displayed either behavior or ideas that have no perceived merit.

I have chosen to be a lifelong learner. My parents' generation did not have the opportunity to pursue an extended formal education. Many times, it was a question of family survival. But they always learned. They taught that we have lessons in everything. It doesn't matter if it was good, bad, or insurmountable adversity. I learned from it.

Life is a continuous and changing classroom. Many lessons are taught but we have to be open and teachable. We must expose our ability to change. We are governed by spiritual laws and scientific laws. It is up to us to choose their impact. I believe they have much in common and can provide a balance and harmony in our lives. Disciples work well in this environment. The key for me is the word *behavior*. Leaders need to understand that human behavior is linked to both. The environment they create enables us to ask questions and grow with the organization. It is then we will find out if we have the talent to make it happen. One of the most honest questions you can ask yourself is, "Am I teachable?" If something new is presented to me, do I have the courage to see the possibility of learning? Often, we confuse learning with formal education. Both are necessary and complement each other.

As we get older we frequently find a comfortable rut for ourselves and camp out for a few years. Being teachable is not relegated strictly to intellect. I believe it requires us to look at the world and decide if what is presented to us will fundamentally change our behavior. We must then decide if our actions will truly impact that behavior.

Is it something we believe in with deep conviction? If so, then do it. If it is something that appears to be a noble cause and others are doing it, then look to something else. Life is too short. We must realize, however, that science and spirituality must be in our portfolio. If we are to lead, then we must be committed to learn. That is the understanding or attitude of leadership and risk-taking.

Working for a Disciple

Here are some points about working for a disciple:

- If you like a learning environment, this is the place for you.
- Prepare to be challenged. Disciples wander the desert of thinking and take their people into new areas. Wear your work boots.
- A disciple will take an organization into territory thought to be unfriendly and will teach a new way. You probably will be expected to also teach the new way.
- If you like safety and the status quo in your thinking, then this leader will cause you angst.
- Disciples are people of integrity and deep personal and spiritual conviction who practice what they preach.
- Disciples expect you to reach. Creative thinking is the norm. The disciple sees things in you that you don't. Get used to it.
- If a disciple asks a question, chances are they already have the answer. This is their way of teaching.
- If you don't want to go back to school, don't work for a disciple.
- Disciples are hands-on. Their organizations learn by doing.
- This is a work environment that asks questions.
- Don't expect a formal classroom. Disciples teach on the fly.
- You will get out of it what you put into an environment led by a disciple. Disciples do not teach you little bits at a time.
- These are people who will think nothing of psychologically

and spiritually backing a dump truck up to a team or meeting and presenting you with an entire load of new possibilities.
- If you love the highs and lows, but want to learn and teach, this is the place for you.

The Gardeners

Hearing the term *gardener* does not conjure up something that is awfully exciting. When I first thought of the gardener I pictured someone up to her elbows in compost, leaves, tools, and sore muscles after a weekend in the yard. One problem with gardening for me is, once you plant you must wait. That takes patience. And having patience as a leader is a virtue. To some leaders it might be viewed as a weakness.

Gardeners cultivate, turn over the soil, plant things, and create chaos before they see the final result. Gardeners in an organization can cause angst. It is as if they—and only they—have been intrigued by someone with the ability to garden. They sense something in the soil.

I like to consider that soil, like the workplace, is a growing environment. Gardeners love to be around a growing environment. I believe that same intuition is present in the workplace. Some leaders walk into a company and sense something in the business. They have that ability to identify where the fertile soil is and what needs to be planted. They have a deep understanding of what needs to be done and where. Their vision is truly linked to science and the human spirit.

This prepping of the soil means they know what ideas and actions need to be planted in order to gain a harvest. Like the crops of the farmer, the gardener knows that it will take time for the crops to grow. And some will take longer than others. It doesn't matter. The gardener's role is to prepare the soil for planting.

If I owned a company and knew changes needed to be made, I would want the gardener leader to be part of the leadership team. Gardeners are part of the entry team. They have their direction and purpose, and must know what must be done and why. Their role is to prepare the organization for change.

If I were an entrepreneur, I would find a gardener and say, "I want to do A, B, and C with that company. Go in and find out where the most versatile areas are and the condition of the company. Tell what will grow first and where. Once you do that, tell me when the best planting season is."

Gardeners, like farmers, are CEOs of the soil. They sense a need for the soil to be worked and then left to rest. It is like employees who learn a new way. They work at getting the new idea and then they leave the information to grow. I believe farmers and sculptors have much in common. Both have a medium to work with, and both mediums offer significant resistance in order to get the final result.

I think if I were to ask a sculptor about a piece of granite, he would dream of a statue of David asleep in the solid mass. Gardeners also sense a hidden piece of art in the land. It is their version of David, but with the gardener, it is something different. His sculpture is a living entity. His piece of art is the planning, nurturing, and development of the human spirit; it is the fundamental of life itself.

Gardeners understand change. They are tuned to the changing of the corporate climate and the need for organizational change. They understand what needs to be planted in the company soil and how to nurture new ideas. Again, they understand how to plant something and let it go dormant for later growth. They understand a caustic environment and are not afraid to turn the soil over for planting new ideas. If necessary, the gardener will say something that others need to hear but may not like it at the time—it is called fertilizer. It may smell bad, but it does wonders for the final product.

One morning, I was listening to the early news on the radio. The commentator was interviewing a woman who was planning her flowerbeds and garden for the spring. The commentator asked her how she knew when the soil was ready to turn over.

Her comment intrigued me because I saw it as relevant to the gardener as a leader. She said, "You pick up a handful of soil, squeeze it, and drop it to the ground. If the soil breaks in two or three pieces, it isn't ready."

I thought about those leaders who are gardeners in their behavior. They know when the soil of productivity is ready in their organization. They will put the pressure on and squeeze the workplace environment and see if it is ready. Employees call that pressure.

The gardener says, "It is time." They can tell if people will not be receptive to the seeds of new ideas. Patience is a true reward.

Working with a Gardener

Here are some tips on working with a gardener.

- If you are someone who has to see the results of your efforts right now, then working for a gardener is not for you.
- Patience is a virtue. Plan for the long haul.
- Gardeners have method, plan, and arrangement in their business plans. Everything is done in its time.
- Gardeners review their plans frequently, if not daily. This is the methodical pulling of the weeds.
- Be prepared to get dirty. Gardeners expect you to get on your hands and knees and work in the soil of the project.
- These are big picture people. They are also realistic in their approach and execution.
- If you like being around projects that will really look good in the end, the gardener environment may be just your ticket.
- If you are not a patient person, then you will not be happy in this environment.
- Gardeners are not spontaneous. They can visualize the final product before it is complete. If you can't do this, then look elsewhere.

Entrepreneurs

Do not cry, whine, and snivel around an entrepreneur. If complacency is something you crave, then this is not the arena for you. Entrepreneurs look for adventure. Sometimes I believe they enjoy the hunt for the new idea more than the actual finish. They love to see their accomplishments come to fruition, but the underlying word seems to be *risk*. Entrepreneurs love the risk. To them, it is a form of adventure.

I have a very close friend, an entrepreneur, who said it best: “I love to hang my toes over the edge. If I don’t risk, I don’t like the challenge.”

I have imagined entrepreneurs as hunters. The challenge of identifying a trail, developing a plan for the hunt, and then taking the risk is almost an adrenaline rush. It is here where they operate the best—taking the risk. They have virtual offices. Any place an idea strikes the entrepreneur is considered her office.

Entrepreneurs not only think—they do. It is often at the same time. These are not people who sit around and let grass grow under their feet. They think, create, modify, leverage, and implement. Time is never an issue. They maximize their own time and if you let them, they will maximize yours. They are not clock watchers. They are idea driven and very competitive. They look both short and long term. It is not uncommon for them to have their money and ideas out years in advance. I have met entrepreneurs who have told me they have investments in markets that have not even been created. They are investing in the real future.

With an entrepreneur, every day is an adventure, different and challenging. These people expect the people around them to be just as challenged. We often say that someone has set the bar awfully high. The entrepreneur sees the bar as a barrier. I would say that entrepreneurs are probably the most dimensional of the behaviors. I use the term *dimensional* to say they can taste and smell new ideas and opportunities.

Working with an Entrepreneur

Here are some tips for working with an entrepreneur:

- You must be comfortable with multiple deadlines. The deadlines may seem unrealistic and the amount of work overwhelming. It is the nature of the game.
- The stakes are high. The entrepreneur knows the power of leverage. That could involve, people, material, and money. When I say leverage, I refer to the strategic positioning of resources.
- These are exciting people. If you relish an eight-to-five job, then working with an entrepreneur is not for you.
- Do not cry, whine, or snivel around an entrepreneur.
- Time is relative to an entrepreneur. If an idea hits, they will run with it and so will you!
- These are people who are really outside the box. You may be expected to think like them.
- Risk is the word. Hours are long and the rewards can be huge.

Hushers

When I was working on the different leadership behaviors I knew what I wanted to say, but I started to draw a blank—I did not know how to say it. Have you ever been working on a problem and everything just seemed to bog down? In other words, you were stuck. I find myself in that situation quite frequently.

What I have learned is that, in those special times, I must give it up. I let it go and, in time, it seems to happen. What I really have to admit is that I do not have all the answers. It is times like that when the answer you are looking for comes from someone else. They don't realize it but they just say something that gives you the answer you need. The key is for me to remain open to the new idea and feel comfortable with it. The expectation can be daunting. The belief in the process is critical.

A while back, a friend of mine was sharing her thoughts on a career change and looking for something she would like to do. In the course of the conversation, she related how the people at her church were giving her some feedback on her talents and abilities.

What she was doing is something very important to any church. This woman had that wonderful ability to stop a child from crying in church simply by picking her up and holding her. Her talent and fame grew to such proportions that the church members called her the official "husher."

When she told me that story I knew I had the word to describe those people who can go into an organization and quiet the unsettled system and the masses. These people are unique. They not only have the ability to quiet a situation, they follow through with a plan or action that keeps the situation stable.

Hushers are great planners and organizers. They have the ability to multitask. They can grasp a situation, stabilize the event, and plan an action. Hushers are invaluable to an organization. They can put their arms around a situation and bring stability and perspective. They work under stress, remain conscious of deadlines, and keep situations in perspective.

Hushers do not like something to be upset unless it is necessary. Hushers are patient—to a point. It is in your best interest to know where that point lies. They have no patience for anyone wanting attention just for the sake of the attention.

Working with a Husher

Here are some things you need to know when working with a husher.

- If anxiety and crisis make you uncomfortable, this is not the place for you.
- Hushers are comfortable in a triage situation and thrive in it.
- Be prepared for immediate directions that are short and to the point.

- Hushers like people around them who think on their feet and are willing to take charge.
- Hushers can plan and execute at the same time. They enjoy people who are instinctive in their thinking.
- Hushers are equal at left- and right-brain thinking.
- If you are a doer and enjoy creativity, then find work with a husher.
- Hushers are big on loyalty. They see loyalty and ethical decision making as critical.
- Hushers do not have tolerance for situational ethics.
- If you like to think, plan, move, and respond all at the same time, then this is an environment for you.
- Around a husher, you may be asked to put your mental arms around a big organizational problem and calm it down.
- Hushers get a lot of attention in times of crisis. You have to be comfortable in that environment.

The Visionaries

When I think of the word *visionary*, several other words come to mind, such as thinker, seeker, futurist, dreamer, and idealist. The Einsteins and Newtons come along just about every other century. They are in that percentile with several zeros to the right of the decimal point, in the population, who are true genius. I have thought about the term *visionary* for a long time and conclude that I don't necessarily believe that one has to be a genius to be a visionary.

If you are around a visionary, then don't bother him with specific detail or an extended list. He will handle it—but in his own time. Visionaries are unique in their process. In one conversation with a friend who I thought was a visionary, I asked him how he looked at the world. His answer was quite simple. He said when he thinks about a problem or an issue, it is like looking in a fog bank. He then said that, over time, the fog just seems to go away and then he sees the answer. If, sometimes, you think a visionary is in another world—he is.

Some of my fondest childhood recollections include the times my father told me I had done a good job. He always tried to show me a better way. At the time, I had this severe case of doing it my way. Not only did I not want to listen, but I felt I had all the answers. I did not have the answers and, in some instances, I did not learn his lesson until years had passed. He did motivate me. Parents tend to do that.

I want to make it clear that motivation is not something that takes place at the moment of demonstration; it takes place at the moment of awareness. Much of what my father taught me did not reach a stage of manifestation until many years had passed. In some instances, it took decades!

Think back to someone who truly had vision. What was it they said or did that caused you to reach that "Aha" moment? Inspirers cause us to reach. It is as if they make us reach into areas of our lives and abilities and cause us to use them in different ways. I often think of the word *suggest* as maybe even seasoned with a hint of intimidation.

I use *intimidation* in a positive way. I see intimidation as something we do to ourselves. It is as if the inspirer shows how we may be limiting ourselves by our own suggestions. In other words, we begin to see that no one is holding us back; it is our own beliefs that are doing so.

Working with a Visionary

- If you are in a hurry, then working for a visionary may also not be the place for you.
- Visionaries take their time. Inspiration may be slow to come. They are always thinking of different possibilities and combinations.
- Much of their work goes on in between their ears.
- Visionaries ask lots of questions and make statements. You may not understand what they are saying, but they do think

out loud. They may ask you a question and you may not be able to answer it. Don't get discouraged. Their workplace is fluid.

- Visionaries are not short-term people; they are thinking out there—way out there!
- Their immediate work environment may seem fragmented and disorganized.
- Expect them to ask you where things are. You will have to have good organizational skills to keep up.
- Be prepared to keep and manage two schedules, yours and theirs.

I share these five behaviors for a reason. First of all, life is not a checklist and these behaviors are not cut and dried. When they appear in combination that is when life gets real exciting. It is also when the Einstein-Brownian theory comes into play. Ideas and projects appear almost chaotic, with productivity and thoughts just ricocheting off each other. Regardless of the combination, the Heisenberg Uncertainty Principle is part of the equation. These behaviors do not stand still and neither should the people who are involved.

I believe these five behaviors provide an environment for employees and associates to enhance and nurture potential. It gives credence to the ability for associates to become adaptive in their personal behavior as the message or messenger. The following are general descriptors of a good leader.

What Makes a Good Leader?

Here are some of the characteristics of a good leader:

- Good leaders have moral conviction. They have a sense of vision for their objective, and the integrity to get there.
- Good leaders have an attitude driven by ethical principles.
- Good leaders do not make everyone happy. That is not their job. They listen, but they alone know they must decide.

- Good leaders have a sense of purpose. They know that they alone are responsible for results.
- Good leaders have defined principles, values, and ethics. They know how to align those qualities on their goals and objectives.
- Good leaders are decision makers. They have a sense of direction.
- Good leaders have sense for things that exist but that they cannot see.
- They have the ability to inspire others to seek out and understand.
- Good leaders understand that a clock has nothing to do with productivity.
- Wisdom tells them that choosing specific life events and overcoming obstacles are critical to inspiration and success.
- Good leaders have a sixth sense for what is right, and faith in their ability.

Questions

Which of the areas best describes you?

- Does one leadership behavior in particular describe you or do you see yourself in several areas?
- If you are in a position of leadership, how would your employees describe you?
- If I asked your employees to describe your leadership style using one of the five mentioned, which one would it be?
- Would you be apprehensive if one of your customers asked you to describe your leadership style?

It is time to take what we have discussed and apply it to our work and our careers. We have new tools. It is now time to use them.

Chapter Fourteen

Suggested Strategies

I don't think God put us on this earth to be intelligent.
I think He put us here to be wise.

As we look at the idea of leadership and its responsibilities, I think we must also look at the way we structure our organizations in order to meet that need. For example, one only has to look at traditional organizational charts to see that most company structures refer to leadership as a method that emanates from the top down.

Western culture traditionally looks at power and authority as coming from above. Western civilization does not have the corner on it either; both the Old and New Testaments and many cultural beliefs set the stage for our organizational perceptions. In the past, authority was extremely powerful and often looked to the universe for the source of its deity. We still carry the tradition today. In the twenty-first century we must look at the advantages of leadership from the bottom up.

True Leaders Live Their Work

We can look at leadership in many ways. My example of leadership from the bottom up includes Mohandas Gandhi and Mother Teresa. Both leaders lived their work. They were not slaves to the geopolitical gerbil cage that is center stage in some organizations—they led from a point of view and had an appetite for attitude. Once that was established, leadership followed. They did not toss out politically correct ideas or visions and wait to see who got on board and what stuck where. Gandhi and Mother Teresa were accessible to their people each day and had a firm understanding of their roles and missions. They were the ultimate definition of adaptation. One does not have to be a Mother Teresa or a Gandhi to have an attitude for leadership. They literally walked the talk.

While, traditionally, we still see leadership as coming from the top down, innovative leaders also understand that many of the needed changes and new ideas come from the bottom up. Both Scripture and science have made their greatest breakthroughs and examples from what occurred on the front line. What we are now looking at is structures in transition.

I see similarities between organizational structures and Newtonian physics. Just as Einstein looked at the universe and started to ask questions, the voices in the wilderness that are looking at the current portfolio of organizational structures ask similar questions.

Einstein concluded that light travels at a constant speed and that, no matter how hard you chase after a beam of light, it still retreats from you at a constant speed.[1] I am sure this, too, will be challenged in the future. It is called knowledge. I believe we are headed in the same direction with the human spirit. If we substitute the speed of light with the human spirit, it is clear that we have foisted the role of traditional structures on the human spirit and called it productivity. If this is true, then some implemented organizational designs actually hinder productivity.

Our methods are relatively new. We have been influenced by the Industrial Revolution and I believe we are still under the management pull of its force. Products, design, technology, and knowledge have increased one hundred-fold over the last century, yet the organizational charts that manage the new knowledge are similar to those of seventy and a hundred years ago. It is a force that keeps pulling true productivity in a different direction. Looking at the workplace today is like taking the Hubble Telescope and looking at one tiny section of the universe.

As we enter the age where our universe, technology, and its laws have a greater influence on our lives, we will begin to see the effects. What is interesting is that many of the laws and principles have scriptural implications. I believe our greatest discovery will be the organizational structure that supports the human spirit and provides the greatest opportunity for the quantum connection.

The human spirit is still adrift in the vacuum of organizational consensus building, and bumping into other entities in its spiritual and scientific journey. I was attending a leadership conference and one of the speakers was relating to the invention of the light bulb. He said if Thomas Edison had had focus groups, then we would have twenty-four-hour dripless candles. The spiritual and physical energy of each human spirit is looking for that adaptive structure that provides the environment where productivity becomes an elegant equation. Einstein proved that both Newtonian physics and quantum theory cannot be right.[2]

Leadership and Support

True leadership and management is a support function whose job is to clear the path for the customer to be served. That is an awesome task. Management's role is to define with precise clarity the vision of the organization and TEACH that principle to all employees. I said teach, and I mean it.

Leaders must be disciples of the message, and they must be the messenger. They are teachers, and must also teach the message to their customers if they want to survive. The traditional organization is facing some of those challenges.

Donald C. Hambick, David A. Nadler, and Michael L. Tushman give some glowing insights in their book, *Navigating Change: How CEOs, Top Teams, and Boards Steer Transformation*. The example they give is from XEROX site-specific beliefs and thinking about what a senior management team ***must avoid***. Their thoughts are as follows:

- Self-managed senior teams do not work.

- Remotely-located teams work less well than teams in physical proximity.
- Consensus leadership does not work.
- Avoid ill-defined team objectives, processes, and rewards that hamper performance.
- Teamwork starts with the CEO.
- Total Quality Management tools and processes can enhance teamwork.
- Roles, responsibilities, and expectations must be clarified.
- An effective governance process must be in place.
- Outside counsel and assistance helps.
- Teams need to be explicitly launched and then maintained over time.[3]

I love these points. I find great satisfaction in knowing that, if a company is not aware of these methods, management has to walk up the stairs to deliver bad ideas. I am not only advocating the way the organization thinks. I believe we must also have physical change in the work environment to support that work force.

Managers should be located on the lowest level possible. They need to be close to the root equations of the organization. They need to understand that their jobs are not a rite of passage, but responsibility—a responsibility they feel every day as they walk into corporate culture. Leadership is the root system of any organization. The leader must know when to be the message or the messenger. A leader's behavior is like a stone that is dropped in the middle of the pond, and the wave of his actions affects all in the organization.

The purpose of a tree is to be planted in good soil for the best growth. Leadership is the organizational root system planted in the ethical soil of ground level support. Its purpose is to produce a stable foundation for employees and customers to be the best they can be. Being a leader requires one to bear a load. One does not appreciate the weight they are to carry unless they both see it and sense its presence.

Twenty-first-century leaders must understand the physical, scientific, and spiritual load they are to bear. This means that nutrition and stability start on the ground floor. Leadership also is the primary equation for any organization. It is similar to the sciences looking for the primary equations that describe the universe. It eluded Einstein, but scientists today are knocking on some pretty interesting doors.

This organizational system has worked in our forests and plant ecosystems. If it has worked in nature since the beginning of time, it can work in the workplace today. How firmly the organization is rooted in its thinking will determine the strength of the company. Management then has the ability to determine the role of the message or the messenger.

The new leader would be required to be adaptive. She would not work her way up in the company—she would work her way down. It would be just the opposite of our current sense of being. Business must learn from science and spirituality. In science, we find our answers in the exploration of the smallest particles. In Scripture, we must look at its application and its impact on the smallest of the small—those who live their beliefs and go unnoticed, those who work for a living. This is quantizing the effects.

Suggested Strategies

I offer some suggested strategies and examples where leaders can apply the Seven Needs for Personal Productivity, the Five-Step Decision-Making Model, and the Leadership Triangle to the workplace.

- If you are a leader or in a position of authority, do not be quick to run to judgment, and find solace in data and information, and stop at knowledge. Look to understanding and wisdom for the ethical and right thing to do.
- As a leader, define, create, and exemplify quality for your employees and its relationship to your product and your

customer. Do not be quick to hold your employees accountable for failed products and poor quality. They only know what you have told them. You control the system. Inspire them to help you change it.

- If you want to be the example, then set it. In this country, the last ones to suffer are at the top. The outcome has become the god. Your employees trust a different deity. If business is bad and profits drop, then set a new ethical example. Employees and customers have the answers. Be brave and ask the questions. Create the symphony.
- Management bonuses have lost their purpose. You owe it to your employees to explain how giving a manager a huge bonus inspires a front-line employee to work harder and inspire teamwork. That is like giving the weatherman a reward for forecasting a good day.
- Your internal communication process is the lifeblood of your organization. Your employees want and need to know what is happening. Be passionate about one-on-one communication. Employees are symphonic instruments. They will follow you into the unknown but they must have faith in you. Tell them the good and the bad. Answers come from the truth and not perception.
- Choose your managers carefully. Look for common sense, talent, skill, discipline, and desire. And hire leaders, communicators, problem solvers, and those with a good work ethic. It is time to choose managers with heart and soul. Set the expectations of your managers to the highest level.
- Ask yourself: Do you train your leaders or do you expect them to come "camera-ready" when you hire them? If you do not have a management-training program then get one and continuously improve it. Your leaders must be the message and the messenger. It is critical that you teach your leaders

the difference between the two and when each behavior is appropriate. If you don't invest in your leaders, why should front-line employees commit to you?

- If a manager does not treat all employees with integrity, dignity, and respect, get rid of him.
- Continuing education of management should be mandatory. They must give back by teaching others. It is not unrealistic to have them publish in trade journals, manuals, and other forms of professional communication.
- Leadership is not a rite of passage. Bad leaders will cost you untold loss of revenue. Autocratic managers who motivate with fear are the largest and costliest line item in your budget. This is not a motivational theory. These are the laws of physics.
- Your numbers will never tell the truth. Numbers are the symptom of a series of events. Remember, they have no conscience. Where does your leadership judgment tell you to go?
- Your expectations can only be as valid as the management team you create. Your task is daunting. Set your expectations and communicate them to everyone. Be clear. What does your organization value and why?
- Continually tell your employees what you believe, how they are valued, and where they are going. If you already have autocratic managers who look for blind loyalty, then you are losing money now! The greatest damage will not be to the customer or product—it will be to the front-line employee. You will pay, and pay dearly.
- Look for people who understand that true productivity lies in the duality of employees being the message of creativity and the messenger of teaching others. This will not be an easy process. If integrity is something you value, then you have no choice.

- All organizations and systems speak to the leaders and employees. Listen to what they are telling you. What signal is your company giving you, and what is noise? Do you know the difference between the two?
- Understand the connections between spirituality, science, and productivity. Your employees bring the first two through the front door of the company. Are you providing the environment for the third? When leadership is educated in the principles of both, everyone wins.
- Provide training and education for management so they can understand and teach Mandelbrot, Mother Teresa, Heisenberg, Einstein, Saint Thomas Aquinas, Moses, Aristotle, and other great thinkers to front-line employees. Have them make formal presentations on the connections. They must practice what they teach.

Questions

- Do you advocate *attitude, leadership, and listening*?
- Your attitude is a key element to success. Are you contagious?
- Does your organization have front-line leaders or front-line consensus builders?
- Is your organization inundated with policies that do not support creativity?
- Should public and private sector leadership training be the same?
- Should they be taught both the scientific and the spiritual principles of leadership?
- Do you have *organizational environmentalists* as leaders?
- Do they understand the Seven Needs for Personal Productivity?

Suggested Strategies for Front-Line Employees

Front-line employees also can apply the Seven Needs for Personal Productivity, the Five-Step Decision-Making Model, and the Leadership Triangle to the workplace. Here are some suggestions:

- Develop your portfolio of skills. If you choose to have a career, let the Seven Needs for Personal Productivity, the Five-Step Decision-Making Model, and Leadership Triangle assist you in developing a plan.
- Define a strategic plan for yourself. What matters most to you in life? What are your priorities? What are you doing each day to help achieve your goals and life plan? This is the foundation of who you are.
- At times, what happens to you will seem unfair. Others will get promotions, pay raises, or the organization may change and leave you behind. Is it fair? No. So what do you do? Rise to a higher level and do your job. Does it get better? That depends on what you need and want from your job and your life goals. What is important to you?
- You are the backbone of the organization. You have the task of dealing with your organization's customers. If the customer is unhappy, you will be the first to know. This is a tough task. This is also your job.
- If your work has average or low pay but good training, education, and experience, and the experience is what you need, then you are being paid a fair wage. Opportunity is your decision. If you complain that you don't make enough money, then develop a financial plan.
- If you need to make changes in your life, then develop a life plan. Both these challenges may appear impossible, but they are not. Over the course of your life, both these steps will give you a pay raise. Any increase in your salary is not something

that is owed to you by your employer. Accept the change in your life. If you think salary is just money, then your challenge is great.

- Always put yourself in a position where you are able to learn. Seek out those people and organizations that have the knowledge, understanding, and wisdom to teach others. Learn from them. Their experience will manifest itself tenfold in you. Always look for a better way to serve your customers and promote communication.
- Avoid the toxic people in your organization and personal life. You know who they are. Do not enter into battles that will lead nowhere. Listen to your heart and do the right thing.
- If you do not like your organization, then you need to make a decision. You are committing an injustice if you condemn and vilify your company but remain there. You will only damage yourself if you remain. Make peace and leave.
- You are responsible for taking control and charge of your life. This is not easy. You have talent and God-given gifts. Life is asking you questions. You have been judged on data, information, and knowledge. Make life-changing decisions based on understanding and wisdom and find a better way. Use them to the best of your ability. This takes attitude, leadership, and listening.

Apply the Seven Needs to Your Career

Ask yourself the following questions:

- Is my current career giving a sense of meaning to and in my life?
- Do I have say-so and input into my destiny?
- Am I getting paid a fair wage? This is not just money—it is overall job satisfaction.
- Is my career enhancing my quality of life?
- Do I have true organizational leadership?

- Am I working for a learning organization? Am I learning?
- Do I know that my job is important to the organization? How so?

If five of the Seven Needs have been missing from your career for over a year, then consider dusting off your resume! What price might you be paying?

The Seven Needs Productivity Circle

So What Must Leaders Do?

You are put in a position to lead. Do so. You must understand that the days of blind faith are gone. You have been given one of the greatest resources on the face of this earth: the human spirit. The external manifestation will be the mind and body. Many will follow because they work and serve with their hearts and souls. Know the difference. They bring spirituality and science to you, and you must tap into both.

Loyalty and respect from your employees is not a right nor is it automatic—you must earn it. Show them a direction; the direction you set is your decision. If you expect your employees to follow, then educate and train and lead them. Define the organization and create the environment. *That is an organizational environmentalist.*

Create a learning environment where your organization teaches employee life-planning skills, potential, and the development of the Seven Needs Productivity Circle. This includes mind, body, heart and soul. Understand and teach the Five-Step Decision-Making Model. That means data, information, knowledge, understanding, and wisdom. Don't let them stop at knowledge to make a decision—encourage them to move to wisdom and make wise decisions.

Become known as a learning organization. More importantly—become known as a learning leader. Understand the difference between the message and the messenger and wave/particle duality. Look for the adaptive nature of your employees. They will look for better ways to do their jobs. Let them learn and your organization will gain the benefits. There is a harmony of science and soul when it comes to the human spirit.

Summary

We are on a twenty-first-century quest for organizational and spiritual discovery. It is a journey that will give us the opportunity to experience immense challenge. It not only will sharpen our skills, it will also present the moments where we can actually define a new work environment. The workplace and organizational design will become more fluid, evolving, and adaptive.

The human spirit has a spiritual and scientific investment, and the implications are critical to organizational relationships. We have spiritual needs. Our quest for science will lead us into exciting frontiers that have significant life-giving implications. Our focus on the universe and study of the heavens presents a wonderful opportunity. We must look at science and spirituality in their duality. This means accepting the implications that truth and discovery can be germinated in a mathematical formula with an example from the book of Genesis.

So, what is on the horizon for the twenty-first-century workplace and the human spirit? We now see ourselves looking deeper than quantum theory and the universe. We hear scientists looking at the universe and consider the word *elegant* as a descriptor. It is here we reach the paradox. Telescopes look into the vastness of space, but leaders fail to look into a greater vastness—the human spirit and the workplace. The word *elegant* is appropriate. I challenge the scientific, spiritual, and corporate leaders to look to each other and design a structure and philosophy for the human spirit and an *organizational environment* where they can work.

I believe every person should have the opportunity to work with mind, body, heart, and soul. My true dream is to someday sit in a room and have a scientist, minister, and business leader observing a group of employees describe the organization they work for and its design, and how they have passion and love for what they do. And when they are finished I can smile, because I finally will have witnessed *the harmony of science and soul.*

Notes

Preface

1. James T. Bond and others, "Highlights of the National Study of the Changing Work Force, Executive Summary," *Families and Work Institute*, no. 3, 2002: 4.
2. Stephen R. Covey, A. Roger Merrill, and Rebecca R. Merrill, *First Things First: To Live, to Love, to Learn, to Leave a Legacy*, reprint ed., New York: Simon & Schuster, 1996).

Chapter One

1. WorldofQuotes.com/author/Theodore-Roosevelt/1/html.
2. Fred Alan Wolf, Ph.D., *The Spiritual Universe, One Physicist's Vision of Spirit, Soul, Matter, and Self* (Portsmouth, NH: Moment Point Press, 1999), 60.
3. Ibid.
4. Ed Oakley and Doug Krug, *Enlightened Leadership: Getting to the Heart of Change* (New York: Simon & Schuster, 1991), 8.
5. Mickey Connolly and Richard Rianoshek, Ph.D., *The Communication Catalyst: the fast (but not stupid) track to value for customers, investors, and employees* (Chicago: Dearborn Trade Publishing, 2003), xii.
6. Connolly and Rianoshek, xiii.
7. Paul Davies, *God and the New Physics* (New York: Simon & Schuster, 1983), 7.

Chapter Two

1. WorldofQuotes.com/author/Mahatma-Gandhi/1/.
2. World Book Online Reference Center, s.v. "Taylor, Frederick Winslow" (by George H. Daniels), http://www.aolsvc.worldbook.aol.com.Articles?id=ar548650 (7 September 2005).

3. Mark 1:9 (New American Bible).
4. Matthew 28:19 (New American Bible).
5. St. Thomas Aquinas, *The Summa Theologica of St. Thomas Aquinas*, 2nd and revised ed., trans. Fathers of the English Dominican Province, literally translated by Fathers of the English Dominican Province. (Online edition copyright 2000 by Kevin Knight). The author thanks Sandra K. Perry, Perrysburg, Ohio, who provided this digital file.
6. Ibid.
7. St. Thomas Aquinas, *Summa Theologica*, http://www.newadvent.org/.
8. Michael Caputo, *God Seen Through the Eyes of the Greatest Minds* (Monroe, LA: Howard Publishing, 2000), 68.
9. Wisdom 9:3 (New American Bible).
10. M.K. Gandhi Institute for Nonviolence, s.v. "Gandhi," 1998, http://www.gandhi@cbu.edu.
11. Hernando De Soto, *The Mystery of Capital: Why Capitalism Triumphs in the West and Fails Everywhere Else* (New York: Basic Books), 189.
12. Ibid.
13. Microsoft® Encarta® Encyclopedia, s.v. "Albert Einstein," 2003.
14. Fred Alan Wolf, *The Spiritual Universe*, 99–102.
15. Isaiah 56:11 (New American Bible).
16. Wisdom 1:1 (New American Bible).

Chapter Three

1. Lewis D. Eigen and Jonathan P. Siegel, *The Manager's Book of Quotations* (Rockville, MD: The Quotation Corporation, 1989), 111.
2. Paul Davies, *God and the New Physics*, 13.
3. Fred Alan Wolf, *The Spiritual Universe,* 101.
4. William W. Scherkenbach, *Deming's Road to Continual Improvement* (Knoxville, TN: SPC Press, Inc., 1991).

5. Henry R. Neave, *The Deming Dimension* (Knoxville, TN: SPC Press Inc., 1990).
6. Ibid., p 152.
7. W. Edwards Deming, *Out of Crisis* (Cambridge, MA: MIT Press, 1982), 15.
8. W. Edwards Deming, *The New Economics for Industry, Government and Education* (Cambridge, MA: Massachusetts Institute of Technology Center for Advanced Engineering Study, 1993), 50–51.
9. Fred Alan Wolf, *The Spiritual Universe,* 42.
10. Microsoft® Encarta® Encyclopedia, s.v. "Revelation," 2003.
11. Thomas Merton, *New Seeds Of Contemplation* (New York: New Directions Publishing Company, 1961), 110.
12. Isaiah 6:9 (New American Bible).
13. Matthew 13:14–15 (New American Bible).
14. Isaiah 6:10 (New American Bible).
15. Wisdom 1:1 (New American Bible).
16. The Internet Encyclopedia of Philosophy, s.v. "Aristotle (384–322 BCE): General Introduction, The Soul & Psychology," www.iep.utm.edu/a/aristotl.htm.
17. Wikipedia, the free encyclopedia, s.v. "Serenity Prayer," http://www.en.wikipediaorg/wiki/Serenity_Prayer.
18. "Contributions to AA: The Slogans, the Serenity Prayer, and the Man on the Bed," *AA Grapevine*, www.aagrapevine.org/about/gvcontributions.php.
19. Sirach 4:24 (New American Bible).
20. Henry Neave, *The Deming Dimension.*

Chapter Four

1. Viktor Frankl, *Man's Search for Meaning* (New York: Pocket Books, 1959, 1962, 1984).
2. Matthew Scully, "Viktor Frankl at Ninety: An Interview," *First Things* 52 (April 1995): 39–43.

3. Paul Davies, *God and the New Physics*, 3.
4. Ibid.
5. Abbot Joseph Wood, "A Letter from the Abbot," *Mount Angel Letter* 53, no. 3 (June 2001), http://www.mtangel.edu/MAL/06%2F01/1mal0601.htm.

Chapter Five

1. Wisdom 7:15, 17–18 (New American Bible).
2. Fred Alan Wolf, *The Spiritual Universe*, 35–37.
3. Isaiah 56:11 (New American Bible).
4. Tom Coens and Mary Jenkins, *Abolishing Performance Appraisals: Why They Backfire and What to Do Instead* (San Francisco: Berrett-Koehler Publishers, Inc., 2000).
5. Ibid.
6. Ibid.
7. Ibid.

Chapter Six

1. James W. Carey, s.v. "McLuhan, Marshall," World Book Online Reference Center, 2005 (World Book, Inc., 29 September 2005), http://www.aolsvc.worldbook.aol.com/wb/Article?id=ar351730.
2. Fred Alan Wolf, *The Spiritual Universe*, 47.
3. W. Edwards Deming, *The New Economics for Industry*, 94.
4. Ibid.
5. Peter Drucker, *The Practice of Management* (New York: HarperCollins Publishers, 1982).

Chapter Seven

1. Thomas Merton, *New Seeds Of Contemplation*.
2. Ibid.
3. Isaiah 56:11 (New American Bible).
4. "Heisenberg Uncertainty Principle," Dr. Darkmatter Presents The

Electronic Universe, http://zebu.uoregon.edu/~imamura/208/jan27/hup.html.

5. Isaiah 57:1 (New American Bible).
6. Hernando De Soto, *The Mystery of Capital: Why Capitalism Triumphs in the West and Fails Everywhere Else*, 5.
7. Ibid., 44.
8. Ibid.
9. "Letter," *Catholic Sentinel*, v. 133, no. 10 (8 March 2002).

Chapter Eleven

1. George Bernard Shaw, "Mrs. Warren's Profession," http://www.quotationspage.com/quote/26793.html.
2. Larry Schwartz, "'Great' and 'Gretzky' belong together," ESPN, http://espn.go.com/sportscentury/features/00014218.html.
3. Wisdom 6:12 (New American Bible).
4. Wisdom 6:8–10 (New American Bible).
5. Wisdom 6:11 (New American Bible).

Chapter Twelve

1. Psalms 5:9 (New American Bible).
2. Kathleen D. Ryan and Daniel K. Ostereich, *Driving Fear Out of the Workplace: How to Overcome the Invisible Barriers to Quality, Productivity and Innovation* (San Francisco, CA: Jossey-Bass, 1991): 21.
3. Ibid.
4. Henry R. Neave, *The Deming Dimension*, 290.
5. Ibid., 292.

Chapter Thirteen

1. Thomas Merton, *New Seeds Of Contemplation*, 110.
2. Bruce Wares, "The Importance of Setting Goals," http://www.bluinc.com/news/theimportance.html.

Chapter Fourteen

1. Brian Greene, *The Elegant Universe, Superstrings, Hidden Dimensions, and the Quest for the Ultimate Theory* (New York: Vintage Books, 1999), 33.
2. Ibid., 3.
3. Donald C. Hambick, David A. Nadler, and Michael L. Tushman, *Navigating Change: How CEOs, Top Teams, and Boards Steer Transformation* (Cambridge, MA: Harvard Business School Press, 1998).

About the Author

Art Bobrowitz has been a passionate student of people and their relationship to quality of life and work issues for more than thirty-five years. As a Wisconsin native, Art moved to Oregon in 1972 and spent over twenty-three years with the Oregon State Police. His primary duties were patrol, training, media relations, and public speaking. His last eight years were spent as a supervisor and teaching at the Oregon Public Safety Academy at Western Oregon University.

Since then, Art has used his thirty-five plus years of management research and leadership experience to launch Compass Rose Consulting, Inc., a management and productivity consulting group. He is the author of *Each Human Spirit: The Transformation of the American Workplace.* He is in high demand as a speaker and trainer and consults with a wide variety of corporations and agencies on productivity, customer satisfaction, communication, and other topics. He continues to write and lecture on issues relating to the workplace and the human spirit.

Art lives with his wife, Roseann, in Keizer, Oregon. He holds a commercial pilot certificate and is active in community issues.

Compass Rose Consulting Inc.

Our attitude and focus is

to inspire and support the human spirit

About the Author